The Competent Leader

A Powerful and Practical Tool Kit for Managers and Supervisors

Peter B. Stark and Jane Flaherty

HRD Press, Inc.
Amherst, Massachusetts

Published by Human Resource Development Press, Inc.

22 Amherst Road

Amherst, Massachusetts 01002

1-800-822-2801 (U.S. and Canada)

1-413-253-3488

1-413-253-3490 (fax)

http://www.hrdpress.com

Production services provided by CompuDesign

Cover design by Eileen Klockars

Editorial services by Suzanne Bay

Contents

CONTENTS

iv

Preface

No matter how you arrived at your position as a supervisor, you now need a whole new set of skills in order to work successfully with your employees. Feeling positive about yourself, making decisions, and solving problems will still be part of your daily life, but you will now need to add the significant and challenging leadership skills of communicating, delegating, coaching, motivating, hiring, and leading.

Your achievement will now be measured in terms of the performance of your staff. Knowing how to work with your employees, therefore, will increase your department's effectiveness. Your employees may turn out to be your most valuable support system as you grow into the successful leader you know you can become.

The Competent Leader outlines and describes the skills you will need to become a strong and competent supervisor and manager. The information we have provided in the text and exhibits is supplemented by *Tips for Success* and *Action Plans*, which appear at the end of each chapter. They include practical suggestions you can put to use immediately.

This book is for those of you who want to not only *survive* in today's competitive environment, but *thrive*.

Acknowledgments

We would like to acknowledge the many employees and members of management teams who have contributed to our knowledge and understanding of effective leadership in organizations. Your insights and candid feedback are the seeds of wisdom in formulating this book.

Specifically, our appreciation goes to the employees and managers we have worked with within the following organizations: Accredited Home Lenders, Action Instruments, American Residential Mortgage Corporation/Chase Manhattan, American Specialty Health Plans, Association of Legal Administrators, Campbell Sales Company, Carlson Companies, Chromalloy, Chula Vista Elementary School District, City of Oceanside, County of San Diego, Eagle Creek Travel Gear, Entergy Operations, Foodmaker Inc., Grossmont Bank, Hallmark Circuits, Hewlett Packard, Institute of Management Studies, La Jolla Beach and Tennis Club, Lightspan Partnership, Los Angeles Dodgers, MailBoxes Etc., Mission Federal Credit Union, Motorola, National Basketball Association, NCR, North Island Federal Credit Union, PETCO, Portland Trail Blazers, Princess Cruises, Quintiles, Ralston Purina, San Diego Convention Center, San Diego Padres, San Diego State University, Texas Utilities, Unisys, University of Phoenix, U.S. Department of Defense, Wisconsin Electric, and Xerox.

We would also like to acknowledge and thank Barbara Hendrickson, our editor, and Jan Christian, for her computer graphics.

Introduction

For the last twenty years, we have had the opportunity to read hundreds of books on leadership, supervision, and management. Each of the books we invested in contained ideas we were able to use in our managerial careers, as well as share with our business clients. So, it would seem that the last thing we need is another book on supervising and managing employees!

However, there are three reasons why we have taken the time to put our thoughts on paper. First, after having the opportunity to train thousands of new and experienced supervisors and managers, we feel we have a solid understanding of what skills it takes to be a successful leader in today's business environment.

Second, we wanted to concentrate on the personal and people skills required to be a great leader. We have found that most people in supervisory, managerial, or other positions of leadership have exceptionally strong technical skills. In fact, people are usually hired and promoted based on how well they perform the "operational" functions of a position. Our experience has been that most people in positions of authority, although strong in technical skills, are not equally strong in their people skills. To continue up the ladder of organizational success, we must be willing to "fine-tune" the relationship-building skills. This book concentrates on these necessary skills.

Third, we wanted to write something on supervision that people would want to read. The books we have used in the past have always received mixed reviews by participants. Some said there was too much information and research to understand, whereas others said, "Where's the beef?" We hope this book will provide you with enough information to improve your skills in managing and leading people, and be easy to read as well. Although the reading is intended to be easy, building the skills and going through the associated growth process described in each chapter will be challenging. It will take hard work on your part.

We use the terms *supervisor* and *manager* interchangeably. Our reasoning for doing so is two-fold. First, we have found little consistency in how organizations decide whether someone is a manager or a supervisor. In one organization, a person with certain responsibilities may be called a supervisor, but in another organization, a person with the same responsibilities may be called a manager—or even a vice president. The second reason we overlap the terms is that we believe the people-related skills required by both supervisors and managers—and even vice presidents—are identical. The responsibilities may be significantly different, but the people-related skills are basically the same.

As we share our ideas, it is important to see this book for what it is: insight from two consultants on the skills needed to be a great supervisor or manager. We are the first to agree that the information will not work in every situation. You will have to adapt the material to meet your unique needs and situations. At the same time, we are also convinced that if managers and supervisors apply the skills we have described, they will eliminate about 90% of the consulting work done in most organizations!

The bottom line: The skills presented here will work, *if* you are willing to learn and then practice them. If you are willing to invest the reading time, as well as the skill-building practice on the job, we promise that you will be proud of the results. You and your employees will accomplish more . . . and everyone will gain more enjoyment from working together. We wish you success!

P.S. When you do a better job as a supervisor, you will also sleep better at night!

About the Authors

Peter Barron Stark specializes in leadership and management training (PBS & Associates, Inc.). For ten years, he owned and operated his own commercial printing company and was able to use these supervisory skills with his employees. Today, he is principal of his own management consulting firm, doing business with organizations throughout the United States and abroad and presenting over 250 seminars, speeches, and workshops annually. As an instructor at San Diego State University, he also shares these principles with students.

Peter has authored two other books: *Goal Setting: Creating Your Life's Dream and Turning It into a Reality* and *It's Negotiable: The How-to Handbook of Win/Win Tactics*. He has been published in *CPA Today* and *Vital Speeches of the Day*, and he writes his own quarterly newsletter, *The Manager's Advisor*.

Jane Flaherty is a Senior Consultant with PBS & Associates. She has over 25 years' experience designing and implementing organizational interventions for the public and private sector. Prior to joining PBS & Associates in 1994, she held positions of increasing responsibility with the Department of Defense Dependents Schools, ranging from classroom teacher to school principal. In addition to organizational development activities, she conducts hundreds of workshops and seminars annually.

Jane serves on the faculty at San Diego State University. She also works with a diverse client base that includes major and small to mid-size corporations, manufacturing firms, service organizations, and government and educational institutions.

Chapter 1

Understanding the Changing Role of Supervision

"Predicting the future is easy. It's trying to figure out what's going on now that's hard."

— Fritz R.S. Dressler

Each year the authors interview hundreds of people involved with organizations as large and diverse as the Department of Defense and as small as entrepreneurial start-up companies. Ranging in age from their early twenties to their late seventies, these interviewees provide insight into the methods used by a wide range of supervisors and managers.

Some supervisors have been truly inspirational; others admitted the need for improvement; and still others were in a state of denial, believing any and all problems were caused by someone else—namely, "the employees." A bewildered manager recently said in one of our seminars, "Did the whole world change and I didn't get it?" Simply put, yes, the whole world did change, and seasoned managers (those with 20 to 30 years of experience) unanimously agree on one thing: The role of the 21st century manager and the skills required to get the job done today are significantly different from the role of the supervisor/manager of the 1940s and 1950s. This chapter reviews some of the factors that contribute to this changing role.

Environmental and Economic Changes

One of the best ways to determine how the role of the supervisor has changed is to study how organizations are being impacted by changes in the environment and the economy.

1. *The most notable shift in our environment has been from an industrial and manufacturing-based society to an information and service-based society.* In 1980, the amount of information entering our society was doubling every ten years. In 1990, the amount of information entering society is doubling every two and one-half years! As we approach the year 2000, it is estimated that the amount of information will double every one and one-half years! With new information entering the workplace at this rate, it is virtually impossible for supervisors to keep current on all the topics affecting them and their employees.

2. *The rapid increase in information flow is causing jobs to become obsolete.* It has been estimated that 50% of the jobs being performed in 1991 did not exist in 1971. That rate of change is not slowing down. We can expect that by the year 2013 essentially all work will be "new." If information is doubling every one and one-half years, 90 percent of the information available to workers in 2013 will be created after 1993. Put another way, all of the knowledge utilized by workers in 1993 represents 10% of what will be available in 20 years.

Historically, the modern world evolved from the Industrial Revolution that began in 18th-century Europe. During the industrial period, the primary key to success and growth, resulting in prosperity, was the ability to efficiently distribute raw materials and products. A secondary key to success was the ability to manage large systems of production. Railroads, the internal combustion engine, interstate highways, and, later, aircraft and airports, eventually produced a global distribution network. The invention of the assembly line and, in the 20th century, the creation of management science enabled societies to produce large quantities of a product at great speed with increasing efficiency and at a low cost.

These enhanced productivity systems were first applied where people had existing work—on the farms. These technologies quickly afforded sufficient gains in productivity to enable workers to leave the farms. This increase in agricultural productivity closed the door on an agricultural-based society and opened the door to the Industrial Revolution. As these systems and techniques merged with manufacturing over a 200-year period, the mass production of goods and materials brought the United States and the world to new levels of wealth and prosperity.

To maximize the country's natural resources and its opportunities to build this massive industrial economy, the needed cities, harbors, railroads, and airports were created. In addition, our ideas about management, organization, education, and work itself were developed to support and maintain this industrial system.

3. *Our economy has shifted from a manufacturing base to a service base.* In 1955, according to an analysis done by Morgan Guaranty Trust Company, manufacturing produced some 30% of all U.S. goods. In 1985, this figure dropped to 21%. By the year 2000, it is expected to drop to 17%. As this happens, manufacturing will become less and less important to the economy as a mechanism for creating wealth. Although there will be fewer manufacturing jobs in 2000, these losses will be more than offset by net new jobs in the service sector.

Exhibit 1.1 illustrates how our economy and environment have evolved over the past 200 years.

Exhibit 1.1: Evolution of Economy and Environment

Factors	Agriculture	Industrial/ Manufacturing	Information/ Service
Dominant Technology	Plow	Machine	Computer
Goal	Survival	Material Wealth	Personal Growth
Output	Food	Goods	Information
Strategic Resource	Land	Capital	Knowledge
Organizational Form	Family	Corporation	Network/Teams
Primary Worker	Farmer	Laborer	Entrepreneur/ Intrapreneur
Nature of Production	Self	Mass	Individualized

4. *Global competition is changing the way we do business.* In the 1940s and 1950s, American-made products were symbolic of high quality. Today, we are struggling to regain our competitive edge. In the 1940s and 1950s, access to information and technology was limited. Presently, 80% of what

3

any organization produces can be equaled by other organizations in the world. Businesses can now choose to compete because access to the information, knowledge, raw materials, and technologies needed to do the core, repetitive tasks is available to anyone who wants it, often over the Internet. The remaining 20% of what any organization produces is based on people. Therefore, all organizations and countries will succeed or fail based on their ability to utilize the remaining 20% that is not available to the competition—their employees.

A byproduct of this global competition is the downsizing—or rightsizing—that took place in most larger-size organizations in the late 1980s and early 1990s. Working for a large organization like AT&T, IBM, Xerox, ITT, General Motors, or even the Department of Defense was once considered lifelong employment. This is no longer the case.

In 1991, General Motors, Chrysler, and Ford cut more than 40,000 North American automotive jobs. *Automotive News* said those jobs were not being replaced in any significant way by Japanese automakers in North America. For all its accomplishments, General Motors today is a humbled colossus, paying in part for what critics call an insulated and bloated management. In December of 1991, General Motors' 11th chairman, Robert Stempel, announced one of GM's most dramatic makeovers. In 1995, GM planned to close 21 manufacturing plants and cut back its workforce by an additional 74,000. A lengthy strike in 1998 crippled its production facilities and weakened GM's position even further.

General Motors is not alone. IBM has eliminated 100,000 jobs since 1986. Kodak initiated an early retirement plan that trimmed 6,000 of its workforce. In 1992, Xerox reduced its workforce by 2,500—20% of its white-collar jobs. AT&T has reduced its workforce by nearly 225,000 over a four-year period. Between 1990 and 1995, the Department of Defense made severe cuts in all its workforces, eliminating nearly half the number of military personnel stationed in Europe as the Cold War came to an end in the early 1990s.

John Stewart, a director of the consulting firm of McKinsey & Co., had this to say: "These jobs are not going to come back after the current recession, because a lot of companies are making fundamental changes in their structure and how they do business." At the height of the downsizing phenomena in 1991, the announced cutbacks of major corporations accelerated to 2,600 jobs each working day. In San Diego County, where the authors are based, over 16,000 jobs have vanished in the past several years from corporations such as Rohr, ITT, General Dynamics, NCR, and Honeywell.

5. *Environmental consciousness and practices are required.* It is virtually impossible to ignore the strong emphasis being placed on environmental consciousness. Corporations must comply with new environmental regulations every year. In 1991, new laws required that daily records be kept on the use of every chemical. The price for non-compliance is steep fines. Cities across the country are now providing separate bins to sort out newspapers, plastics, and aluminum products for recycling. Companies are proud to print their literature on recycled paper. Some organizations refuse to use Styrofoam cups. From all indications, this environmental consciousness will continue and intensify in the years to come.

6. *Technological advances are coming faster than ever before.* Technology is advancing so rapidly that it is difficult for even the experts to keep up. A computer specialist was asked, "How can consumers be sure that they are getting a 'state-of-the-art' computer?" The computer technician's interesting reply was, "If a computer has progressed enough for us to sell it on the retail market, it's already obsolete!" The computer has changed the way we do business. It is not uncommon in a $20 million organization to find limited clerical support personnel. It is also increasingly more common to find a computer on the desk of every executive.

   Other miracle advancements significantly changing the way we do business are the fax machine, the cellular phone, e-mail, pagers, networked computer systems, and the Internet. When the fax machine made its debut in the mid-1980s, it became possible to receive documents anywhere in the world in a matter of moments. This has caused us to redefine our concept of time. Delivering a proposal to a firm 3,000 miles away used to take days. Today, it takes place almost instantly. The cellular phone now makes it possible to be in constant phone communication with anyone, just about anywhere. Advances in technology allow almost instant ability to communicate with anyone in the organization via e-mail, no matter how remote the location. Access to the Internet has leveled the playing field by giving anyone with a computer and a modem a powerful tool to conduct research, advertise products, and stay current with the latest in just about anything!

7. *Laws, laws, and more legal stuff.* Legal issues are an ongoing and growing concern for organizations. From the employee lawsuits regarding workplace harassment and equal opportunity to laws that dictate the particulars for how we do business, the legal process has affected almost everyone. As organizations struggle to interpret the intent and impact of laws governing

5

the workplace, policies have changed considerably. In a recent sexual harassment briefing we were conducting for a client, one participant said, "Is it safe to say anything at work?"

Workforce Composition Changes

In addition to environmental and economic changes, our workforce has also dramatically changed. Several major trends have contributed to this.

1. *In the last fifty years, the most significant change in our workforce has been the number of women on the job.* In the 1950s, less than 35% of American women worked outside the home. In 1960, less than 40% of them did. The social changes during the late 1960s and early 1970s, coupled with genuine financial necessity, allowed women to gain a foothold in the business world. This entry into business essentially redefined their role in paid employment as the norm, rather than the exception. By 1985, 61% of all married women with children were part of the labor force—more than twice the 1960 rate of 28%. This trend is continuing. Between 1985 and the year 2000, white males, who only a generation ago made up the dominant segment of the workforce, will comprise only 15% of the net additions to the workforce. The majority of new entrants will be women and minorities. The Department of Labor estimates that by the year 2000, about 48% of the workforce will be female.

   Women are still heavily concentrated in lower paying occupations, but they have made substantial progress in obtaining jobs in the managerial and professional specialties. According to the U.S. Department of Labor Women's Bureau, in 1984 women held 33.6% of managerial and executive positions and nearly half (48.5%) of all jobs in the professional occupations. By 1994 they held 48.1% of managerial and executive positions and accounted for over half, 52.8%, of all workers employed in professional occupations. By the year 2000, 61% of all American women will be employed. In 1998, women working full time still earn only 76.4 cents for every dollar earned by the average working man. Even in traditionally female occupations where women outnumber men, women still earn less than men.

   Within Fortune 500 companies and other major institutions, women are still in the lower echelons. According to the Administrative Management Society, women comprised over 60% of all white-collar workers in 1986. However, they only represented 10% of those persons classified as managers and held only 2% of all top-level executive positions.

Recently, however, women have been making significant progress and have actually fared better than men in the workplace. Between 1980 and 1985, for example, employment rates for women grew at an average of 2.4% a year, while the same rates for men increased at less than 1.0%. During the same period, women saw their incomes rise at an average rate of 5.6%, while men watched theirs decline by 0.7%.

2. *The average age of the workforce is increasing.* Between now and the year 2000, the number of workers between the ages of 35 and 54 will increase by more than 25 million, and the median age for employed Americans will rise to 45 years, up from 36 years in 1987. By the year 2005, more than 15% of the workforce will be over age 55. Never before has such a large segment of our workforce been so near to retirement age.

3. *The number of available workers is decreasing.* Today many employers are finding themselves in the unaccustomed position of scrambling for workers. Between now and the year 2000, the number of young workers aged 16 to 24 will drop by almost two million, or 8%. This decline is already affecting many businesses. Companies in the service industries, such as fast-food places and hotels, are experiencing increasing difficulty in hiring and retaining employees. To take up some of the slack, many fast-food chains have begun campaigns to hire senior citizens. Companies in the high-tech industries are experiencing major shortages of engineers and have turned to offering, in addition to attractive salaries, a whole range of incentives and benefits designed to attract and retain qualified employees. Many engineers in these fields know they are a valuable asset and, in some cases, jump ship as soon as the next highest bidder is willing to offer more. Recently, we have heard of cases where engineers have retained agents to locate positions and negotiate salaries for them!

4. *The number of minorities in the workplace will continue to increase.* By the year 2000, members of American minority groups—especially African-Americans and Hispanics—will be less of a minority in the workforce than ever before. According to a 1993 report of the U.S. Bureau of Labor Statistics, by the end of this century, African-Americans will make up over 12% of the total workforce; Hispanics will account for 10%, and Asians another 4%. Over the next several years, almost one-third of all new entrants into the labor force will be minorities—twice their current share. In California, it is estimated that by the year 2005, more than 50% of the population will be comprised of people of color who as a group will be speaking more than 80 languages. Finally, 80% of the net labor force growth will be white women, people of color, and immigrants.

5. *The education gap is widening.* The United States currently has the most highly educated workforce in its history. More people are completing high school, going to college, and entering continuing education programs. In 1964, 45.1% of workers had high school diplomas. As recently as the late 1980s, 86% of 25–29 year olds had high school diplomas. Never before have more people in the workforce attended college. Estimates are that by the year 2000, at least half of our workforce will have some college education.

On the other hand, the number of less-educated people in the workplace is increasing, as is the number of people who are considered functionally illiterate. While it is difficult to accurately measure illiteracy, estimates suggest that approximately 20 million people are illiterate. Approximately 25% of those who graduate from high school cannot read past the eighth-grade level. In a recently released workplace survey taken by two management professors at Old Dominion University in Norfolk, Virginia, 63.5% of the 1,328 firms responding said they have workers who lack basic skills—the ability to read, write, and comprehend English—needed to perform the required and essential tasks.

In today's high-tech workplace, college education is not always a requirement for a high paying job. Individuals with specific technical or vocational training are in high demand, helping organizations with all aspects of the technology required to conduct business in today's fast-paced, interconnected world. In the Southern California area, qualified applicants can expect a starting salary in the range of $28,000 to $42,000, with no college education required.

6. *Workers are packing up and going.* Fifty years ago, packing up your family and moving was a big deal. In the 1940s and 1950s, changing jobs was unusual. Statistics tell us our parents probably had only two or three distinct careers. We will probably have five to six. Our children will probably have eight to ten different careers, six of which have not even been conceived yet! Today, because of our transportation systems, it is not uncommon for a worker to move from one state to another or one job to another because of better opportunities elsewhere.

These workforce trends make it even more difficult to be a successful supervisor. Aside from getting the job done, other issues arise: a worker who is older than the supervisor, a worker who does not understand English or does not read, a worker who has more formal education than the manager, and co-workers who encounter cultural conflicts. Perhaps most significantly of all, there are many men still unsure about how to relate to women in the working environment.

Changing Workforce Values

One of the most striking ways to study how the role of the supervisor has changed over the last 50 years is to look at the values of the workers they supervise. A list of typical work values in the 1940s and 1950s is illustrated in Exhibit 1.2, as well as some of the critical values of today's workforce. What a contrast!

Looking at the two lists of values, it becomes clear that today's worker is no longer happy to just have a job. Today's workers want work to be meaningful and fun, and want to be recognized for their contributions. This need for job fulfillment is expressed not only by workers, but by supervisors and managers themselves. Occasionally, we hear disgruntled managers say, "Workers today have no values!" Typically, the manager, a Baby Boomer who worked long, hard hours to get where he or she is today, has difficulty understanding the priorities of Generation X, which include the need to be recognized, workplace flexibility, equality among team members, and an employer who recognizes the employee's need to have a balanced life. Simply put, employees born between 1960 and 1980 who are now in or just entering the workforce have very different values than the previous generation.

Exhibit 1.2: Values of the Workforce/Past and Present

Values of the 1940s–1950s Workforce	Values of Today's Workforce
Family	*Benefits*
Good craftsmanship	*Concern for health*
Happy to have a job	*Education*
Job stability	*Flexible schedule*
Loyalty to boss	*High concern for self*
Loyalty to company	*Input appreciated*
Patriotism	*Interesting work*
Savings account	*Need for time off*
Technical ability	*Open communication*
	Opportunity to advance
	Personal growth
	Recognition

While there may be a tendency on the part of the manager to discount these values as being "soft," self-serving, or not loyal to the employer, taking a quick look at the facts will help us understand why today's workers are bringing with them a very different set of values.

First, we jokingly say employees today listen to radio station "W.I.I.F.M." or, "What's in it for me?" Workers are keenly interested in how much you pay and what benefits you offer. They see themselves as providing you, the employer, with a needed commodity, and want to be fairly paid for what they offer. Some harsh economic facts are driving Generation X's financial concerns. According to Claire Raines in her 1997 book, *Beyond Generation X*, the following conditions are faced by young employees today:

- Poverty among "twenty-somethings" has increased by 50% since the mid-1970s.
- In the 1950s, young homeowners could make the monthly mortgage payment by using 14% of their income. Today it takes 40%.
- Americans work an average of one month per year more than they did ten years ago, yet real wages have steadily declined since 1973.
- Home ownership may be unrealistic for many members of Generation X. The median price of a home (adjusted for inflation) has increased 78% in the last 30 years.
- In the 1960s, one out of ten college graduates took a job that didn't require a degree. Over the next 15 years, one in three graduates will have to settle for jobs that don't match their credentials.
- Fortune 500 companies are laying off workers at an unprecedented pace. The trend is expected to worsen in the next century.

In addition to financial challenges, younger employees look to the future they will be inheriting and see pollution, crime, racial tension, and AIDS, leading to a sense of powerlessness. Experienced managers often see these skeptical employees as "jaded" and note that they don't share the same sense of optimism that the manager did when he or she started working.

Perhaps one of the most difficult issues for today's manager, though, is this generation's lack of respect for authority and limited interest in titles. This generation was the first to grow up, under the guidance of Dr. Spock, in an egalitarian home atmosphere. Both parent and child had rights and provided input into family affairs. Further, this was the first generation that spent long hours on their own, after school, waiting for parents to return home after work. The need to fend for themselves has resulted in more self-reliant, autonomous employees.

Based on these values, what skills did it take for a supervisor in the 1940s and 1950s to effectively manage his or her workers? If the worker was loyal to the boss, loyal to the company, and thankful to have a job, the skills needed to manage might look like those outlined in Exhibit 1.3. Based on today's values, let's review the skills needed to be a successful manager in today's world.

Exhibit 1.3: Skills to Manage Employees/Past and Present

Skills Needed: 1940s–1950s Supervisor	Skills Needed: Today's Supervisor
Ability to control	Clarifying expectations
Delegation	Coaching and counseling
Directive	Communication
Problem solving	Confidence
Strong authority figure	Consulting
Technical expertise	Creativity
	Delegating
	Enabling
	Empowering
	Leadership
	Listening
	Mentoring
	Motivating
	Negotiating
	Organizing
	Problem solving
	Questioning
	Team building

How is that for a list of what is required for supervisors to do their jobs effectively? One seminar participant stated, "You almost need to be a psychologist to get the job done." In many ways, he is right. Supervising today is much more difficult than it was back in the 1940s and 1950s. Technical expertise is still required of supervisors, just as it was 50 years ago. But today, being technically sound is no longer enough if one wants to be a successful supervisor.

Ten years ago we could look at the list of what today's workers want and agree that it would be nice if we could provide a work environment like that. We might even agree that it would be theoretically the right thing to do. Today, however, we are faced with a new reality: If you are managing a business where the majority of your front-line employees are members of Generation X, your business will not be successful and may not even survive *unless* you manage them well. Given the changing values younger employees bring with them to the workplace and the fact that it has become increasingly more difficult to hire qualified employees in the late 1990s (and incredibly expensive to replace them when they leave), it makes sense that effectively managing the workers of today is not an option. It is essential.

The challenge for all supervisors today is to gain the attention, trust, enthusiasm, and commitment of their employees. It is no longer adequate to assemble, organize, and manage capital, raw materials, and a workforce within a tightly defined system of production. What is required is the leadership skill to create work environments of creativity, innovation, and enthusiasm so that once in, our employees are committed and loyal, and stay with us. In the following chapters, we will discuss the skills that help build relationships, encourage motivated employees, and foster a creative environment. The remaining chapters are devoted to enhancing your skills toward becoming a confident, successful leader in today's environment.

Chapter 2

Building Your Confidence and Self-Esteem

"Our own attitudes have far more to do with how happy we are than do any external circumstances."

— *Dr. Nathaniel Branden*

Since most managers and supervisors have not had much training or practice in people skills, it is not uncommon to find supervisors with "people problems." When these people problems arise and the problems are not easily solved, the supervisor may begin to question if he or she has what it takes to accomplish the job. Some feel completely unprepared for the job of supervision. It is also common to hear lead people in organizations say that they do not want to become a supervisor because of the tough problems supervisors have to tackle. When we begin to question our ability to be a good supervisor, our self-esteem—how we feel about ourselves—begins to fade.

Being a great supervisor starts with *you*. The way you feel and see yourself affects every aspect of your role as a leader. William James, the great philosopher and psychologist, once observed that the greatest discovery of our age has been that by changing the inner aspects of our thinking, we can change the outer aspects of our life. As another sage puts it, "We aren't what we think we are, but what we think, we are!" The higher your self-esteem, the better your chances are of being a great supervisor and a great leader. This chapter discusses the importance of self-esteem and what you can do to raise your self-esteem to an even higher level.

As a first step to enhancing self-esteem, we can begin with a self-assessment. This is an opportunity for you to take an honest look at yourself and assess how you feel about your abilities as a supervisor. In which aspects of supervision do you have a high degree of confidence? In which aspects are you unsure or feel a lack of confidence? The Self-Esteem Assessment in Exhibit 2.1 gives you a starting point to determine your strengths as a supervisor and leader, and provides you with a springboard for setting goals and improving skills.

Exhibit 2.1: Assessment Tool for Self-Esteem

Self-Esteem Assessment

On a scale of 1 to 10 (10 being the highest confidence score, 5 being an average confidence score, and 1 being the lowest or no-confidence score), rate how you feel about yourself in each of the 16 areas. Use any number between 1 and 10 to accurately describe your feelings. For example, if you feel just slightly above average on your communication skills as a supervisor, you might rate them as a 6, but if you feel more confident, rate them as an 8.

As a supervisor, I feel the following levels of confidence in each category, ranging from 1 to 10, 10 being the highest level of confidence.

1. _____ My relationship with people who report to me.
2. _____ My relationship with my boss.
3. _____ My verbal communication skills.
4. _____ My written communication skills.
5. _____ My technical skills to get the job done.
6. _____ My ability to motivate others.
7. _____ My ability to solve problems in my department as they arise.
8. _____ My ability to coach and counsel people so they improve their performance.
9. _____ My relationships with co-workers.
10. _____ My ability to effectively organize my tasks and my work area.
11. _____ My ability to accomplish my organizational goals.
12. _____ My ability as a leader.
13. _____ Others' level of trust in me.
14. _____ My level of trust in my employees.
15. _____ My ability to interview and hire the right people.
16. _____ My ability to effectively delegate tasks and responsibilities.

Next, identify your top three areas of strength and your three areas for improvement.

Areas of Strength	Areas for Improvement
1.	*1.*
2.	*2.*
3.	*3.*

What Is Self-Esteem?

Self esteem is quite simply how you *feel* about yourself. How we feel about ourselves critically influences virtually every aspect of our lives. Our self-esteem influences everything from the way we function at work and our personal relationships and role as parents to what we accomplish in life. Every response we make in life, every goal we set, is shaped by who and what we think we are. Thus, self-esteem is the major key to our success and our failure, and is key to the level of our accomplishment as a supervisor or leader.

Nathaniel Branden, in his classic book *How to Raise Your Self-Esteem*, describes our self-concept as who and what we consciously and subconsciously think we are—our physical and psychological traits, our assets and liabilities, and, above all, our self-esteem. Our self-esteem is the evaluating component of our self-concept: whether we like or do not like ourselves, whether we feel good or bad about ourselves. Another way to describe this evaluating component of our self-esteem is *the way we feel about ourselves*.

As you look around at your fellow human beings, you will find it hard to ignore the reality that very few people are happy and fulfilled and leading purposeful lives. Many seem unable to cope with their problems and the circumstances of daily living. The majority, settling for the average, have resigned themselves to living a life of mediocrity. As a result, feelings of inadequacy cause them to blame society, people, circumstances, and surrounding conditions for their failures and disappointments. On the other hand, people with high self-esteem lead more fulfilling lives, expect the best, and accept full responsibility for their lives.

Self-esteem has two components: (1) a feeling of personal competence and *(2) a feeling of personal worth*. In other words, self-esteem is the sum of our self-confidence and self-respect. Self-esteem, on whatever level, is an intimate experience; it resides in the core of our being. It is what you think and feel about yourself, not how someone else thinks or judges you. The tragedy is that so many people look for self-confidence and self-respect everywhere *except* within themselves, and so they fail in their search. Unless you perceive your own true worth as a person or supervisor, you cannot come close to achieving high self-esteem. Only to the degree that you can truly acknowledge your own unique importance will you be able to free yourself from self-imposed limitations.

Great teachers and leaders throughout time have come to the same conclusion: You cannot look to someone outside yourself to solve your problems. If we are to increase our self-esteem, we will have to increase the behaviors in our life that enhance our self-confidence and self-worth. As Eleanor Roosevelt said, "Nobody can make you feel inferior without your consent."

To have high self-esteem is to feel confidently appropriate to life—that is, competent and worthy in the sense that you can master what you set out to accomplish. To grow in self-esteem is to grow in the conviction that one is competent to live and is also worthy of happiness. As a supervisor, this means you are competent at getting the job done and are worthy of having the position of responsibility. With these feelings, you can face life with greater confidence and optimism. This confidence will help you to reach your goals and to experience fulfillment. As you grow in self-esteem, you will expand your capacity for happiness and increase the possibility of setting and achieving higher goals.

The Cycle of Self-Esteem

When we are born, it is the only time in our life that we truly have a blank slate in terms of self-esteem. From our first day in the world, we begin to form self-esteem. We receive information from our parents and significant others that begins to shape how we feel about ourselves. Whether high or low, positive or negative, we develop feelings about ourselves that are reinforced by others.

How this self-esteem helps or hinders us internally is by self-talk. Every thought we think is conveyed by communicating with ourselves in words. Try to describe your positive attributes without using words. It is difficult to think a thought without using words.

It is this self-talk that forms the basis for how we communicate with the outer world. Our inner thoughts, whether positive or negative, impact our communication with others. It is easy to judge how people feel about themselves by listening to the words they use to express themselves. It is your communication with others that determines how they respond to you. As a supervisor or manager, if you lack confidence in your ability to be an effective leader of your team, it is almost certain your followers will also sense your lack of confidence. It will

16

affect every aspect of your relationship with your followers. The chances are that their respect for you will dwindle and their productivity and motivation may decline as well. One thing is absolutely certain: Supervisors and managers with low self-esteem have more problems with their workforces than supervisors and managers with high self-esteem.

The last part of this cycle, as illustrated in Exhibit 2.2, is the way that others respond to your verbal and nonverbal communication and how these responses reinforce your self-esteem. Supervisors and managers with high self-esteem communicate that fact to others and others respond to them in a congruent manner. People with low self-esteem manifest the opposite traits in the way others relate to them. We have all met supervisors who seem to be continually "dumped on." It is possible that they are sending out signals that generate this negative response from others.

If we are going to enhance our self-esteem, we must realize that the process starts with our own thoughts. As we change our self-talk and our thinking, we will change the way we feel about ourselves and how we communicate with others. This, in turn, will change the way others respond to us. Positive communication from others tends to reinforce positive self-esteem. It can be a positive cycle or a vicious cycle. Fortunately, the cycle starts with us!

What Contributes to Self-Esteem?

There are six common contributors to our self-esteem:

1. *The most dynamic of the contributors are the ideas, beliefs, and values that we have accepted from our parents.* Because most adults have not concentrated on the importance of having high self-esteem, their negative concepts, values, and beliefs are passed on like a contagious disease to their children through attitudes, actions, and reactions. If parents feel inadequate and inferior in any sense, we, as children, will inherit those same feelings of inadequacy. On the other hand, parents who value high self-esteem pass on a great gift of confidence and self-esteem to their children.

    In defense of all our parents, they did the best job they knew how or were capable of doing. Now, we must do everything in our power to put our lives on the positive self-esteem track and not put the blame on our parents or anyone else. At this point, blaming does not help to improve one's self-esteem. It is just wasted energy that should be spent improving ourselves.

2. *A second leading contributor to our self-esteem comes from the significant others in our lives.* Whether they are teachers, bosses, lovers, children,

Exhibit 2.2: Cycle of Self-Esteem

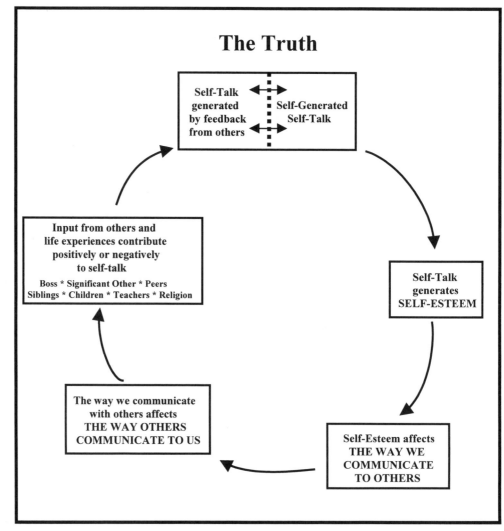

The Truth

Self-Talk generated by feedback from others ⟷ Self-Generated Self-Talk

Input from others and life experiences contribute positively or negatively to self-talk
Boss * Significant Other * Peers
Siblings * Children * Teachers * Religion

Self-Talk generates SELF-ESTEEM

The way we communicate with others affects THE WAY OTHERS COMMUNICATE TO US

Self-Esteem affects THE WAY WE COMMUNICATE TO OTHERS

Copyright: PBS & Associates, Inc.

peers, or people we hold in high regard, our self-esteem is molded by how these people act and react toward us.

We can all think of a teacher, boss, coach, parent, or friend whose actions or behaviors had an impact on how we felt about ourselves. Whether it was our ability to play the piano or a sport or how well we did in school, others' actions toward us impact us. Here's one example:

"I remember, as if it were yesterday, how my eighth-grade math teacher told me in front of all my classmates that she did not think I had the mental capability to tackle ninth-grade algebra. I listened to Miss Carroll and took what was called Business Math. It was full of students who made the kids in the algebra class look like geniuses. Although it put me a year behind my class for the rest of my junior and senior high career, I learned all sorts of practical skills like balancing a checkbook, calculating interest rates, and how to run a business profitably. Like many reflections in life, it was devastating at the time, but a blessing in disguise."

If we are in a position to influence others (i.e., teachers, supervisors, or managers), we will influence those who look to us for leadership and inspiration. Our employees will intuitively sense any lack of self-worth and inevitably begin to amplify what they identify and associate with us.

As a leader, you have the ability to make your workforce feel on top of the world—or you can make them feel incredibly inadequate. We have seen people with high self-esteem totally devastated by a boss. Supervisors and managers with low self-esteem are usually difficult people to work with and for. They find it much easier to enhance their own low self-esteem by tearing down others. Low self-esteem managers will try to make others feel less intelligent, less motivated, and less competent in an effort to make themselves look better. Working for this type of boss is a painful experience. There is no excuse for treating someone with a lack of dignity or respect. High self-esteem managers treat everyone with dignity and respect.

3. *A third contributor to our self-esteem is the habitual comparison of ourselves to others.* Most forms of competition are hostile. They may seem friendly on the surface, but the prime motivation is to be or do "better than" the next person. We usually compete with others only when we are unsure of ourselves and our abilities. Competitive people feel that others are better than they are and they set out to prove otherwise. They struggle to surpass those they feel are superior.

People with high self-esteem, on the other hand, do not feel the need to compete. They do not need to look and see what others are doing and do not have the need to be "better than" the next person. Recognizing their capabilities for what they are, they strive for excellence in their own lives. Their only competition is with themselves—to achieve greater personal growth. The key is to set your own standards. This example from one of the authors illustrates how to set your own standards:

"In 1990, I applied for professional speaker accreditation from Toastmasters International. Toastmasters is a worldwide organization that promotes public speaking and communication skills. Out of Toastmasters' 180,000 members, only 40 people had ever been awarded the accreditation. In 1986, I tried for the accreditation but did not make the final cut when I gave my speech at the International Convention. In 1990, I went about the process differently. I set a goal not to win the accreditation, but to give the best speech I could possibly give. The result was that I significantly reduced my nervousness before the convention presentation because I was only concerned with my own performance. The byproduct of this inner goal was that I also was awarded the accreditation."

4. *A fourth contributor to our self-esteem is our religious or spiritual upbringing and teaching.* Depending on the household you were brought up in and the house of worship you attend, religion can be a very positive influence or you may carry with you feelings of guilt, worry, and shame. People with high self-esteem use their spiritual and religious teachings to serve them in a positive way.

5. *A fifth contributor to self-esteem is setting realistic goals.* In working with people who have low self-esteem, we notice a tendency to set either very high goals or to set no goals. Dr. David McClelland, a Harvard researcher, shows that even high achievers set only moderate goals, just out of their reach. When they achieve them, it reinforces their positive self-esteem. On the other hand, when your goals are set unrealistically high and you do not achieve them, it reinforces negative self-esteem. A subsidiary effect of unrealistic goals is that people with low self-esteem will eventually stop setting goals. When they stop setting goals, they slowly begin to lose the feeling of mastery over their environment, and this once again reinforces a negative "I failed" attitude. People with high self-esteem set realistic and attainable goals.

6. *The sixth, and last, contributor to our self-esteem is society.* We live in a society where most people are quick to tell you what you cannot do, rather than encouraging you to take your success to even greater heights. People will tell you about your faults and weaknesses before they will expound upon your strengths. When entrepreneurs start their own business, they can

focus on negative thoughts and horror stories about being an entrepreneur, such as the belief that eight out of ten new businesses fail and that the chances of making it past the three-year mark are slim. Or they can choose to focus on success stories, such as those of Microsoft, Dell Computer, and Starbucks Coffee.

High-self-esteem people associate themselves with other positive people. People with high self-esteem look at the positive side of life and do not have a need to put others down.

What Are the Benefits of High Self-Esteem?

If you have ever been in a relationship with someone who has poor self-esteem, you know that life can be very difficult for you and the other person. Whether it is your boss, friend, lover, or significant other, the effect of low self-esteem has deep roots. With poor self-esteem, life can be difficult at its best. Fortunately, we can improve our self-esteem. If you are willing to take the time to work at developing your self-esteem, there are many benefits.

1. *You will feel happier about life.* When you feel more positive about yourself, it is only natural that you will be able to better cope with life and its interesting twists and turns. When you have high self-esteem, you can maintain an "I can do it" or "I can get through it" type of attitude. These are the people who live by Reverend Robert Schuller's words, "Tough times never last, but tough people do."

2. *You will be more motivated and ambitious.* People with high self-esteem tend to set more goals and seem to accomplish more with their lives. These same people have the feeling that they make a difference in their world. Whether it be their work environment, their families, or their civic accomplishments, people with high self-esteem know they make a positive difference.

3. *You will have better relationships.* When you have high self-esteem, you tend to treat others better. You can do this easily because you feel good about yourself. When you treat others better, they will treat you better in return. This relates back to the cycle of self-esteem mentioned earlier. When you have high self-esteem, it dictates what relationships you will even enter into. If you are treated poorly by someone, your self-esteem thermostat will tell you that you deserve to be treated better and you will look elsewhere for your rewards.

4. *You will live life more humorously.* Have you ever had an incident in your life that devastated you? Maybe it was a relationship that soured, an embarrassing situation, or a task that you did not perform as well as you would have liked. Usually, when one of these situations occurs, we feel terrible. We feel like we failed! Then, as time passes by, we slowly start to see the situation as humorous. In fact, years later, we can sit around the dinner table and share the entire incident in the form of a joke. The benefit of having high self-esteem is that you have the ability to see the humor sooner.

5. *You will be more open to change and risk-taking.* Whether it is new ideas, situations, opportunities, or challenges, when you have high self-esteem, you are more willing to experience new things. Anything new requires learning. Along with learning comes mistakes. People with high self-esteem look at mistakes as learning and use this learning to grow. Sir Thomas Watson of IBM once said, "If you want to succeed, double your failure rate!"

6. *You will be more comfortable giving and receiving compliments.* When paying someone a compliment, how many times have you heard the reply, "Oh, it was nothing" or "It's just an old thing I threw on"? When someone downplays a compliment, the person who gave the compliment is not rewarded. By belittling the response, the person receiving the compliment has invalidated the other person. People with high self-esteem find it easy to say either a simple "Thank you" to compliments or a sentence of "Thank you, I appreciate your compliment." With this type of response, the complimenter will feel comfortable giving compliments again. People with high self-esteem find it very easy to give compliments. By giving others compliments, others like them better and this reinforces their growing sense of self-esteem.

7. *You will be more open to criticism.* Supervisors with low self-esteem do not have the ability to listen or accept feedback from their employees. When you have high self-esteem, you will find it easier to accept feedback from others. You recognize their responses as learning experiences and incorporate what you learn into making yourself a better person. People with low self-esteem spend their time defending their actions, blaming others, and making excuses about why things have to be the way they are.

8. *You will be better able to think for yourself.* Supervisors with high self-esteem are able to incorporate the opinions of others, assimilate the information, and form their own definite feelings, opinions, and positions. With high self-esteem, you have a strong sense of what is right and wrong and

that makes your decision making an easier process. With strong self-esteem, you will find it easier to be more assertive and stick up for what you believe is right.

9. *You will not need constant approval and recognition from others.* People with low self-esteem feel a stronger need to do and say things that will win the approval of others. Some people spend their entire lives trying to win the approval and support of others. Others stay in bad relationships far too long. They are afraid to take bold steps and be on their own, for fear of what the change may bring.

10. *You will have the ability to accept people, including yourself, as they are, not as you would like them to be.* When you have high self-esteem, you have the ability to walk in the other person's moccasins. With high self-esteem, you will not feel a strong need to change your life for another person's approval. You will also be less inclined to try to change others.

Twenty Steps to Higher Self-Esteem

In the preceding pages, we learned about self-esteem—what it is and how we develop it—and about the benefits of obtaining high self-esteem. Now let's look at what we can do to raise our self-esteem. There are hundreds of little things you can do on a daily basis that will enhance your self-esteem.

What follows are twenty of our most important suggestions for supervisors. Do not be concerned with trying all twenty at the same time. We recommend that you write each of these suggestions on an individual 3" × 5" card and work on only one or two points each week. After you have concentrated on each point for a period of four to six weeks, that specific point will begin to become a part of your life. In other words, you will have replaced the self-defeating habits of your past with these good habits. The result is a higher degree of self-esteem that will permeate and penetrate your entire life.

1. *Live for today.* One phrase we'd like to cut from the English language is "if only." "If only" I could get one more promotion, could make a certain income, could close a certain sale, could become a husband or a father. "If only" I could afford a bigger house or a fancier car, "if only" my boss would get off my back, "if only" I could motivate this one employee . . . *then* I would really be happy.

   It is important to have a purpose, to set goals, and to strive for future success. But it is equally important to be happy with your life right now. Do not put your self-worth and self-confidence out of reach until some future date. Most people learn only too late that the quest is irrational; the longing will always be for "something more." Focus on what is good right now. Each day ask yourself, "What am I thankful for?" and "What can I do *today* for myself?"

2. *Set goals.* In order to gain mastery over your environment, it is important that you be able to accomplish the things in life that you feel are important. Setting and achieving predetermined goals is one of the most important roads to travel if you are going to increase your self-esteem. Setting goals is intimately associated with living actively. It is through actions that an attitude of self-responsibility is developed. Ask yourself, "What actions can I take to increase my self-esteem or advance my career, investments, and relationships?" "What actions will bring me closer to my goals?" When you set goals, you will realize you do have control in your life, you will be more motivated, and you will be proud of your accomplishments.

3. *Associate with others who have high self-esteem.* You will encounter negative people who will always look at the downside or point out the negative in any situation. Some will even purposely try to drag you down. When you associate with other individuals who have high self-esteem, you will reap the benefits they have to offer. They tend to be happier with life and deal easier with change and adversity, and will offer you support and unequaled encouragement. Choose your friends and associates wisely.

4. *Dress and look your best always.* You can tell a lot about how a person feels by looking at the way he or she dresses. We are not suggesting that you always wear a fashionable suit to work. We are suggesting that you take the time to dress and groom appropriately so you feel good about how you look. People respond to us, in part, by our appearance. It goes back to the vicious cycle of self-esteem. By feeling good about your appearance, you send a message to others that you care and like yourself. The response from others will reinforce these feelings. How you look on the outside deeply affects how you feel on the inside.

5. *Set your own standards.* By setting internal standards, you will be comparing you to you. This means we have to believe in our own uniqueness. When we appreciate the true nature of self-esteem, we see that it is not competitive or comparative. Genuine self-esteem is not expressed by being better than others or diminishing others so we can elevate ourselves. It is developed by setting personal goals, challenging ourselves, and feeling proud of our accomplishments. You decide what standards are important to you.

6. *Be honest with yourself.* Unfortunately, the appropriate use of self-honesty is not automatic; rather, it is an active choice. How we use our consciousness, the honesty of our relationship to reality, and the level of our personal integrity will influence our self-esteem. If you choose to fake the reality of who you are, you will mislead others, as well as yourself. You may do so because you feel or believe that who you are is not acceptable. You value a delusion in someone else's mind above your own knowledge of the truth. The penalty is that you go through life with the frustrated sense of being an impostor. This means, among other things, that you sentence yourself to the anxiety of wondering when you will be found out. The lies most devastating to our self-esteem are not so much the lies we tell as the lies we live. Good self-esteem demands congruence—which means that the self within and the self projected to the world must be in accord.

Remember that self-esteem is not determined solely by worldly success, physical appearance, popularity, or any other value not directly under our control. Rather, it is a function of our rationality, honesty, and integrity, all operations of the mind for which we are responsible. Be honest with yourself. Acknowledge your special talents and gifts. Be aware of your faults or weaknesses and decide what and how you want to improve.

7. *Look people in the eye.* Before you can look others in the eye, you need to be able to look yourself in the eye. When you look into a mirror, you need to feel good about *you*. Most people will tell you that they like people better who are able to look at them eyeball-to-eyeball. Research has shown that people who look others in the eye are perceived as more honest, trustworthy, and credible. Those three adjectives are valuable to anyone.

8. *Volunteer your name first.* Whether you are introducing yourself or answering the telephone, you tell a lot about yourself by volunteering your name first in a conversation. You are telling others you have self-confidence and self-respect, and are proud of who you are. Others, in turn, will respond to you with a higher level of respect.

9. *Take full responsibility for your life.* Men and women who enjoy high self-esteem have an active orientation to life, rather than a passive one. They take full responsibility for the attainment of their goals. They ask the questions, "Where do I want to be?" and "How do I get there?" They do not wait for others to fulfill their wants and dreams. Self-responsibility is indispensable to good self-esteem. Avoiding self-responsibility victimizes us in our own lives. It leaves us helpless. We give power to everyone except ourselves. When we are frustrated, we look for someone to blame; we find oth-

ers are at fault for our unhappiness. In contrast, the appreciation of self-responsibility can be an exhilarating and empowering experience. It places our lives back into our own hands. In short, people with high self-esteem take responsibility for their own existence.

10. *Treat everyone you meet with dignity and respect.* From the president of your corporation to the janitor who cleans your office, from your significant other to the person who waits on your table when you eat out, treat everyone with dignity and respect. With this attitude, people will go out of their way to help you. Friendships are easier to attain and you will find most people will like you better. As a side benefit, you will never have to worry about offending the wrong person. Being liked by others once again enhances our self-esteem.

11. *Think for yourself.* Often what people call "thinking" is merely recycling the opinions of others, not true thinking. Thinking independently—about our work, our relationships, the values that will guide our lives—is part of what is meant by living consciously. Often, you will find yourself bowing to the wishes of others. It takes a conscious effort on your part to think through the situation, form an opinion, and then steadfastly execute your opinion.

12. *Develop your imagination.* The starting point of all change is when we begin to change our imagination, which has been limiting our awareness. It is possible to do this because we make our own world. Creating higher self-esteem begins in our subconscious mind and imagination. As Professor William James pointed out, ". . . it begins with changing the inner aspects of our thinking." We know from experience that an outward change will come after we change from within. By changing our imagination, we change our awareness and, therefore, our reactions to people, circumstances, and conditions.

13. *Improve your communication skills.* Communication is the tool that connects us to others. Clearly expressing your ideas allows you to be understood. Listening allows you to grow, learn, and open up to other people and ideas. Communication is the glue that binds friendships, marriages, and successful relationships at work.

There are hundreds of available ways to improve your communication skills: books, tapes, seminars, Toastmasters, etc. Find one and take some time to improve your ability to connect with others. You will see that as your confidence in your communication skills improves, so will your self-esteem.

14. *Remember, all successful people have experienced failure.* Most people who have accomplished anything great have experienced many failures. The difference is that these successful people view failure differently than most. They use the failure as a learning experience and benefit from it. Dr. Warren Bennis, author of the book *Leaders, The Strategies for Taking Charge*, describes how all the great leaders he interviewed had at least one devastating experience in their lives. Gail Sheehy, in her book *Pathfinders*, describes the same phenomena. The difference in the people these two authors describe is the way each viewed the failure in their lives. They viewed it as a learning experience.

    Thomas Edison failed 10,000 times to get the incandescent light to burn; Ty Cobb, the all-time base stealer in major league baseball, was tagged out more than any other player in the history of the game; Babe Ruth holds the all-time strikeout record; Henry Ford was broke at the age of 40; and Lee Iacocca was fired by Henry Ford II at the age of 54. The great news is that each one of these people is remembered for their successes, not for their failures. You, too, will be remembered for the number of times that you succeed. And the number of times you succeed will be in direct proportion to the number of times that you fail, but keep on trying.

15. *Take a self-esteem inventory.* Change always starts with awareness. To increase your own self-awareness, take a self-inventory. Make a list of all your positive attributes. Most people undervalue their assets. Each year, it is important to acknowledge your strengths, your areas for improvement, and your significant accomplishments for the past year. With your attributes on paper, you will find it easier to value yourself, feel proud of strengths, and set new goals for areas of improvement.

16. *Develop the habit of positive self-talk.* Your self-esteem is shaped by the way you communicate with yourself. The sooner you can change the way you communicate with yourself, the sooner your communication with others will change as well. When you change your communication with others, it changes the way others respond to you and this reinforces your positive self-talk. As your self-talk is enhanced and becomes more positive, your self-esteem will follow in a positive manner. Assess your self-talk. Are you being kind to yourself? If you don't like what you hear, change your negative self-talk into positive self-talk. Focus on positive belief in yourself.

17. *Be a volunteer or a mentor.* Give back. Help others as you have been helped. Give some of your time to those who could benefit from your friendship or expertise. Whether it is a person or an organization, you will

27

feel good after you have touched another in a positive way. It usually costs you very little and you have a lot to gain knowing you have helped someone.

18. *Try it until you make it!* Many people ask, "How can I exhibit the behaviors of a person with high self-esteem when I do not feel that way?" Unfortunately, many do not realize that behaviors that generate good self-esteem are also expressions of good self-esteem. Behaviors that are expressions of good self-esteem are also generators of good self-esteem. If you practice each one of the behaviors we have just reviewed, you will begin to develop higher self-esteem. What it takes on your part is acting out each of these behaviors listed on the preceding pages. Even when you do not feel like manifesting high self-esteem behaviors, TRY IT! If you *act* like you have high self-esteem, high self-esteem will follow. The only secret to enhancing and maintaining high self-esteem is to practice, practice, and practice some more.

19. *Accept change.* The one thing we can most certainly count on in this world is change. It's the one constant. Be aware that change is inevitable. You can choose to resist change and view it as negative. If you take this perspective, you set yourself up for constant disappointment. However, you can also view change as an opportunity. With any change, you can look for the good, for an opportunity to grow.

20. *Focus on what you want, not what you do not want.* People with high self-esteem focus on what they want in life, not what they do not want or what they want to avoid. If you want a new job, an improved relationship, or a slimmer you, do not focus on being stuck where you are, the negative aspects of the relationship, or your current weight. Put your sights on the new job: What will it be? Where will it be? What will you be doing? Focus on how the relationship will be better: Is there better communication? Do we have greater mutual respect? Are we having more fun? And the slimmer you: How will you feel? What will you look like? How will others react to you? Remember, you will get what you expect. So expect the best.

28

Tips for Success: Confidence and Self-Esteem

1. Recognize that your self-esteem and self-image impact every aspect of your role as a supervisor.

2. Stop valuing your self-worth by comparing yourself to others. Set your own standards and then strive to achieve those standards.

3. Set realistic and obtainable goals. It is the fastest way to raise your self-esteem. When you set a goal and achieve it, you will feel that you have mastery over your environment.

4. Associate with high-self-esteemers. You *do* have a choice as to whom you associate with. Individuals with high self-esteem can help you build your self-esteem.

5. Laugh sooner. If you have ever experienced a crisis or a failure, you know that at some point you will be able to laugh about it. The goal is to laugh sooner.

6. Give and accept compliments. When you give sincere compliments, people like you better. When you accept compliments, it demonstrates high self-esteem.

7. Ask for and accept feedback from others. When people care about you enough to offer feedback, either positive or negative, you have the opportunity to grow.

8. Take full responsibility for your actions. Empowered people with high self-esteem know they are responsible for their decisions and actions.

9. Use positive self-talk, because what you *think* about comes about.

10. Remember, successful people have experienced failure. Successful people with high self-esteem do not view failure as failure, but rather as an opportunity to learn how to do things differently.

Action Plan: Building Your Confidence and Self-Esteem

Three steps I can take to enhance my self-esteem and when I will begin each step:

Action Step 1:

Target Date for Initiation:

Action Step 2:

Target Date for Initiation:

Action Step 3:

Target Date for Initiation:

Chapter 3

Leading Organizational Change

"The trouble with the future is that it usually arrives before we're ready for it."

— *Arnold H. Glasow*

Being a leader in an organization during the turbulent past decade has been challenging and, at times, has perhaps seemed like an overwhelming task. During the past ten years, every organization has felt the impact of change. Some organizations have experienced rapid growth; others have felt the effects of downsizing. Expenses have gone up and profits declined. Customers have increased their demands for quality products. Their expectations and standards for service have escalated. Many markets have expanded, and just as many have crumbled. Organizations have experienced greater competition and advanced technological demands. All indicators are that organizations will continue facing challenges created by sharp economic swings, keen competitive pressures, globalization of the marketplace, and the reshaping of businesses worldwide. Simply put, change is here to stay. Change is the reality today and those organizations and people who will not change will not survive what some have called "The Age of Instability."

For a multitude of reasons, changes in our economy or environment have forced supervisors and organizations to respond with a resulting change in the way they do business. Whether we like it or not, organizational changes result in supervisors having to implement those changes. In addition to the other more traditional skills we possess as supervisors, it is critical that we understand our roles as leaders or change agents during these rapidly changing times. Having an understanding of the way change affects our organization and recognizing the resulting impact of the change on the individuals within our organization are critical. One familiar comment from supervisors and managers is, "Employees do not like to change." Our ability to deal positively with change, in large part, determines our effectiveness as leaders during these rapidly changing times.

Unfortunately for managers and supervisors, it's a given fact that employees do not all respond to change with the attitude, "Fantastic, another organizational change and I'm excited to be a part of it!" We have found that when change is introduced to an organization (or better yet, rumored), employees will respond in one of three ways.

1. First, some of the strongest-willed employees will fight organizational change, even when deep down inside they recognize that the change is in the best interests of the organization. Strong-willed employees are like dinosaurs. They may be well on the way to extinction, but they will fight change each step of the way.

2. The second type of employee takes a "let's wait and watch" approach to change. These employees will not fight an organizational change because they do not think that the change will have a direct impact on them. They dig their heels deeply into the sand and hope that the change will eventually pass them by. These employees are like rabbits on the highways at night. They sit and are mesmerized by the lights. Unfortunately, some rabbits get hit. Employees who ignore change can become victims of the process as they sit on the sidelines and watch the passing parade.

3. Last, the third group of employees are the ones who are able to accurately assess the future and possess the flexibility to adapt accordingly. These employees are like dolphins. Dolphins are one of the brightest mammals in the ocean. They possess the skills needed to adapt to any environment. They are comfortable swimming in a pool of carp. They are equally confident swimming in a sea of sharks. They successfully adapt to a constantly changing environment. Dolphins are always thinking ahead, planning their next strategy. They learn from, and respond appropriately to, their rapidly changing environment.

Reasons People Resist Change

Given that change is here to stay and has a direct impact on the way we do business within our organization, why do some people seem to dig in their heels and need to be dragged along, resisting making changes in their behavior and attitude at all costs? The following ten reasons best describe why some people have a tough time changing their mindsets and behavior:

1. *Fear of failure or success.* Some employee resistance to change is rooted in fear. During periods of change, an employee may feel the need to cling to the past because it was a more secure, predictable time. Employees may be afraid to commit to a change in the way they do things out of fear of not being successful. If what they did in the past worked well for them, they may resist changing their behavior out of fear that they will not achieve as much in the future.

2. *Creatures of habit.* Doing things in the same routine, predictable manner is comfortable. Asking people to change the way they operate or think requires them to move outside their comfort zone. "We've always done it this way, so why do we need to change?" becomes the rallying cry for people who have difficulty changing their routines. In some cases, employees may ignore or deny the change simply because it requires them to experience something beyond their normal method of operation. They are not interested in discomfort.

3. *No obvious need.* "If it has been working all this time, and working well, why do we need to change?" Like the old expression, "If it ain't broke, why fix it?" employees within an organization may only see a change from the perspective of the impact it has on them and their particular jobs. Not seeing the big picture, they may resist the change because they fail to recognize the positive impact of the change on the organization as a whole. They find the talk about change disruptive and totally unnecessary.

4. *Loss of control.* Employees working in familiar routines develop a sense of control over their work environment. They know what works and what doesn't. Therefore, they are confident about their contribution to the organization. For some employees, asking them to change the way they operate creates a feeling of being powerless and confused during the transition.

5. *Concern about their support system.* Employees operating within predictable routines know their support system will back them up during challenging times. When organizational systems and structures are changed, some employees may resist the change because they lack confidence in their support system. They fear change because they fear working for a new supervisor or fear working with other employees they don't know, and on unfamiliar projects. Feeling insecure about their support system, they are hesitant or resistant to change because they fear that if they try and fail, there will be no one there to support them.

33

6. *Closed mind.* For a variety of reasons, some employees seem to approach all change from an attitude of "Please don't confuse me with any further facts or supporting documentation about this proposed or required change—I've already made up my mind!" Employees with this attitude resent being asked to change. They approach the change process with their minds firmly made up, muttering "No way!" during discussions and explanations of the future.

7. *Unwilling to learn.* Some employees, hesitant about trying new routines, express their resistance by being unwilling to learn anything new. They may say, "I already know all that I need to know," or "I don't need to know." Like resistant employees who have already made up their minds that the change won't be productive, employees reluctant to learn something new impede the organization's growth and adaptation to change. They also hinder their own personal growth and development.

8. *Fear that the change may not be better.* If things have been going well, some employees resist change because they fear that the change will not result in improvement. Focusing only on their part of the operation, they may fail to realize that change is needed in order for the organization to stay competitive. They may dig in their heels and resist forward movement because they are satisfied with the way things are going; they don't think that a proposed change will result in an organizational improvement. Their current status is quite sufficient, and they wish to maintain business as usual.

9. *Fear of the unknown.* Employees may resist a change within their organization because it is something unfamiliar. Not knowing much about the specifics of the change, they think about a worst-case scenario, which can be very scary. Rather than find out more, they let fear of the unknown become their rationale for not giving the change a chance. These employees may actually acknowledge that a problem exists, and they might agree that a change could improve an existing problem. They, however, assume that the change might actually make things worse and fear the outcome! They will put up roadblocks in the movement toward change.

10. *Fear of personal impact.* Viewing change from a personal standpoint, some employees may respond by asking how the change will benefit them directly. Will it make their job easier? Will they have to work harder? Will the change put their job security in jeopardy? Will the change force them to work with different people or learn a new job? These are all initial reactions supervisors encounter when they announce an organizational change to employees.

Typical Employee Responses Regarding Change

During times of organization change, you will notice employees reacting to change with a variety of responses. It is important for a supervisor tasked with implementing organizational change to be able to understand employee reactions when change is implemented and recognize that these are normal reactions and part of the process employees go through during periods of organizational change. The following reactions are some typical responses to organizational change:

1. *Not me!* Typically, when an employee is asked to do a different job or change the way they currently do a particular job, they respond out of denial with "Not me!" They may begin to tell their supervisor about someone else better suited for the job, or deny that they are capable of making the proposed change. This initial reaction is a result of the employee's satisfaction with the current status quo and fear of what unknowns the change may create for them personally.

2. *What will this do to my job security?* "What's in it for me?" is often an employee's first response upon learning about a proposed organizational change. It is natural for employees to see change from the perspective of their own job security. Employees wonder what will happen to their job if technological advances are introduced or if downsizing prompts a restructuring of the organization. Employees are also concerned about what financial impact the changes will have on them personally. Will the change result in less work for them, or even do away with their job altogether? It is normal for employees to view organizational change *first* from the perspective of their own job security and *second* from the needs of the organization.

3. *Anger.* Some employees are so resistant to change that they become frustrated and angry. Their anger may be repressed, causing an increase in stress, or overt, resulting in emotional outbursts. Whether repressed or overt, anger is a typical reaction to change. Anger results from employees feeling that their job security is being threatened, or that they sense a loss of control over their work environment.

4. *Gossip.* Gossip, always an organizational challenge, often escalates during periods of organizational change. Employees who respond to organizational change with frustration, anger, and disbelief often resort to vicious gossip or "back-stabbing." Feeling a sense of loss of information, power, and control, people often respond by gossiping to others in the organization. This gossip is detrimental to the positive forward thrust that should accompany organizational change.

5. *Who's in charge here?* During times when organizations are restructuring, it is natural for employees to question leadership. If employees are concerned that they will be working for a new supervisor, there will undoubtedly be unrest during the transition period as they anticipate changing allegiance from one leader to another. When employees have not been communicated with and when they do not see the positive results of the changes, it is normal for them to question the wisdom of the organization's leadership.

6. *Panic!* Some employees, finding comfort in a predictable routine, panic at the mere mention of change. For them, upsetting the routine and making changes in the way they normally proceed with their jobs can cause panic. It can also make them physically ill. They may resist change at all costs— not out of stubbornness, but out of sheer panic at the thought of how the change will impact them personally. They may be so plagued with the feeling of panic that they are not able to rationally deal with the change.

7. *I quit!* Some employees may actually be so resistant to the idea of organizational change that they elect to quit rather than make the needed changes. Unfortunately, changes going on in one organization are typical of changes going on in other organizations. Electing to stand on one's principles and fight change by quitting often makes the point, but usually at great cost to the employee making the point, *not* to the organization.

36

Don't get discouraged. Not all employee responses to change are negative! The following positive responses to change come typically from employees who feel a high degree of self-esteem, personal competence, and self-confidence. They see change in an entirely different perspective, and when in alignment with the supervisor, they even help support and sell organizational change to other employees. These employees typically have the ability to remain open-minded in response to change and see change as having a positive influence on both them personally as well as on the organization. Here are some of their responses:

1. *This is a challenge!* Employees viewing change as a challenge feel that they can rise to the occasion. They feel that they have what it takes to be a contributing team player when the change affects their work world. They remain open to new ideas, ask questions, and feel confident in their ability to acquire the knowledge needed to complete the task. They exhibit a "can do" attitude in their approach to change. They may admit that the task is difficult, the procedure is a bit cloudy, and the outcome is unknown or questionable, but they are committed in their desire to rise to the challenge!

2. *Enthusiasm.* Some employees naturally approach life and challenges more enthusiastically than others. These employees possess a gift: Instead of trying to pick apart proposed changes and find all the ways they won't work, enthusiastic employees see change as a natural part of an organization's evolution. These are employees who understand the bigger picture. They understand the value in making change. They visualize what could be, and they have a positive vision about the company's future. Enthusiastic employees can affect others with their enthusiasm. Supervisors lucky enough to have enthusiastic employees need to support and nurture these employees because they can help make the implementation of change much more palatable for other employees.

3. *Maybe I could adjust to this change.* Some employees don't embrace change enthusiastically or jump out of their seats ready to accept a challenge resulting from organizational change. Instead, they may watch from the sidelines, but they remain open-minded. They may not commit initially, but after a period of observation, agree to give the change a chance. They remain open-minded enough to entertain the thought that they could adjust to the change. While they may not be eager participants in the change process, they give the new ideas and processes a chance. They express a willingness to learn new techniques and procedures and do not sabotage change activities.

Understanding Why People Respond So Differently

In the previous pages, we've looked at why employees are resistant to change and what some of their typical responses are when the change is implemented. We've seen that responses can range from fear and panic to enthusiastic support for the change. What is it about people that makes them respond to change in such a variety of responses? The following list comprises some of the reasons why people react to change so differently.

1. *Family upbringing.* The way your family reacted to changes in their environment when you were growing up partially determines your attitudes about change. If you lived in the same home throughout your school years, attended the same church, shopped at the same stores, and traveled the same routes daily, you may have more difficulty dealing with change than a person who lived in several different neighborhoods. If the people within your neighborhood all embraced the same values and ethics during your formative years, it may be more difficult for you to appreciate the diversity of today's workforce. Finally, if you were fortunate enough to have been

raised in a family that experienced changes positively and tackled them as challenges that would result in a positive outcome, you will have a more optimistic outlook about change than a person raised in a home where change was viewed as an unwanted evil that upset the predictable family routine.

2. *Past successes and failures.* To a great extent, how we have experienced changes in the past determines how we view the change process in the future. If our past experiences during times of change have been mostly positive, we will have a more optimistic outlook about the change process. But if we have experienced failure during periods of change, those failures may shadow our outlook about future changes. We may view any change as being negative, based solely on past negative experiences.

3. *Personal mental well-being.* It's a known fact that people with high self-esteem and self-confidence are better equipped to deal with changes in both their personal and organizational life. They can see the change process from a broader perspective. They have confidence not only in themselves, but in the leadership above them. Self-confident people have an understanding of their part in the change process and see the value of dealing with change positively. Insecure people, on the other hand, internalize the change process and see it as being threatening. They view the process as having a negative effect on them personally. Finally, employees with a positive mental outlook have the ability to see the change process as providing greater opportunities for them and enhancing their personal and career growth. They view change as bringing them more, not less!

4. *Communication.* How the change process is communicated to people within the organization is a critical factor that determines how people will react to the change. When upper management plans and communicates effectively with all employees, change is better understood and more readily accepted. Changes that are mandated with little communication, however, are often poorly received. Balking at change when the process is mandated is a natural response to having something shoved down your throat. On the other hand, when the reasoning behind the change is fully communicated, employees are much more likely to buy into the change.

5. *Ability to control the situation.* People are more likely to understand and implement changes when they feel that they have some control over the situation. Soliciting input from employees will keep the doors of communication open and create more of a feeling of control for the employee. If employees know that their input is desired and seriously considered, they will feel that their contribution matters. Knowing that their input makes a

difference helps employees feel that they have more control during periods of change. No one likes to ride the winds of change without feeling, to some extent, that they have control over the situation.

6. *Job satisfaction.* How happy employees are with their jobs, in part, determines their reactions during times of change. Employees who experience a high degree of job satisfaction are better able to weather periods of change. They are more positive in their approach to their work and can see change as an organizational necessity that must be faced. Unhappy employees, on the other hand, view change as just another annoyance in a long list of complaints about their work. Chances are that whatever the change, disgruntled employees will view it as having a negative impact on both the organization and them personally.

7. *Level of trust.* The level of trust within any organization helps determine reactions during turbulent times. In organizations where there is a high degree of trust and where respect and dignity for each individual employee is valued, there is less resistance to change. However, in organizational environments where there is a high degree of distrust, change is viewed as just one more trick by management. In such organizations, change will be resisted, not because employees may find it unwarranted, but simply because they mistrust everything management does. Such employees become confused. They see the necessity of change but they don't trust the change agents.

8. *Age, gender, and values.* How we react to change also is determined, in part, by our age, our sex, and our values. Generally, but not always, people tend to become more resistant to change as they age. The older they get, the more comfortable it is for them to operate within known parameters and predictable routines. Also, males and females may face the same change with different reactions, based on their previous experiences. What we value also plays a big part in determining how we react to change. If we value stability, status quo, and control over our environment, we may be more resistant to change than someone who values risk taking and exploration, and who is excited about future unknowns.

9. *Timing.* The timing of changes also impacts a person's reaction to change. If the change occurred at a time when the employee was financially secure, the change may be viewed positively. However, if the change occurred during a time of financial insecurity, the same change may be viewed as having a negative impact on the individual. How fast an employee receives word of the change also impacts the response. If changes have been long rumored

or thoroughly communicated within the organization, the employee may more readily accept the change. If, however, the employee is suddenly confronted with the change, he may be resistant and, in a worst-case scenario, may even try to sabotage the change process.

We've explored why people resist change, described typical reactions to change, and explained what makes people react to change so differently. You may be tempted, at this point, to be discouraged regarding your own ability to drive organizational change. Don't give up. Fortunately, there are several specific actions and straightforward approaches managers and supervisors can take to help navigate their employees successfully through organizational change. These guidelines can make times of change some of the most rewarding and productive times in your leadership history!

Guidelines for Organizational Change

1. *Involve employees in the change process.* We are firm believers that employees are not so much against change as they are against being changed. Anytime managers are going to implement organizational change, there is always a lag between the time the change has been discussed at the management level and the time the change is going to be implemented. Managers believe that they are the only ones who know about the changes that are going to take place. Unfortunately, employees are already undermining the decisions with negative informal communication. Our experience has been that the rumors and gossip surrounding proposed changes are often exaggerated and seem to generate additional erroneous information each time they are passed from one employee to another! The sooner you involve employees in the process, the better off you will be implementing the change. A formal communication channel will be more effective at implementing change than a negative informal one.

2. *Interview employees.* It is critical that managers and supervisors understand what employees are feeling regarding the change. It is only when you accurately understand their feelings that you know what issues need to be addressed. Implementing change requires the ability to sell. It is difficult to effectively sell without understanding your buyer's needs, concerns, and fears.

3. *Ask questions, don't tell.* We are fond of the statement, "You can tell tough employees, but you can't tell them much." People who do not deal well with change generally are the same employees who cannot be "told" any-

thing. For this reason, we recommend asking them questions rather than telling them why the changes are taking place.

Recently, we worked with an organization that was implementing a major change the management hoped would improve both their profitability and customer service. Moving from a system where a specific individual is responsible for a specific customer to a team of individuals who would be responsible for satisfying customers would change the way the organization had done business for the past thirty years. Management told employees why the changes needed to take place until they were blue in the face. Employees were adamantly opposed to the change. As a last resort, management switched strategies and decided to ask the following question: "If we keep going without any change, is our organization going to flourish in the next ten years, or will *not* changing undermine our success?" Ninety-five percent of employees stated that *not* changing would lead to the company's demise. With this new data, management got all the employees involved in helping to design the specific change strategy that would be implemented.

4. *Get the informal leaders involved—those who support the changes and those who do not.* Most managers and supervisors get the "positive" informal leaders involved in helping implement changes. They have a reputation for supporting management, regardless of the change. The mistake many managers make is not involving those who are more negative in the beginning stages of the change process. When they are left out of any change efforts and ignored, they lack commitment and may even try to sabotage the change. By involving them, their behaviors are likely to change. Knowing what their objections and concerns are regarding the change will also help you design your change strategy. If you can meet their concerns, they will help in selling the change to the rest of the organization.

5. *Don't cover all the bases yourself.* Too often managers and supervisors feel they must use self-protective measures, especially during organizational change. They start by trying to oversee all activities. You should concentrate on effective delegation during the early stages of the change process. Effective delegation is particularly good for two reasons. First, it helps you manage and maintain your workload. Second, it gives your employees a sense of involvement. That positions them to share in the responsibility for change.

6. *Raise expectations.* Now, more than ever, you should ask more from your employees. While it may be more practical to expect less in terms of performance, this is the time to raise your levels of performance for both yourself and your employees. During change, employees are more likely to

change their work habits. Reach for the opportunity and push them to try harder and work smarter. Require performance improvements and make the process challenging, but remember to keep goals realistic so you eliminate frustration and failure.

7. *Ask employees for their commitment.* Once the change has been announced, it is important that you personally ask for each employee's commitment to successfully implement the change. It is equally important that you tell the employee that if there are problems, you want to hear about them. Charles Kettering put it this way, "Problems are the price of progress. Don't bring me anything but problems." Remember, if a negative employee does not tell you about problems, you can be sure he will be telling other employees about why the change will not work.

8. *Overcommunicate.* The change process usually means that normal communication channels in the firm won't be working as well as they usually do. During this time, your employees will be hungrier than ever for information and answers. You can "beef up" communication in two ways. First, *give employees an opportunity to give you input.* Start by becoming more available and asking more questions. Get employee opinions and reactions to the changes. Maintain your visibility and make it clear that you are an accessible boss. Just letting your employees know that you don't have any new information is meaningful information to them. Second, *strive to be specific.* Clear up rumors and misinformation that clutter the communication changes. Remember, it is almost impossible to overcommunicate.

9. *Be firm, but flexible.* As you introduce a change, it is important that you see the change through to completion. Abandoning it halfway through the change process accomplishes two things. First, it destroys your credibility. Second, it tells every employee that if you take the stance of a dinosaur, the change will pass by, even if you lose your job and become extinct in the process. Remain flexible because you may have to adapt to a myriad of situations to successfully implement your change.

10. *Keep positive.* Your attitude as a manager or supervisor will be a major factor in determining what type of climate is exhibited by your employees. Your attitude is the one thing that keeps you in control. Change can be stressful and confusing. Try to remain upbeat, positive, and enthusiastic. Foster motivation in others. During times of transition and change, try to compensate your employees for their extra effort. Write a little note of encouragement and leave it on an employee's desk. Leave a nice message on their voice mail. E-mail a word of thanks or encouragement. Take them aside and tell them what a great job they are doing. Listen to their com-

ments and suggestions. And try to instill organizational change as a personal challenge!

The best way to predict the future is to invent it. Consider what changes are coming, what needs to happen, and how you can contribute! Instead of changing with the times, make it a habit to change just a little bit ahead of the times.

Tips for Success: Organizational Change

1. Be a role model for leading the new change. Gain a reputation for leading your team forward, not defending the past.

2. Hold yourself accountable for successful implementation of change. Maintain high personal standards and hold others accountable to agreed-upon team standards.

3. Develop a compelling positive vision of the future. While you may not have all the details, the more positive your vision, the greater the chance for your success. Also, the clearer your vision, the easier it is for your employees to follow your lead.

4. Set clear, specific goals and communicate the goals to each member on your team so they know the target and understand how their individual effort contributes to the team's success.

5. Double your communication efforts during periods of rapid organizational change. Overcommunicate to make sure that employees feel they are getting enough communication regarding the change.

6. During times of change, focus on ensuring customer satisfaction, both internally and externally. This focus reminds all members of the team what your real purpose for existence is.

7. Show unwavering commitment to the success of your team and your organization. Expect the waters to get choppy during times of fast change. Hang on. Ride the waves. Your tenacity will be a source of inspiration for your team.

8. Get in the habit of rewarding the messenger, even if the news is not good. During times of change, you want to know, firsthand, what your employees are thinking and feeling. Their insights will help make you a more informed, better decision maker.

9. Expect resistance. Robert F. Kennedy said, "Twenty percent of the people are against any change!"

10. Don't drag your heels and resist change. Move fast! All the research shows that fast change is easier to deal with than slow change.

Action Plan: Leading Organizational Change

Three steps I can take to introduce or support change and when I will begin each step:

Action Step 1:
Target Date for Initiation:

Action Step 2:
Target Date for Initiation:

Action Step 3:
Target Date for Initiation:

Chapter 4

Setting Goals and Planning Actions

"The tragedy of life doesn't lie in not reaching your goal. The tragedy lies in having no goal to reach."

—*Benjamin E. Mays*

In working with thousands of supervisors in diverse settings, we have noted that along with other positive characteristics, great leaders always have a set of clearly defined goals. We have also noted the reverse. Supervisors who struggle in their relationships with their employees and have difficulty getting their teams motivated often have only one goal: "Just let me survive one more day!" It's a known fact that individuals and teams who set and achieve goals accomplish more, feel better about themselves, and are more confident in their abilities. Goals can be powerfully motivating.

The accomplishment of anything great begins with clear goals. While most people would readily agree with this statement, it is amazing how many people lack goals in both their personal and professional lives. Some studies have found that up to 90% of the population do not set goals. Often, these people do not really know what a goal is or how to go about setting one. Well-defined goals are part fantasy and part pragmatism. If you can dream, conceive, and believe, then you can achieve your goals.

There is a procedure for setting and reaching your goals. The following pages describe the goal-setting process. You will learn what it takes to be a great goal setter and goal achiever. Whether your goals are financial, business, educational, family, physical, social, spiritual, or recreational, you will be successful if you follow this process.

It is important to realize that achieving any goal will take persistence, commitment, and a willingness to forego temporary pleasures for the pursuit of your goal. Goals will give you a well-defined purpose, a sense of accomplishment, and a feeling of mastery over your environment. This, in turn, will lead to a high self-confidence that will permeate your entire life. Without goals, you are like a ship without sails and a rudder. You are truly at the mercy of the wind. You will drift, but you will not drive. Without goals, you spend the majority of your time reacting to instead of creating your environment.

Whether you choose to be a great goal setter or a ship floundering at sea, it is important for you to realize one thing: Whatever you do with your life, you write your own ticket!

Defining Success

It is important to realize that *you* are a success in life if *you* are able to realize what *you* deem an important and worthwhile accomplishment. Success is a very personal journey. It is different things to different people. What are *you* after? What is important to *you*?

Abraham Maslow, in his book *Motivation and Personality*, states that, "No matter how old you are, the day you cannot sit down and come up with a want list, you are in trouble; you are on the way out."

You must first recognize you are different from others. Your wants are different, your needs are different, your life is different, and therefore, your goals will be different. So, what is success? It is about (1) doing, (2) participating, (3) progressing, and (4) learning. These processes are all personal achievements.

Unfortunately, the vast majority of people look at success as a comparison: "Am I doing better than my parents, my neighbors, my associates, or myself compared to last year?" Your success cannot be a comparison of you to others, your environment, or your past. To truly be a success, you must accomplish pre-set goals that are meaningful to you.

When you set and accomplish goals, you gain a sense of mastery over your environment. With the feeling that you can accomplish what you set out to do, you will become successful. If you *must* compare, look at your success as a comparison of yourself to your potential. Most people never realize that success has more to do with an internal mental environment than with external physical surroundings.

So, set meaningful goals, achieve your goals, and breathe the feeling of success.

Why People Don't Set Goals

1. *Lack of goal-setting knowledge.* In 1953, Yale University professors surveyed the graduating class to find out how many people had goals. They found out that (1) only 3% of the class had goals that were well-defined, (2) 10% had goals, but they were not specific, and (3) the remaining 87% had no formalized goals, just vague ideas of what they wanted to accomplish in their lives.

   These dramatic results were unveiled more than twenty years later when Yale University did a follow-up study in 1975. Researchers found that the 3% of the class who had written specific goals had accomplished more in their lives than the remaining 87% combined!

2. *Not clear about what they want.* In the great Lewis Carroll novel, *Alice in Wonderland*, Alice turns to the Cheshire cat and asks, "Which way do I go from here?" The cat replies, "Where do you want to end up?" When Alice states that she's not quite sure where she wants to end up, the cat rightfully replies, "Then it does not really matter which way you go."

   One of the differences between successful supervisors and unsuccessful supervisors is their purpose in life. If you do not know where you are going, then you will probably end up "somewhere." But, if you do have specific goals and a clear-cut specific plan for your life, then your chances for achieving your objectives within or near the time frame you have set for yourself are extremely high.

3. *Fear of failure.* Many people have a fear of setting goals—a fear that they may not accomplish what they set out to do. Because of this fear, they do not set concrete goals. If you do not set goals, then you are truly not living up to your potential. The best way to overcome any fear is to do the task you fear most. Therefore, by becoming an avid goal setter, you will gain a lot more out of life.

4. *Negative attitude.* If you have a negative attitude toward life, you are not likely to be a goal setter. People who are successful goal setters have a great positive mental attitude. Your ability to control your attitude on a daily basis is proof of your success. Those who achieve significant results in their careers and in their lives recognize the importance of viewing the glass as *half full* instead of as *half empty*. Your success is a result of your motivation, and your motivation is your own personal responsibility. Probably the most important factor in developing internal motivation is to increase your desire for the motives, goals, or objectives you believe you want.

5. *Poor self-image.* Your self-image is the *picture* you have of yourself, or how you *see* yourself. This picture contributes to your self-esteem or how you *feel* about yourself. If you see yourself as a failure or as someone who cannot achieve what you really want, you will feel unempowered and unmotivated to even try to accomplish a goal. So, the easy way out is to avoid setting goals in the first place. Successful goal setters work on their self-image and self-esteem first. Review the concepts presented in Chapter 2, *Building Your Confidence and Self-Esteem.* Use some of those ideas to build your self-esteem. The better you feel about yourself, the greater is your belief in yourself and your abilities. This strong belief in self will give you the internal push to begin and succeed with the goal-setting process.

6. *Limited thinking.* Another reason why people do not set goals is because of "limited thinking." That is, they have a narrow perspective on what they can achieve. Some people box themselves into a narrow thought process. This imaging box does not allow them to see beyond the box or expand their thinking to new horizons. Limited thinking perpetuates the status quo of no growth.

    A classic example of this concept at work is the story of the old fisherman. Each day he would walk out to the end of a pier with a rusty old rod, a crusty reel, a yellow bucket, and a dirty stick that was snapped off at exactly ten inches. Each day he would cast his line into the water and bring up fish. When he reeled one in, he would hold the fish up to his stick. If the fish was bigger than the stick, he would throw it back. If the fish was smaller than the stick, he would keep it.

    Since keeping the little ones and throwing back the big ones was not what other fisherman did, someone asked him why he felt compelled to do the opposite. He replied, "It's because of my frying pan. It's only ten inches."

    Limited thinking kept the fisherman from looking beyond the familiar. Successful goal setters think big and look beyond what they currently have. So, don't let the big fish get away!

7. *Procrastination.* How long have you been promising yourself that you would take a course, learn a new language, start an exercise program, stop drinking or smoking, write or call someone, or start a certain project? If you are like most people, you probably never get around to doing a lot of things you would like to do. You really mean to, but you find yourself making excuses like: "I am too busy this week" or "I will get to it as soon as I finish this project."

Why do people procrastinate? Are they shy, lazy, indecisive, indifferent, or fearful? Do they have low self-esteem? Are they unclear about their goals? All of these characteristics can play a role in fostering procrastination. The most important step in overcoming procrastination is the first step. It does not matter how small the first step is; what matters is that a first step is taken. Whatever you want to do in life, you can "win it." Just take the first step and begin the journey.

The Goal-Setting Process

Step One: Create a Vision

We will discuss the power of a vision in Chapter 20. Successful leaders know the practical value of the visioning process. They also know that creating a vision is the first step in goal setting. Before you begin to set a goal, you need a clear mental *picture* of what it is you want to achieve. This picture is your vision of success. Creating a vision is the ability to see beyond *what is* to the picture of *what could be*.

To start the visioning process, you must get in touch with your true desire. What is important to you? What matters? What do you care about? What do you really want? A vision comes from the heart. It must be truly meaningful to you.

Once you are clear on what you want, begin to form the picture. Create a mental picture of what you want. Make the picture clear, specific, and detailed. See yourself in the picture. What are you doing? What are you saying? Wearing? Who else is with you? How are people treating one another? How do you feel about yourself? About the others around you?

The visioning process requires quiet reflection. Step back from your busy, fast-paced environment and relax. Visioning requires imagery and creativity. The more relaxed you are and the farther away you are from day-to-day tensions, the easier it is to create, the easier it is to visualize. Many people have a difficult time creating a vision because that vision may be so far removed from reality. Yet it is that very distance or gap between the vision and current reality that propels you toward achieving the vision.

This concept was first described by Robert Fritz in his book, *The Path of Least Resistance*. Fritz calls it *structural tension*. There are two components to structural tension. One is the vision or the picture of what you want. The second component is *current reality* or what you have now. As Fritz maintains, "The difference or discrepancy between what you have (current reality) and the result you want (vision) creates structural tension."

Structural tension is useful because it seeks resolution. In other words, to resolve the tension between your vision and current reality, one or the other has to give. As Fritz puts it, structural tension may be resolved in either of two ways. It may be resolved through a change in current reality, so that your outward circumstances come to correspond more closely with your vision. On the other hand, the tension may be resolved through a change in your vision, so that you alter the result you want in order to correspond more closely with what you have now.

In summary, to achieve your vision, first crystallize the vision. Make it real, in your mind and in your heart. Then, acknowledge current reality. Feel the tension between the two. Allow yourself to be propelled toward your vision. Use the structural tension as an ally to move you to what you truly want.

Step Two: Decide on Actions

Now that your vision is clear, you can begin to determine the actions that must be taken to achieve the vision. These actions become the specific goals that are to be accomplished. A goal is a target, an end, or an objective. It is the accomplishment of these targets or goals that brings you closer to your vision.

For example, if your vision is to achieve a more prominent position in your organization or to move higher on your career path, you would first go through the visioning process and become crystal clear on what it is you actually want. You would know exactly what it would look like and how it would feel. Then ask yourself, "What do I need to accomplish to get to my vision?" One action may be to go back to school and complete a degree program. If you need the degree to achieve the vision, it becomes one of your key goals.

At this point in the goal-setting process, simply list the various actions you must take to achieve the vision. As we move through the next steps, we will discuss how to write effective goal statements.

Step Three: Identify Roadblocks

Now that you know what it will take to achieve your vision by outlining key actions or goals, you can begin to identify the barriers or roadblocks that may get in your way. It may sound negative to spend your time and energy thinking about barriers or problems, but there are two good reasons for this. First, if you are able to think about what problems could stop you, you can also begin to generate plans to get around the problems if they should arise. And second, when they do come up, they do not paralyze you. Many people have had their goals undermined when problems surfaced. Sometimes people will even tell you they thought the problems would arise, but they did nothing to prepare for it.

For example, a supervisor sets a goal to reorganize his or her department. The full reorganization never takes place because as soon as the supervisor introduces the changes, the employees start to block the process. When asked if he or she thinks the employees may make the process difficult, the supervisor responds affirmatively. If you know that it is going to be a problem, you should create a plan to effectively deal with and eliminate that roadblock. If we think through which problems might stop us, we are seldom blind-sided by roadblocks.

Back to our example of going back to school to get your degree. Some of the roadblocks you could anticipate in this goal might include (1) not enough time, (2) fear of going back to being a student, and (3) financial constraints. For each of the roadblocks you identify, develop some strategies to get around the problem. It may include (1) changing your own thinking, (2) getting help from others, or (3) committing to specific time blocks to do what you need to do. Keep the vision in mind and then overcoming the roadblocks will not be so tough.

Step Four: List the Benefits

If you spend time listing the problems or roadblocks you could encounter, you will find it much easier to generate a list of benefits you would receive when you achieve the goal. The question that then needs to be answered is, "Do the benefits make the goal worth achieving?" If the answer is *yes*, you know that it is worth tackling the problems to achieve the benefits of goal attainment.

Continuing with our example, some of the benefits of going back to school and obtaining a degree might be (1) improved chances for promotion, (2) increased salary, (3) enhanced self-esteem, and (4) the feeling of accomplishing something you have wanted to accomplish for many years.

As you list the benefits, you will want to make sure the benefits outweigh the problems you will encounter. If the benefits do not outweigh the problems, the problems will stop you. Focus on the benefits. They will help you get through the tough times!

Step Five: Write the Goal

The research on high achievers shows that successful goal setters write out their goals. There is something almost magical about writing down goals. Without writing down the goal, it is merely an idea or a wish. Writing it down helps to bring it to life.

Here is a simple, yet effective guideline for writing good goals. It is called the **S-M-A-R-T** model. Each letter of the **S-M-A-R-T** model refers to a characteristic of effective goals:

Specific. Good goals are specific. They detail exactly what is to be accomplished. Don't be vague or general. Write out specifically what is to be accomplished.

Measurable. You must be able to measure the success of your goal. In other words, how will you know when you are successful? Whether the goal is broken down into number of units produced, salary earned, days worked, pounds lost, chapters completed, or number of classes attended, you need a way to quantify your results. Measuring your results helps to keep you moving toward your goal. Yes, it is a great motivator!

Attainable. Research shows us that high achievers set goals that challenge their abilities, but that are not unrealistically out of reach. When you set challenging, but attainable goals, you will experience success and increase your self-esteem. Be realistic about your goals. It is not unrealistic to go back to school for a degree. It is unrealistic to expect to get a doctorate in only one year. Make your goals a stretch, but make them a more guaranteed stretch!

Relevant. Do not forget that your vision is the driver for your goals. Make sure that your goals are relevant to the vision. The accomplishment of each goal should move you closer to realizing your vision. Keep your goals moving on the track to your desired future.

Time-bound. Good goals have a time frame. When you set a specific time frame to get something done, it will always take you that amount of time or even less time to complete the task than if you had no time frame at all. One example of this is when you prepare to travel or go on vacation. Usually, when you are leaving on a trip, you have all sorts of tasks that need to be accomplished before you leave. You may be rushed, but you will always get the tasks done. You have to because you are leaving. If you were not leaving, those same tasks may take you two or three times as long to accomplish. Life is short! Set a time frame because you will always accomplish more.

Step Six: Design an Action Plan

Now that you have your goals and they are **S-M-A-R-T** goals, you know exactly what you want to achieve and by when. The last step in the goal-setting process is to design a specific action plan to achieve the goals. This is a step-by-step breakdown of the small actions you will take to achieve each goal and when you will take them.

Back to the degree example. Let's say your goal is stated like this:

I will complete my M.S. degree by December of 2001.

Your specific action plan might look like Exhibit 4.1. Each time you complete an action, check it off or scratch it out and then celebrate. You are on your way to achieving your ultimate goal!

Remember, the secret to achieving goals is your willingness to do whatever it takes to get there. It means that you are willing to sacrifice in order to accomplish your goal. It means that you are willing to confront problems and roadblocks and work around them. It means that you will write out your goals and ensure that they are **S-M-A-R-T**. It takes work. It also means that you will reap the benefits—that you will bring your vision to life!

Exhibit 4.1: Specific Action Plan

Goal: To complete my M.S. degree by December of 2001

Specific Actions	By What Deadline
1. Call the university and get an application	May, this year
2. Call my former college so transcripts can be sent	June, this year
3. Complete application and send it in	July 15, this year
4. Set up meeting with university counselor	August 1, this year
5. Register for classes	August 22, this year

Setting Goals with Employees

If you are setting goals that involve your employees, here are some suggestions that will help you create successful goals that employees will feel motivated to achieve.

1. *Involve employees in the goal-setting process.* One of the classic pitfalls supervisors stumble into is setting goals *for* their employees versus *with* their employees. People want to contribute to the goals for which they will be held accountable. Dumping your goals on employees without their input is a de-motivator. Have your employees create their goals with you. You will be surprised at the level of commitment and personal ownership you will see.

2. *Ask how the employee can accomplish the goal before you tell how.* Ask your employees for their ideas on how to accomplish the goal before you give your input. Even if you take the risk of asking the employee if a certain goal is possible and the employee telling you it is not possible, you are still better off. If you dictate the goal to the employee without allowing any input, the employee is still going to harbor the feelings that the goal cannot be accomplished. If you get their input on how the goal can be accomplished, you may get some new, creative, and better approaches. The key here, as with all good communication, is to listen.

3. *Ensure the goal's feasibility.* If you set a goal with your employees to have the departmental budget completed by the end of the month, you must make sure the employees have access to the tools and information they need to complete the task. Set your employees up for success by ensuring that they have what they require to do the job. This goes back to making sure that the goal is realistic and attainable.

4. *Make the goal challenging.* Tasks that are not challenging are not motivating. One of the most fundamental motivations for any employee, especially one who is basically competent at his or her work, is challenge. Challenge creates motivation to achieve goals. If you allow mediocrity to continue in your department, you are undermining your own success.

5. *Make sure the goal is relevant.* Most people do not want to accomplish a goal just for the sake of accomplishing a goal. They want to understand the purpose, or why they are doing a particular task. Employees need to understand how the work they are doing is connected to the larger purpose of the organization. People will extend themselves for work they see as important.

Though not all work has earth-shattering significance (like that of a doctor, fire fighter, paramedic, etc.), most of it can be put into terms of *significance to others.* In business, you are either supporting a customer or supporting someone internally who is supporting a customer. Either way, if you do not do your job, the service to the customer is likely to suffer. Without customers, the organization will suffer. As the organization suffers, so do profits. As profits suffer, layoffs begin. Eventually, the organization is likely to die.

Most jobs do have significance. If there is no significance in a particular job, there is probably no need for the employee. Make sure you take the time to explain the importance or relevance of the goal. Remember, good goals are relevant.

6. *Recognize success.* Make sure to recognize your employee's success. We all want to know that our work is acknowledged and recognized. This does not take much time, but it will buy you a great deal. Employees want to please supervisors. Take the time to acknowledge them with a written note, a pat on the back, or a simple "good job," and you will have a cadre of loyal, hard-working employees.

Tips for Success: Goals and Actions

1. Set goals. Most people do not set goals. Those who do are far more likely to accomplish what they want in life.

2. Adopt a positive attitude. People who achieve significant results and have a sense of fulfillment in their lives view the glass as half full instead of half empty.

3. Do it now. Successful goal setters take action *now*. Remember, the most important step in overcoming procrastination is the first step, no matter how small.

4. Clarify your vision. What do you truly want? Create a clear and specific mental picture. Use this vision to guide you in the goal-setting process.

5. Write S-M-A-R-T goals (Specific, Measurable, Attainable, Relevant, and Time-bound).

6. Design a specific action plan with target dates for completion.

7. Get your employees involved in the goal-setting process. Their involvement will foster significant personal motivation.

8. Be sure the goal is possible. Does the person have the tools and information necessary for successful completion of the goal?

9. Discuss the significance of the goal. Believe it is a goal that should be accomplished.

10. Recognize success. Any achievement deserves recognition. Whether it is a personal, team, or employee accomplishment, take time to acknowledge and recognize success.

Action Plan: Setting Goals and Planning Actions

Three steps I can take to improve my goal setting and when I will begin each step:

Action Step 1:
Target Date for Initiation:

Action Step 2:
Target Date for Initiation:

Action Step 3:
Target Date for Initiation:

Chapter 5

Managing Time to Accomplish Your Goals

"The only way there is true equality in this world is when we all have the same amount of time. Some people just accomplish more."

—Peter B. Stark

I just don't have the time. How many times have you heard this comment? How many times have you used it yourself? Each time we do not accomplish something we should have, or intended to, this attitude seems to surface.

Many managers and supervisors frequently feel the pressure of a lack of time. Picture this: You have spent your entire morning in a meeting. An unproductive meeting at that. You get out of the meeting, return phone calls, and then eat lunch. After lunch, you attend another two-hour meeting. At the conclusion of the meeting, you return more phone calls. At 3:30 p.m., an employee comes into your office and needs to review a project she is working on. At 4:30 p.m., you realize you have to leave to go pick up the kids from pre-school. All of a sudden, panic strikes. You realize that you have a report due by tomorrow afternoon. You have two choices. You can take it home with you and complete it tonight after the kids go to bed (significant others do not endorse this alternative) or you can delegate it by dumping it on one of your employees. Either choice is not ideal.

What happened? You literally ran out of time—time needed to complete a very important project in an effective manner. The reasons? Lack of priorities, unclear goals, interruptions, unproductive meetings, disorganization, inability to say "no," and possibly ineffective delegation.

The 168 Hour Limit

Another great cliche in time management is *if there were only more hours in the day*. Wishing there were more hours in the day is just that—a wish. There are two facts we know about time. First, there are exactly 24 hours or 1,440 minutes in every day. That amounts to 168 hours in a week and 8,760 hours in a year. Second, we all have the same amount of time. Rich people cannot buy more. Forgetful people cannot lose it. Scientists cannot invent more time. Powerful people cannot yield influence and gain more. When it comes to time, it is the only aspect of life where there is true equality. So the challenge is not one of where to find more time. You cannot do it. The real question we need to be asking is this: How do we manage the things that we do in the 168 hours that are available each week?

The following is a typical breakdown of how activities can consume our time:

Time at work (9 hours per day)	45
Travel to work (1 hour per day)	5
Eating meals (2 hours per day)	14
Sleeping (7 hours per day)	49
Bathing and dressing (1 hour per day)	7
Total	**120**

What this means is that we have 48 hours to spend on other activities. Things such as:

Family time   _____

Leisure activities   _____

Religious/spiritual worship   _____

Paying bills   _____

Personal growth   _____

Activities for children   _____

Grocery shopping   _____

Yard work   _____

Cleaning the house   _____

Maintaining the car   _____

Watching television   _____

Reading the newspaper   _____

Free time   _____

If the typical breakdown of activities is fairly accurate for you, then you have approximately 48 hours to spend on other activities. If you have a career that takes more time, say 55 hours in a week, then you only have 38 hours to divide up for other activities. If you have a new baby or very young children in your family, you may have even fewer hours for other activities.

Conducting a Time Management Audit

If you are going to be successful at managing your time, then it is critical that you know how you spend your time. If we are focusing on accomplishment, then it is important that you realize when you are productive and when you are not. The best way to conduct a time audit is to record your time, activity by activity, as you progress throughout the day. To conduct a time audit, follow the seven steps listed below:

1. List boundary times. For example, list what time you get up in the morning and what time you go to bed at night.

2. Then write down/fill in activities that are conducted on a ritual basis: things like taking a shower, reading the paper, driving to work and back, or eating meals are things that you do on a consistent daily basis.

3. Shade in meetings and other large blocks of time where you spent your day.

4. Outline all other activities that made up your day.

5. Compute the length of time you spent in that activity.

6. Circle anything you accomplished or completed.

7. Summarize the areas where you did not make the best possible use of your time.

One problem with this kind of time audit is that when you forget to record your activities as you complete them, you may find that you have blank spots during your day. If someone asked you what you did in that time slot, you may find it necessary to reply, "I worked . . . I think."

A sample time audit might look something like this:

5:00	am	Get up and fix the coffee	10	minutes
5:10	am	Take a shower, get dressed	30	minutes
5:40	am	Read newspaper	15	minutes
5:55	am	Organize day (home office)	30	minutes
6:25	am	Fix breakfast for family	35	minutes
7:00	am	Help get children ready for school	30	minutes
7:30	am	Take children to school	20	minutes
7:50	am	Drive to office	10	minutes
8:00	am	Staff meeting	1	hour
9:00	am	Return phone calls	15	minutes
9:15	am	Write article for company newsletter	30	minutes
9:45	am	Listen to John whine about the policy change	30	minutes
10:15	am	Solve a problem for an angry customer	10	minutes
10:25	am	Leave for a 10:30 meeting	5	minutes
10:30	am	Attend meeting on the XYZ project	2	hours
12:30	pm	Lunch	45	minutes
1:15	pm	Return phone calls	15	minutes
1:30	pm	Update boss (unexpected)	1	hour
2:30	pm	Handle a customer problem	10	minutes
2:40	pm	Write a proposal for the ABC Company	1	hour
3:40	pm	Take care of three phone calls	15	minutes
3:55	pm	John back for clarification . . . more whining	10	minutes
4:05	pm	Work on Mary's performance review (overdue)	25	minutes
4:30	pm	Walk to Andy's desk to update the ABC project	15	minutes
4:45	pm	Return two phone calls	10	minutes
4:55	pm	Talk with Larry about football game (unexpected)	15	minutes
5:10	pm	Organize desk	10	minutes
5:20	pm	Leave to pick up children from day care	30	minutes
5:50	pm	Get home, decide what to have for dinner	15	minutes
6:05	pm	Prepare and eat dinner	55	minutes
7:00	pm	Clean up after dinner	15	minutes
7:15	pm	Help children with homework	45	minutes
8:00	pm	Watch television with family	30	minutes
8:30	pm	Get children ready for bed	30	minutes
9:00	pm	Decide to watch TV but fall asleep	2	hours
11:00	pm	Wake up and go to bed	6	hours
5:00	am	Get up and start the routine all over again		

What are the benefits of conducting a time audit? It lets you see how you really do spend your time. Some of the learning points from this audit are:

- I spent four hours in meetings during the day.
- I spent 40 minutes of my day listening to John whine.
- I wasted 15 minutes walking to Andy's desk when inter-office mail would have worked just fine.
- Mary's review was the most important task I had to complete and I still did not get it done.
- The ABC proposal could have easily been delegated if I had planned ahead.

In this exercise, I just estimated that I probably missed two hours of my time. What's scary is that this was a typical day for me. So what's two hours a day? When you think about the big picture, minutes turn into hours and hours quickly turn into days. For example, let's say you find that you waste just 15 minutes each day. At the end of the year, that adds up to 11 full eight-hour days of productivity. Thirty minutes wasted equals 22 full eight-hour days. One hour a day equals 44 full eight-hour days, and last, if you find two hours, like I did, *that* equals 88 full eight-hour days of productivity.

A blank page is provided so you can complete a time audit. You are welcome to make multiple copies if you would like to chart more than one day. We recommend that you conduct a time audit at least four times a year.

Exhibit 5.1: Time Audit

Daily Time Log

Note: Do not try to account for each minute of the day. Account for 15-minute blocks of time.

Day of Week: M T W TH F		Date:	
Time	**Activity**	**Time**	**Activity**
6:00		1:00	
6:15		1:15	
6:30		1:30	
6:45		1:45	
7:00		2:00	
7:15		2:15	
7:30		2:30	
7:45		2:45	
8:00		3:00	
8:15		3:15	
8:30		3:30	
8:45		3:45	
9:00		4:00	
9:15		4:15	
9:30		4:30	
9:45		4:45	
10:00		5:00	
10:15		5:15	
10:30		5:30	
10:45		5:45	
11:00		6:00	
11:15		6:15	
11:30		6:30	
11:45		6:45	
12:00		7:00	
12:15		7:15	
12:30		7:30	
12:45		7:45	

Was this day: _____ Typical? _____ More busy? _____ Less busy?
Comments: _____

_____

_____

Successful Time Management and Task Accomplishment

You will find the following four steps helpful in managing your time.

Step One: Create a Master "To Do" List

This is a critical step. Many managers and supervisors try to keep track of all their tasks by leaving reminder notes for themselves. Yes, 3M Post-it notes work great for reminders. Little slips of paper and telephone message slips are other great reminders. The problem with this method is that little pieces of paper get lost. It can also be confusing. So, take all your tasks and record them on one "master" piece of paper. This first step is critical in helping you get organized.

Step Two: Prioritize Your Tasks

One thing is certain. Despite what many managers think, you can only do one task at a time. And we need to do the most important task first. The following five categories may be helpful in breaking down your priorities:

Category A—Highest priority (critical to my success and urgent)
Category A tasks are easy to distinguish. If you do not get them done, they will have a negative impact on your performance review. Whether it is your boss, an employee, or a client, if you do not get these tasks completed, the person who needed the task accomplished might lower your performance rating if he or she were to give you one. If you were supposed to solve a customer's problem and did not, the chances are that the customer would tell someone else in your organization about the problem. If your boss found out, he or she would feel you were not doing your job. Many supervisors and managers have lost their jobs or customers because they did not recognize a task as Category A.

Category B—Proactive (helpful to my success but not urgent)
A great example of a Category B task would be going to a time management seminar. It is not critical that you go right at this moment. However, by going, you may find better ways to manage your time. By managing your time better, you accomplish more. By using some time each day for Category B tasks, you will eliminate some of the fires that come up on a daily basis. Thus, you will have more time for your Category A tasks.

Category C—Routine ordinary tasks (time discretionary and time-bound)
Category C tasks need to be completed on a routine basis. A report is a great example. It has a specific date and time when it is due. You could work on the report at night after dinner. You could do it first thing in the morning. It is at your discretion when you complete the report. The only time the report becomes

a Category A task is fifteen minutes before it is due. Another example would be scheduling your employees to work. You could work on the schedule any time during the week. If you procrastinated up to the day when the new schedule was supposed to start, then it would become a Category A task. With proper time management, however, it should have remained a Category C task.

Category D—Routine ordinary tasks (not time-bound)
These are the tasks and projects that you would like to complete but there are no penalties or time constraints if you do not. A great example is that many of us have a stack of papers or other documents on our desk. Sometimes it is a big stack; other times it is a small stack. What we know is that most items in the stack fall into Category D. Every once in awhile, something ends up in our D stack by mistake (like a bill from the telephone company), and we feel the penalties of a miscategorized task. With D's, you can almost always delegate or dump. Give the project to someone else or throw it out. If it has been in your D pile for a month, it will not make much difference who does it or if it gets done at all.

Category E—Leisure time
Everyone needs to spend some time each day or week doing something that is relaxing or pleasurable to them. Leisure is different things to different people. For some people, going to the beach and enjoying the sunshine is relaxing. For others, this same activity is stressful. Pick what works best for you and spend some time each week or each day in a relaxing activity.

Step Three: Sub-Categorize Your Priorities

Once you have determined which tasks are your Category A priorities, then the next step is to determine which is the highest priority, the most urgent item of the A's. Label that task A1. Then take the second highest priority in Category A and label that A2. Do the same for the rest of the Category A's, B's, C's, and D's. An example of how this prioritization may look follows:

A1	Complete Mary's review
A2	Complete the proposal to the Henley Company
A3	Return phone calls
B1	Hold a staff meeting
B2	Clean off my desk
C1	Prepare budget comparison (due in two weeks)
C2	Return call to Larry
D1	Go through the stack of junk on my credenza
D2	Read old magazines

Four Tips to Help You Maintain Your Priorities

1. *Do your A's first.* Many supervisors find it a lot easier to do C's. The classic line is, "I will get these C's off the list first and then I will get to the A's." The problem is that you run out of time before you get to complete your A's. C's will not cost you your job. A's will, so do them first.

2. *Work on your B's each day.* We have found it helpful to work on a B each day. The easiest thing to do is to say you never have any time to move your B's up. An example of a B might be to create a model or template for one of the types of projects you are required to complete. If you had the model or template, others in the department could complete the task for you. You never seem to find the time to do this task, but if you make the time, it will free up hours every time this type of task surfaces in the future. Although you do not think you have the time to complete the template, you always find the time to complete the actual task. Make time each day to work on a B.

3. *Place less emphasis on C's.* Unfortunately, C's are usually easier to complete than A's. For this reason, the natural tendency is to do C's first. This is an error that many supervisors and managers make. We say to ourselves, "I will just get these few things out of the way, then I will complete the tough task." Each day, it is important to consciously prioritize each task. Returning an angry customer's phone call (an A) needs to take precedence over reviewing your monthly budget (a C). Once our tasks are prioritized, we need to do the highest priority, most-urgent item first.

4. *Use the GUTS theory on D's.* Everyone has a few D's. The best example is the pile of things you have stacked up in places like your desk, credenza, or some other slightly out-of-the-way location. With D's, you can practice the GUTS theory. GUTS stands for:

   G = Give it away to someone else

   U = Use it

   T = Throw it away

   S = Save and file it

   It you will practice the GUTS theory, you will eliminate a lot of clutter from your life. The problem with unattended D's is that they eventually multiply and will psychologically overwhelm you. Every time you walk into your office and see your stack of D's or a cluttered drawer or shelf, it bothers you because you are reminded of what you have not done. Use GUTS and you will keep your D's to a manageable level.

Step Four: Identify Your Time-Wasters

What wastes your time? The following are typical time-wasters. Place a check by the ones you feel cause you to waste the most time.

____	Misplacing something	____	Opening junk mail
____	Socializing	____	Unclear directions from boss
____	Watching television	____	Procrastination
____	Correcting others' mistakes	____	Tough employees
____	Paperwork	____	Unproductive meetings
____	Putting out "fires"	____	Interruptions
____	Commuting to/from work	____	_____
____	_____	____	_____

Once you know where you waste your time, following the suggestions in this chapter will help you overcome these time-wasters and make the best possible use of your time.

Are You a Procrastinator?

Recently an employee told us that her supervisor suffered from a severe case of "T.N.T." Not being familiar with that condition, we inquired and learned that "T.N.T." translates to "I'll do it **T**omorrow, **N**ot **T**oday." The supervisor was a noted procrastinator!

What's one task that you should accomplish now but (for whatever reason) you have been putting off for tomorrow or some other distant time in the future? All of us, from time to time, have procrastinated doing something that we know should be accomplished. By definition, procrastination is the intentional and habitual postponement of a task in order to do a task of less importance. If we have a legitimate reason for postponing a task, then by this definition, it is not procrastination. For example, if you decide not to work on the department budget today because the corporate budget is not going to be finalized until tomorrow, you may have a legitimate reason for postponement. You do not want to do the work twice. But if you choose not to work on the budget because it is tedious and you would rather reorganize your files, the chances are good that you are falling into the procrastination pit.

List three tasks where you are presently procrastinating:

Task One: _____

Task Two: _____

Task Three: _____

According to data we have collected in seminars, the following are some of the most common excuses why people procrastinate. Place a check by the excuses you have used in postponing some of your tasks.

_____ It's not due yet.

_____ I work better under pressure.

_____ The task is boring.

_____ I hope it will take care of itself.

_____ The task is tedious.

_____ The task is too complicated.

_____ I do not feel motivated to do it right now.

_____ I think I will have a drink first.

_____ I think I will eat first.

_____ I think I will watch a little TV first.

_____ I think I will take a short nap.

_____ I'm too busy.

_____ It's too early/late in the day to start that now.

_____ It needs further study.

_____ It is too nice a day to be spending it doing that.

_____ I will wait until Friday . . . next week . . . next year.

_____ It's too late now.

_____ I'm not sure where to begin the task.

_____ I do not want to spend more money.

_____ Before I start I need to . . .

_____ I am waiting for someone else to get something back to me.

_____ They might tell me no.

_____ I really do mean to do it but I keep forgetting.

67

Characteristics of Procrastinators

1. *Procrastinators know they have a problem and know they need to take action.* Procrastinators generally feel guilty every time they look at the task that needs to be completed. Procrastinators often have a good idea of exactly what needs to be done. However, great procrastinators continually postpone the very action that will relieve their guilt.

2. *Great procrastinators always promise to take action at some indeterminate time in the future.* The hallmark of procrastinators is that they do not ever take immediate action unless there is a crisis concerning the task. The self-talk of a procrastinator generally uses the phrase "I need to" rather than "I will." For example, a procrastinator feels comfortable saying, "I need to clean out the garage." A more goal-directed individual might say, "I will clean out the garage by noon tomorrow."

3. *Great procrastinators like to make the performance of the procrastinated task contingent on something else.* This makes the delay seem rational and justifiable. For example, a procrastinator might say, "I will take a vacation as soon as the pace slows down." Unfortunately, for the true procrastinator, the pace never slows down. In this scenario, the delay tactic is a convenient excuse rather than a legitimate reason for the delay. Most procrastination involves self-deception. We try to rationalize why we have not yet com-

pleted the task. When we procrastinate, we usually feel guilty or awkward because we acknowledge the fact that we are not weighing the penalties of not completing the task or the benefits of completing the task accurately. For example, if you presently are working in a declining industry, it may be in your best interest to actively look for a job in a new industry. The benefit of doing this is that you most likely will find a new job when you take action. The penalty for not taking action is that you might be laid off. When we accurately assess the benefits and the penalties, we probably would not have procrastinated the task of looking for a new job.

Real Reasons People Procrastinate

There are some definite reasons why people procrastinate. Here are some possible reasons that you may need to address before you can reduce procrastination in your life.

1. *Physical exhaustion.* When you are physically exhausted, it is difficult to do the things you enjoy, let alone do a task you have no desire to do. This may sound confusing, but when you procrastinate, the mental strain and guilt tend to make you physically *more* tired. The benefit of going to sleep is that you do not think about your procrastinated tasks. The penalty occurs when you have things you should have done "hanging" on your mind, so you do not sleep as well. When you complete procrastinated tasks, you will actually sleep better at night.

2. *Desire for perfection.* Some people do not want to start a task unless they can do it perfectly. Although not starting a task because you cannot do it perfectly may be a legitimate reason, it can also be used as an excuse. Most authors would never write a book if it had to be perfect in content and grammar. For some individuals, perfection is a reason not to start a task. For other individuals, perfection is the reason to get up tomorrow morning and continue working on the task.

3. *Depression.* If you have ever experienced a bout of depression, you know it is virtually impossible to get started on any task. The reason depression works so strongly in reinforcing procrastination is because depressed people usually have a negative vision. Tomorrow does not look very exciting, so what good is it going to do to take any action today? I have to have a positive vision that tomorrow is going to be better in order to complete this procrastinated task today.

4. *Manipulation of/dependence on others.* If you put off balancing your checkbook each month and your significant other is uncomfortable not knowing

how much money you have, then he or she will balance your checkbook for you. In this case, there is actually a positive payoff by procrastinating this task.

5. *Analytical ability.* If someone gave you a complex set of mathematical problems to complete, would you put off this task? There is a good chance you would if you did not have a strong background in math. When we lack understanding or knowledge, we tend to procrastinate.

6. *Forgetfulness.* If you do not have an effective "things to do" list or calendar system, you will find that you forget what needs to be done. If you legitimately forget a task, that may be a legitimate reason.

7. *Lack of desire to assume responsibility.* If you do not want to be responsible for the success or failure of a completed task, you might postpone the accomplishment of that task.

8. *Anxiety.* If you have a fear or anticipate a negative outcome, you will tend to procrastinate a task. For example, a supervisor who puts off confronting a problem employee because of fear and uneasiness that the encounter might get emotional shows anxiety. The anxiety reflects an anticipated fear of the employee. We put off tasks that are unpleasant.

Eight Steps to Overcoming Procrastination

1. *Decide what is causing the delay.* To win the battle with procrastination, it is critical that you figure out what is causing you to delay the task. Look back over the list of excuses and real reasons on the previous pages and see which ones apply to you. Once you pinpoint the cause, it is easier to generate a solution.

2. *Change your attitude.* Most people are not excited about completing a task that has been put off. It is this very lack of excitement and enthusiasm that creates a need to put off the task in favor of one of lesser importance. In fact, you will find that with most procrastinated tasks, you use negative self-talk. If your self-talk consists of statements like, "I don't even know where to start" or "This task is boring," it will most likely have a negative impact on the outcome. You are much better off focusing on the benefits of completing the task rather than the negative aspects of getting started on the task.

3. *Conquer your fears.* Sometimes we put off a task because we fear the outcome. An individual puts off going back to school because he is much older than most students and is not sure how well he will do. A good way to overcome your fears and get on with life is to analyze what might be the worst possible thing that could happen. After you recognize the worst

possible outcome, then ask yourself, "Can I live with the worst possible scenario?" Most times, we can live with the worst possible outcome.

4. *Make a master procrastination list.* To know what really needs to be done, analyze the different areas of your life and make a list of all the things you are presently procrastinating. Then, next to each procrastinated task, estimate how much time it will take to complete. Some tasks will only take minutes, others will take hours and days, and still other tasks may take years. After you analyze the amount of time needed to complete the tasks, then prioritize an order for completion.

5. *Organize a plan for completion.* After you have prioritized your tasks, the next step is to organize a plan to complete each project. Break down each project into smaller tasks. For example, if you presently have a large pile of magazines you need to read, it may be easier to accomplish the task by taking the following steps: First, separate them into piles by the different magazines you subscribe to. Second, work on only one type of magazine at a time. Third, flip open each magazine to the table of contents and highlight the articles you want to read. Fourth, tear out the articles that are important to you and throw out the rest of the magazines. Fifth, set a goal to read or review articles for fifteen minutes at a time (at least once or twice a day) until you have completed the task.

6. *Act now.* There is only one real solution to winning the battle with procrastination. Like the Nike ad, "Just Do It!" Let's say you have to write an article for your corporation's newsletter. The article will take approximately one hour to write. At this moment, you only have fifteen minutes before you need to be at a meeting. You can still act now. In fifteen minutes, you could put together an outline of the article.

7. *Do the toughest part first.* A young boy was sitting at the dinner table staring at some green peas that he did not want to eat. The problem was that his mother had said, "You cannot leave the table until you finish all your dinner, and that includes your peas." After watching his son stare at the green peas for over an hour, the boy's father shared this pearl of wisdom: "Son, if you have to swallow a frog, don't sit there and look at it." And so is the case with procrastinated tasks. They normally do not get better with time. They are very similar to green peas: If you don't like them hot, you probably will like them even less when they are cold. Another father had this piece of advice, "If you do one thing you dislike each day, life will be a lot easier."

8. *Reward yourself.* When you accomplish a task you have been putting off, reward yourself. Rewards differ from person to person. For one person the reward might be drinking beer; for another person, it might be walking on the beach.

Tips for Success: Time Management

1. Organize your work environment. Does the environment you work in work for you or against you? The more your environment is organized, the more productive you will be.

2. Establish place habits. It is estimated that the average American spends six months of his or her life looking for items that are lost, misplaced, or just plain missing. Think how much time you could save if everything you needed had a specific place, just like your screwdriver or flashlight.

3. Create a master daily "To Do" list. Each day you need to create a *new* "To Do" list. The tasks may take longer than you like, but if each task is on your list, it will eventually be done. (There are several types of computer-generated organizers that do an excellent job.)

4. Prioritize your tasks. Once you have prioritized your tasks, then do your highest-rated, most urgent items first.

5. Set goals. Without a specific set of goals, it really does not matter how you spend your time. (For more information on the specifics of goal setting, refer to Chapter 4.)

6. Cluster common tasks. When you return to your office after a meeting, there will be several phone messages on your voice mail. You can quickly cluster the messages and return them within five minutes. Clustering common tasks saves time.

7. Delineate time blocks. Block off a portion of time and work on only that task during the specified time frame. This technique works great on tasks where you have been procrastinating.

8. Stop procrastinating. Make a list of all the things in your life that you have been postponing. Then set a goal with a specific plan and time frame to accomplish those procrastinated tasks.

9. Delegate where appropriate. It is often more appropriate and efficient for someone else to accomplish the task. (For more information on effective delegation, refer to Chapter 7.)

10. Take the one-minute acid test. Ask, "Is what I am doing right now the best possible and most important use of my time?" Also ask, "Five years from now, what will be the most important to have completed, task A or task B?" These questions also help you put things in proper perspective.

Action Plan: Managing Time to Accomplish Your Goals

Three steps I can take to implement time management skills and when I will begin each step:

Action Step 1:

Target Date for Initiation:

Action Step 2:

Target Date for Initiation:

Action Step 3:

Target Date for Initiation:

Chapter 6

Communicating Effectively

> "I know you believe you understood what you think I said, but I'm not sure you realize that what you heard is not what I meant to say."
>
> —Sign on an executive's desk

Communication in the 21st century: mobile phones bouncing messages off satellites, fax machines sending complete proposals around the world in minutes, electronic mail relaying critical messages to hundreds of people simultaneously, teleconferencing around the world, interactive videos providing training at employees' desks. All these incredible high-tech advancements in communication, and two people standing face to face, speaking the same language, cannot seem to understand one another!

Of all the advancements made in communication technology, human communication continues to be the most challenging. The climbing divorce rate and the increasing number of runaways testify to the difficulties of marital and family communication. National and international crises point to the problems of communication among cultures and nations of the world. Government misunderstands the people and the people cannot seem to get their messages across to their elected leaders. Managers say that their employees do not follow instructions and employees say that their bosses do not listen. No wonder the line from the classic movie *Cool Hand Luke* has become such a catch phrase: "What we have here is a failure to communicate."

Communication is blamed as the root of relationship problems and acknowledged as the key to successful relationships. Divorced couples cite "poor communication" as the greatest contributor to their marital problems; and when successful couples are asked the reason for their success, the most frequent comment is "We communicate."

The same concept applies to the business environment. When employees are asked to describe their best and worst bosses, guess what item is at the top of both lists? You guessed it—communication!

Exhibit 6.1 lists some of the most common traits of "best" and "worst" bosses.

Exhibit 6.1: Description of Bosses

Worst Boss	Best Boss
Doesn't care about others	*Gives feedback*
Poor communicator	*Good communicator*
Doesn't listen	*Listens*
Gives mixed messages	*Speaks clearly*
Tells instead of asks	*Solicits input*
Self-focused	*Other-focused*

Research has consistently shown that the ability to communicate is the one characteristic judged by supervisors and managers to be most critical in determining promotability. In one study of 88 profit and nonprofit organizations evaluating the importance of 31 skills, interpersonal communication and listening skills were rated as the most important. A manager's number one challenge can be summed up in one word: communication.

In another survey of over 8,000 people in universities, businesses, government agencies, and hospitals, virtually everyone felt that he or she was communicating at least as well as and in many cases *better* than almost everyone else in the organization. Most people readily admit that there are communication problems in their organizations, but the problems are almost always associated with those "other people." Thus, while proficiency in communication skills is critical to managerial success, most individuals do not feel a strong need to improve their own skill level.

What We Know about Communication

There are certain aspects of communication that impact our day-to-day lives.

1. *No matter how hard one tries, one cannot avoid communicating; you cannot **not** communicate.* Many times we think we are not communicating because we are not verbally communicating. Not true: We are always communicating, whether we want to or not. We communicate nonverbally—with our eyes, facial expressions, gestures—and even by the color of our skin. During 30 minutes of discussion, people can exchange approximately 800 different nonverbal messages. The messages we send without words have a greater impact than when we speak.

   Dr. Albert Mehrabian, a noted UCLA researcher in the field of nonverbal communication, found that only 7% of our feelings and attitudes are communicated through our words. An astonishing 38% are communicated via our vocal intonation and the remaining 55% through our nonverbal expressions. And that is only a small part of the picture. The communication channel that we have the most control over and best understand, *our words*, has the least impact on the total message. And the channel we have the least control over and understand the least, *nonverbal communication*, has the most impact on our message. Whether we want to or not, we are always communicating.

2. *Communicating does not necessarily mean understanding.* Can you think of a time when you were convinced that you got your message across but later found out quite the opposite?

3. *Communication is irreversible.* Once you have communicated a message and it has been received, either verbally or nonverbally, it is irreversible. Have you ever said something that you have regretted? Or wished you had said something and did not? When dealing with employees, it is critical to choose words and messages carefully, because they will have a lasting impact. Unlike writing a letter where we can erase what does not sound right, our verbal and nonverbal communication is forever.

4. *Communication is affected by physical and social settings.* When we interact with someone, it is not in isolation but within a specific physical and social surrounding. For example, when our boss talks to us from behind his or her desk about a memo, the conversation will probably be quite different than the one that takes place during lunch at the corner deli.

   Another example of how our communication is "setting-controlled" is in a courtroom. Not only do we speak differently, but the physical layout—with the judge elevated above the other participants—also sends strong communication messages.

5. *Communication is dynamic.* Communication is an ongoing and ever-changing process. As participants in communication, we are constantly affected by other people's messages and, as a consequence, we undergo continual change. Every time we interact with someone, we leave that moment with new information . . . and a changed relationship.

Making Communication Work

Effective communication skills form the foundation for successful management and supervision. Our communication skills are so fundamental that it is easy to sometimes forget their significance. Because we communicate a lot, we often assume that it means we communicate well. You cannot lead without being able to communicate your ideas or without being able to understand those you are trying to lead.

All critical management skills require effective communication. Whether you are leading, coaching, delegating, building a team, making decisions, counseling, hiring, or doing just about any management activity you can think of, you will need to communicate. Effective communication involves (1) speaking clearly, (2) listening for understanding, and (3) fostering an open communication climate. In this chapter, we will look at each of these communication factors and offer valuable tips that you can use to improve your communication ability.

Speaking Clearly

As a manager, one of your primary responsibilities is to get the right message to the right person to get the results you expect. Because the communication process is so complex, getting your message across is not an easy task.

Think of all the things that can get in the way of you getting your message across to another person so that that you will get the results you expect. Here are some of the barriers or roadblocks that can get in the way: lack of understanding (on your part or theirs), interruptions, noise, emotional state (yours or theirs), bias, prejudice, boredom, resentment, language problems, culture, physical environment, lack of trust, poor listening habits, mixed messages, and unclear priorities.

To work your way around these barriers, consider the following ideas:

1. *Think through what you want to say before you say it.* Begin by focusing on your intention or goal. Be clear about what you expect as a result of

your communication. Do you want an employee to do a certain job? Do you want a co-worker to support you on a particular project? Do you want your boss to give you more information? In your mind, clearly define what you want to accomplish. Once you are clear about what your communication goal is, you can focus on the message you need to get across.

Your message must be tailored to the needs of the receivers or listeners. Consider the receivers' point of view. What information will they need? What will their opinions be? How are they likely to respond? Once you have thought through some of these issues, you can formulate a clear statement that is more likely to be well-received by the listeners.

2. *Once you have made your point, ask each listener for feedback.* Make sure that each listener has understood your intention and specifically what it is you want. You can get this feedback by observing and asking. Observe the listener's behavior. Is it in agreement? Does he or she appear to have questions or disagree? Also pay attention to the nonverbal cues you are receiving.

In addition to observation, ask for feedback. Ask the listeners what questions they have. Ask for their opinion or for their input. Check to make sure that they understand your message. If the message is somewhat complex, you can ask them to paraphrase what they currently understand to make sure you are both on the same wavelength.

77

3. *Speak clearly and concisely.* Some people believe that wordiness is a sign of knowledge or power, but it actually gets in the way of effective communication. Being overly verbose is a distraction. Many people will simply tune out a speaker who is too wordy. Keep your words and sentences short and to the point. Pay attention to how others are responding to you. If you notice signs of restlessness—loss of eye contact, fidgeting, or daydreaming—you have lost your listeners and may be going on too long. Move on to your next point and summarize the discussion. Keep your responses short and direct. A good rule of thumb is to keep answers under a minute.

4. *Speak with enthusiasm and expressiveness.* If you are trying to convince others or to motivate a team or individual, your ability to be enthusiastic is critical. Be aware of your tone of voice. Are you speaking in a monotone? If so, this is one of the quickest ways to lose the listener. Add variety to your voice by varying the speed, rate, and tone of your voice. Be conscious of emphasizing key words and phrases to get your message across better. Make sure that your level of enthusiasm is appropriate for the topic and the listener. Too much enthusiasm at an inappropriate time can come across as

phony or insincere. Adding examples, personal stories or experiences, and analogies or metaphors always makes your message more interesting.

5. *Develop a natural and informal style*. People are more likely to listen if you appear natural and informal in your discussions. Many employees complain that their bosses are stiff or formal when communicating. If you want to open up communication, be yourself. Let others get to know you by being yourself. Speak with your employees as you would to a friend. This informal approach will help you to build trust and credibility with others.

6. *Be sincere*. Your employees, co-workers, and your boss can see right through you! It is important to always be sincere in your communication. This includes letting others know when you are unsure or do not understand. It also includes telling the truth and being as direct and honest as you can be. When others truly believe that you speak from the heart, you are beginning to create a trusting relationship. Others will be honest with you in return. When two people or a team of people are open and honest with one another, the chances of getting and receiving clear communication will increase tenfold.

Listening for Understanding

Communication is a two-way street. In addition to speaking clearly, the effective communicator is a good listener. Listening involves not only hearing the speaker's words, but also understanding the message and its importance to the speaker, and then communicating that understanding to the speaker.

Most of us are not good listeners. There are many reasons for this. To begin with, we are not taught to be good listeners. Think of your formal education. Did you ever have a course in listening? You had plenty of courses in the other communication skills, such as reading and writing. You may have even had a class in public speaking. But very few of us have had lessons in how to *listen*.

In addition, we think many times faster than we speak. An average speaker will vocalize approximately 135 to 150 words per minute, but the receiver can comprehend as many as 500 to 600 words per minute. This time differential makes it easy for the mind to wander and take side trips away from the topic at hand.

Another reason why listening is so difficult is that we have a tendency to "half listen" while we are working on a reply. How often have you caught yourself formulating a reply and even starting to speak before the speaker has even finished his or her sentence?

Other factors that get in the way of effective listening include (1) noise or other disturbances, (2) mental or emotional distractions, (3) finding the speaker or topic boring or uninteresting, (4) prejudice or bias, or (5) simply an unwilling-ness to truly understand another point of view.

To overcome these barriers, try some of the following tips for improving your lis-tening ability:

1. *Develop an attitude of wanting to listen.* Being a good listener starts with a positive attitude toward listening. If you are not in the right frame of mind for listening, you will miss valuable information. Even if you do not feel like listening, remember that you can always learn something from everyone and that listening is a critical component to establishing trusting relation-ships. Good leaders always want to listen because they know the value of continuous learning. They also know that you cannot continue to learn if you do not listen.

2. *Reschedule a conversation if you cannot give it your undivided attention.* If you are unable to devote yourself to listening, for whatever reason, tell the speaker that you are unable to fully listen to him or her at this time. However, because you want to give your undivided attention, you would like to reschedule the conversation. Most people are more than willing to reschedule. In addition, many people will be impressed with your honesty and with the fact that you care enough to set aside time for them. When you do actually meet with the speaker, make sure to eliminate all distractions and give your full attention.

3. *Focus your attention on understanding the other person's meaning, not on formulating your response.* A good listener is "other-focused" rather than "self-focused." Your goal is to understand the other person. To do this, give them your undivided attention, ask questions for clarification, and check your perceptions for understanding. Focusing your attention on the speaker will also help you to listen without interrupting.

4. *Show the speaker that you are listening by using "attending skills."* A crit-ical part of the listening process is letting the speaker know that you are interested and that you are attending to his or her message. These are some of the attending skills you could use:

   ♦ Maintain eye contact to show interest and to observe the speaker.
   ♦ Lean forward slightly to communicate concern and to better comprehend the message.
   ♦ Come out from behind a desk or any other physical barrier.

- Nod your head to indicate understanding.
- Smile when the speaker uses humor.
- Allow for pauses—don't feel you have to fill the space with your words while the other person takes time to collect his or her thoughts.

5. *Use open-ended questions to open up communication.* Open-ended questions facilitate the conversation and provide an invitation to respond back and forth. They also let the other person know that his or her thinking is important to you. Open-ended questions cannot be answered with a simple "yes" or "no." These kinds of questions begin with words like "Tell me," "What," "How," "Explain," and "Describe."

6. *Use paraphrasing to verify understanding.* A paraphrase is a brief rephrasing of the speaker's words. Paraphrase by restating the speaker's information in your own words. Paraphrasing shows the speaker that you are listening and that you understand what he or she has said. It also ensures that your interpretation of the message is correct.

   Examples:

   "You think the XYZ program is not a good idea because . . ."
   "It sounds like your major concerns on this project are . . ."

7. *Use reflective statements to convey that you understand the speaker's feelings.* Reflective statements are short declarative statements that reflect the speaker's feelings or emotions without indicating agreement or disagreement. The purpose of reflecting is to let the speaker know that you understand how they *feel* about a particular topic or issue. Reflecting helps to establish rapport with the speaker, as well as provides an opportunity for the speaker to simply vent or "let off steam."

   Examples:

   "You're excited about this opportunity to work with the new software."
   "You seem worried about not being able to make the schedule."

8. *Summarize conversations to ensure understanding and provide closure.* A summary statement is a concise restatement of the key points discussed during a lengthy conversation. The summary brings the conversation to a close. It may also include a recap of specific actions or agreements made.

   Examples:

   "It seems that we agree that the project has gotten off track and that we will take the following steps to correct the situation . . ."

"As I understand it, you feel that we should bring the marketing people in on this proposal. As we discussed, I will contact them and set up a meeting for next week to discuss their involvement."

Fostering an Open Communication Climate

Speaking clearly and listening for understanding are the first steps to being a more effective communicator. In addition, good managers, supervisors, and leaders take specific actions to create a climate that is conducive to open and honest communication. In this open communication climate, people feel free to give their input and ideas, information is shared freely, conflicts are openly discussed and worked through, and people are more willing to express innovative ideas and to take risks.

The basis of the open communication climate is trust. The leader establishes an environment of trust within and among all the people in the group. To begin to build or expand trust in your organization and to foster an open communication climate, try some of the following tips.

1. *Keep your employees informed.* We all want to be "in the know." Take time to keep your employees informed about what is happening within the organization. Let employees in on the "big picture" and the reasons for management decisions. The more people feel informed about their organization, the better they feel about their participation in that organization. Managers who tend to hide information from their employees will soon lose credibility and will certainly not be included in important informal information loops. When you do not have the answer or are unsure of the reason for a particular decision, be honest with your employees and do whatever you can to get more information to them as soon as possible.

2. *Use a "real" open door policy.* Most managers say they have an open door policy. However, employees often quickly find out that although the door may be open, the mind is closed! If you have an open door policy, it means that you welcome people to come to your office with their ideas, comments, complaints, and suggestions. It also means that you are open to actively listen to and honestly respond to those who come to see you.

3. *Encourage others to express contrary viewpoints.* Let people know that you expect them to challenge and disagree with you. When they do, let them state their case. Do not interrupt. Ask questions to ensure that you understand their point of view. Look for areas of agreement and be willing to see others' perspectives. Once you have a clear understanding of others' views,

clarify the points that you support and those you cannot support. Provide a thorough explanation as to "why" you disagree. Help other people understand your perspective by speaking clearly and providing examples and illustrations to clarify your points.

4. *Don't "shoot the messenger."* Nothing destroys trust and credibility more than this one. Unfortunately, this is a common problem in many organizations. A good leader understands that in today's complex organizations people are required to relay messages. These messages may be from other groups within the organization, members of management, special groups or task teams, or employee or labor groups. All messages should be received calmly and no blame must be placed on the messenger. If you shoot the messenger one too many times, not only will the messenger not come back again, but everyone else will do whatever it takes to keep information from you.

5. *Encourage employees to share information.* If your employees rely solely on you to keep them informed, you will quickly become overwhelmed and the employees will not get all that they need to do a quality job. Let your staff know that you expect them to share information on a regular basis. Set aside time in staff meetings simply for information sharing. Actively involve others in giving updates and sharing other relevant information. When employees come to you for information that someone else can handle, redirect the employee to go to one of their colleagues for that information.

6. *Use a variety of tools to disseminate information.* Help get the word out by using a variety of tools to communicate. Get your employees' input and suggestions regarding communication tools. You could use such tools as the following:

   a. Departmental bulletin board
   b. Organizational or departmental newsletter
   c. Suggestion box
   d. Special information-sharing meetings
   e. Video or teleconferencing
   f. Electronic mail

7. *Promptly respond to communication from others.* A general rule of thumb is to get back to people within a maximum of twenty-four hours. A better rule of thumb for some of the people would be to get back within four hours. When someone sends you a note, letter, or phone message, get back as soon as you can to let that person know what you are doing about the concern. Even if you cannot respond with a complete answer or solution right away, you can let them know that you are working on it and that you will get back ASAP. Then, do what you said you would do!

8. *Keep your manager informed.* Managers differ in the amount of information they wish to receive from the people they manage. Take the time to discover what your boss expects from you. How often does he or she expect to hear from you? Does he or she prefer written information (reports or status updates) or a weekly face-to-face meeting? What types of decisions does he or she expect to be consulted on? When can you make decisions on your own? How much detail does he or she like? These and many other questions must be answered so you can respond appropriately to your boss. If you cannot readily find the answers to these questions, set up a meeting with your boss to go over these kinds of issues. Remember, no boss likes surprises. Find out what your boss needs and keep him or her informed and up to date.

Tips for Success: Communication

1. Think through what you want to say before you say it. Remember: You cannot *not* communicate.

2. Speak clearly and concisely. Also speak with enthusiasm and expressiveness.

3. Be sincere. Most people have a good "insincerity detector."

4. Develop a desire to listen. Demonstrate this by focusing on the sender's message, not on formulating your response.

5. Use the "open door" policy with your employees.

6. Show the speaker that you are listening. Demonstrate this by using attending skills such as eye contact and leaning forward.

7. Use open-ended questions to open up communication. However, use reflective statements to make sure you understand the speaker's feelings.

8. Summarize conversations to ensure understanding and provide closure.

9. Don't shoot the messenger. Encourage or reward people who have contrary viewpoints or who bring you bad news.

10. Keep your boss informed.

Action Plan: Communicating Effectively

Three steps I can take to improve speaking and listening and when I will begin each step:

Action Step 1:
Target Date for Initiation:

Action Step 2:
Target Date for Initiation:

Action Step 3:
Target Date for Initiation:

Chapter

7

Delegating to Succeed through Others

"Never tell a person how to do things. Tell them what to do and they will surprise you with their ingenuity."

—*General George Patton*

Most managers and supervisors have heard about delegation. We have read about it. We know that it is important for supervisors to practice. But like many of the skills presented in this book, very few managers or supervisors take the time to study and practice how to be an effective delegator. The most frightening thought about delegation is that when you delegate something, you are putting your reputation and your career path in the hands of other people. They can damage you if they are not the right people, if you have not trained them properly, or if you fail to delegate properly. The concept of delegation is vitally important to supervisors and managers if they are going to be effective in their jobs.

R. Alec MacKenzie, a leading author on the subject of time management, defines managing and supervising as getting things done through people. Delegation essentially is giving people things to do. Thus, by definition, the two are inextricably interwoven. It is difficult to be an effective supervisor without being an effective delegator, and vice versa.

There are many benefits to effective delegation.

1. *Delegation expands the results from what one person can accomplish to what many people can accomplish.* By involving other people through effective delegation, we have the potential to get more things accomplished

in our area of influence. In addition, we are likely to get new ideas and approaches to problems by tapping the input and brain power from others.

2. *Delegation frees up our time to get the most important things accomplished.* Many of the tasks that supervisors and managers do can be completed by their employees. By delegating routine and ongoing tasks, managers will have more time for more critical tasks, for leadership activities, and for innovation and problem prevention.

3. *Delegation develops our employees.* So many times we do not delegate tasks because we feel our employees are not capable of doing the task. Until we delegate the task to them and develop their skills, knowledge, and competence, however, we will continue to feel that our employees lack the capability. When we delegate tasks to employees, we in effect say, "You've got what it takes to do this job." This will enhance levels of trust between the employee and supervisor. Delegation is a critical employee development tool.

4. *Delegation helps empower our employees by taking the decision-making process to the appropriate level.* In the 1940s and 1950s, many managers felt that the quality of a decision improved the higher up the organizational chart it was made. We know now that decisions involving problems at different levels of the organization are often better if they are made by the people who are actually doing the work. Making decisions at levels where employees are making the product or dealing with customers fosters motivation and a sense of ownership for the task at hand.

Operating versus Managing Tasks

When we asked supervisors why they were promoted to supervision, most said it was because of their operational skill or ability to do the job they were doing well. They were good at the "doing" tasks that got the job done. Most organizations do promote the person who is the best at getting the job done. Examples of this are numerous. The best salesperson is promoted to sales manager. The best teacher is promoted to principal. The best cook tries to open his or her own restaurant. The best worker, engineer, or computer specialist is made the supervisor. If the worker in the new position does not learn new supervisory and management skills, the tragedy is often double. This means that the company loses its best worker and, at the same time, sets up a supervisor for failure.

Dr. Lawrence J. Peter and Raymond Hull developed the *Peter Principle* to describe this process. Peter and Hull extended this principle even further to state that people rise to their own level of incompetence if they are not willing to learn new skills to fit the new job. Exhibit 7.1 is adapted from Louis Allen's Theory of

Operating Priority. This model graphically shows how the need for managing and supervising skills increases as you move up in an organization.

Exhibit 7.1: Louis Allen's Theory of Operating Priority

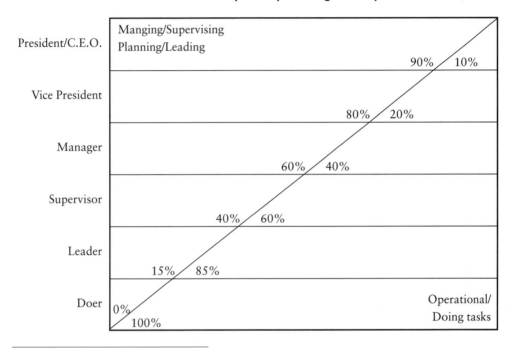

From *The Time Trap*, R. Alec Mackenzie.

As we rise further up the ladder in organizations, our responsibilities change from less emphasis on the operational (doing) tasks to more emphasis on the leadership tasks (managing, planning, leading). Getting bogged down in the "doing" functions rather than the planning, managing, and leading functions is one of the primary downfalls of many supervisors.

Louis Allen also states that when a supervisor is given an operational function and a managing function at the same time, the average supervisor will choose to do the operational function first. Most supervisors prefer the operational functions because (1) they are more familiar with them, (2) they are usually easier for the supervisor, (3) they have immediate results, and (most importantly) (4) the supervisor has been rewarded with a promotion for successfully performing the operational tasks. The past experience and success actually hinders the current effectiveness as a supervisor.

It is important to realize that the percentages in each of the categories shown in Exhibit 7.1 are not fixed percentages; they are simply estimates. The ideal ratio between *managing time* and *operating time* will vary, depending upon your management level and your particular organization. One reality remains constant: The higher you progress in management, the more time you should spend in managing, planning, problem-solving, and leading kinds of tasks and the less time you should spend on operating tasks.

Take a moment to complete the Delegation Assessment in Exhibit 7.2. It will help you rate yourself as a delegator in your current work structure.

Exhibit 7.2: Delegation Assessment

How Are You at Delegating?

How well do you delegate? As a supervisor, answer each question according to your current work structure by circling either a *Yes* or *No* response.

1. Yes No I give my employees new tasks, even though they may make mistakes.
2. Yes No My employees get promotions at least as frequently as other people with equivalent responsibility in our organization.
3. Yes No I very seldom take work home or work late at the office.
4. Yes No My operation functions smoothly when I am absent.
5. Yes No I spend more time on planning and supervision than working on details.
6. Yes No My employees feel they have sufficient authority over personnel, finances, facilities, and other resources.
7. Yes No My follow-up procedures are adequate.
8. Yes No I do not overrule or reverse decisions made by my employees.
9. Yes No I never bypass my employees by making decisions that are part of their jobs.
10. Yes No I do not do several things that my employees can—and should—be doing.
11. Yes No If I were incapacitated for six months, there is someone who can take my place.
12. Yes No My key employees delegate well to their own employees.
13. Yes No When I return from an absence, there is not a pile of paperwork requiring my action.
14. Yes No My employees take initiative in expanding their authority with delegated projects without waiting for me to initiate all assignments.
15. Yes No When I delegate, I specify the expected results, not how the tasks are to be done.

Scoring Key: Give yourself one point for each *Yes* answer. A good score is anything above 12.

Why We Don't Delegate

Most supervisors and managers know that delegation is important to their success. So, why don't they delegate more? Over the years, we have compiled a list of the most common responses to why people do not delegate. Review this list in Exhibit 7.3 to provide insight into your own delegation practices.

Exhibit 7.3: Reasons for Not Delegating

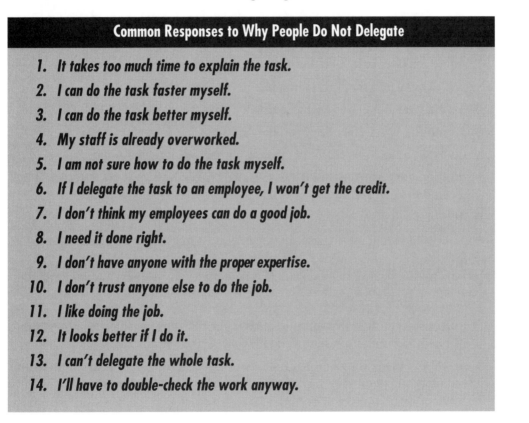

Common Responses to Why People Do Not Delegate

1. It takes too much time to explain the task.
2. I can do the task faster myself.
3. I can do the task better myself.
4. My staff is already overworked.
5. I am not sure how to do the task myself.
6. If I delegate the task to an employee, I won't get the credit.
7. I don't think my employees can do a good job.
8. I need it done right.
9. I don't have anyone with the proper expertise.
10. I don't trust anyone else to do the job.
11. I like doing the job.
12. It looks better if I do it.
13. I can't delegate the whole task.
14. I'll have to double-check the work anyway.

With all these reasons we have for not delegating, it is no wonder that we are hesitant to delegate. The following poem, written by an author known as "anonymous," brings a humorous light to our hesitancy.

Functions of a Supervisor

As nearly everyone knows, a supervisor has practically nothing to do, except,

- ➤ to decide what is to be done;
- ➤ to tell somebody to do it;
- ➤ to listen to reasons why it should not be done, why it should be done by someone else, or why it should be done in a different way;
- ➤ to follow up to see if the thing has been done;
- ➤ to discover it has not been done;
- ➤ to inquire why it has not been done;
- ➤ to listen to excuses from the person who should have done it;
- ➤ to follow up again to see if the thing has been done, only to discover it has been done incorrectly;
- ➤ to point out how it should have been done;
- ➤ to conclude that as long as it has been done it might as well be left where it is;
- ➤ to wonder if it is time to get rid of a person who cannot do a thing right;
- ➤ to reflect that he or she probably has a significant other and a large family, and certainly any successor would be just as bad and maybe worse;
- ➤ to consider how much simpler and better the thing would have been done if one had done it oneself in the first place;
- ➤ to reflect sadly that one could have done it right in 20 minutes, and now one has to spend two days to find out why it has taken three weeks for somebody else to do it wrong!

Common Mistakes in Delegation and How to Avoid Them

When managers decide to delegate, they often make mistakes that can negatively impact the employee's ability to do the job. After reviewing the following common mistakes, determine how you can avoid making these errors.

1. *Promote an attitude to the workforce of "I can do it better myself."* Most supervisors started out by doing the job so they often think that they are

still the best person to "do the job"—even though they have been promoted out of the job and into supervision.

Even if the supervisor can do a better job, the choice is not between the quality of his or her work and the quality of the employee's. The choice is between the benefits of the employee learning to perform that single task and the supervisor spending that time on planning, delegating, coaching, supervising, and developing an employee. Believe in your employees' abilities. They just might surprise you!

2. *Failure to keep employees informed about plans the supervisor has for the operation.* Some supervisors delegate tasks without providing all the necessary information to do the task successfully. Many supervisors leave out the *big picture*—the information about future goals, plans, and important organizational decisions. Employees must be fully informed to make the best possible decisions for the organization.

3. *Failure to require, receive, and/or utilize progress reports.* When you do not have a method to check on the employee's progress, two things happen. First, you communicate to the employee that the task delegated to him or her is not important. Second, you may set yourself and the employee up for failure. Agree with the employee on specific times to check progress at certain intervals from the beginning of delegation through completion. Remember, these checkpoints are designed to help the delegation process, not hinder its success.

4. *Unwillingness to let employees supply their own ideas.* When you do not ask for your employee's ideas and opinions, you are communicating that you do not value the employee. You are also limiting your opportunity to gain new information. Remember, if you always do what you've always done, you'll always get what you've always got! Encourage employees to be creative and give their ideas about ways to complete the task.

5. *Tendency to "dump projects."* Projects are usually "dumped" on someone because the supervisor has not taken the time to properly plan the delegation. At a moment's notice, the supervisor assigns the project to the employee. There are two negative outcomes: (a) the chances that the project will be done incorrectly increase immensely, and (b) the employee loses motivation because the supervisor did not take into consideration the employee's strengths or ability to get the job done. To ensure that the delegation is successful, take time to plan the delegation, pick the right person for the job, and discuss the task and its expected outcomes.

6. *Failure to give the employee credit for shouldering responsibility.* Typically, supervisors who do not delegate like to take all the credit in their area of influence. When an employee does take responsibility, no praise or recognition is passed to the supervisor. Acknowledging an employee's success may be viewed as threatening to the supervisor. With feelings of insecurity, this same supervisor will usually fail to back up an employee when he or she does make decisions. Give credit where credit is due. You will not only gain an enthusiastic employee, but also a loyal one!

7. *Inattention to project completion.* Not recognizing a project's completion will practically guarantee that the next project delegated will be completed late, if at all. This then reinforces the supervisor's negative feelings about delegating in the first place. Take a moment to acknowledge task completion. You can also use this opportunity to praise a job well done or to refine or train new skills.

8. *Lack of respect for the employee's ambitions.* Supervisors who do not delegate usually do not have an interest in developing their employees. This leads the employee to feel that the supervisor does not care about him or her. When we feel that the boss does not care about us, we lose our motivation and respect for the supervisor. So, get to know your employees. Find out their strengths, weaknesses, and their ambitions. If possible, support those ambitions. Help them grow.

Deciding What to Delegate

There are four basic steps in deciding what tasks you presently do that could be delegated:

1. Analyze your job

2. Categorize your activities

3. Estimate the percentage of time you spend in each category

4. Decide what to delegate and to whom you will delegate the task

Step One: Analyze Your Job

The easiest way to analyze your job is to make a list of at least ten tasks that you perform on a daily basis. The more complete the list is, the better understanding you will have of the tasks you may want to delegate. Use Exhibit 7.4 as your guide sheet.

Step Two: Categorize Your Activities

Categorize each of your activities into one of the following four categories: RO for routine or ongoing activities, FF for fire-fighting or problem-solving activities, PR for proactive or initiative-taking activities, and ED for employee development or "helping-people-to-grow" activities. This information should also be recorded in the appropriate column of Exhibit 7.4.

Step Three: Estimate the Percentage of Time in Each Category

The estimated percentage of time you spend on each activity has already been recorded on the chart in Exhibit 7.4. Now transfer those amounts into this section, remembering that the total should add up to 100%.

RO ACTIVITIES	_____
FF ACTIVITIES	_____
PR ACTIVITIES	_____
ED ACTIVITIES	_____
TOTAL:	100%

The typical supervisor spends 50% of his or her time on routine activities, another 30 to 40% on "fire-fighting" activities, and only 10 to 20% on proactive initiative-taking and employee-developing activities. To gain more time for problem prevention and employee development, you must first decide which routine activities you can delegate and to whom.

Step Four: Decide What to Delegate and to Whom

Study the information you have gathered so far, concentrating on the RO tasks. Which of these, as well as any of the others, could you delegate? Use Exhibit 7.5 to list the tasks, to whom, by when, and the average number of minutes each day you will save if you delegate the task.

The reason we ask you to list the approximate number of minutes you will save each day if you delegate the task is because most people do not realize how a few minutes each day begins to quickly add up. Exhibit 7.6 shows how minutes quickly add up to full 8-hour days when considered on a yearly basis.

If you were able to delegate just one task that takes 60 minutes each day, at the end of the year you would have 44 full 8-hour days to be spent another way. That is almost a full month of extra productivity to carry out more important leadership tasks.

Exhibit 7.4: Preparing for Delegation

First, list ten of the activities you do on your job. Second, decide which category each activity falls into: **RO** for routine, **FF** for fire-fighting, **PR** for proactive, or **ED** for employee development. Finally, estimate the percentage of time spent on each activity.

	Activity	Category	Percentage
1.			
2.			
3.			
4.			
5.			
6.			
7.			
8.			
9.			
10.			

Exhibit 7.5: Planning Your Delegation

List the tasks you could delegate, to whom, by when, and the average number of minutes each day you will save if you delegate the task. In determining to whom to delegate the task, consider employee development and learning. Are you selecting the appropriate person for the task?

	Task	To Whom	By When	Minutes Saved
1.				
2.				
3.				
4.				
5.				

Exhibit 7.6: Time Value of Delegation

Minutes Each Day the Task Takes	Number of 8-Hour Days per Year
15 minutes each day	11 full 8-hour days each year
30 minutes each day	22 full 8-hour days each year
60 minutes each day	44 full 8-hour days each year

Another way to look at this is to ask, "How much is my time or my employees' time worth?" To find out what that means to you, study Exhibit 7.7. Locate your approximate yearly income on the left side of the exhibit and then see what saving an extra hour a day could mean to your success and your organization's profits. When we look at the value of our time, it usually adds up much faster than we think.

Exhibit 7.7 Delegation Savings

Yearly Income	Per Hour	One Hour a Day All Month	One Hour a Day All Year
$20,000	$ 9.62	$202.02	$2,501
$25,000	$12.02	$252.42	$3,125
$30,000	$14.42	$302.82	$3,749
$35,000	$16.83	$353.43	$4,376
$40,000	$19.23	$403.83	$5,000
$45,000	$21.63	$454.23	$5,624
$50,000	$24.04	$504.84	$6,250
$60,000	$28.85	$605.85	$7,501

Income divided by 2080 (52 weeks × 40 hours) for per hour rate. Month as 21 days. Year as 260 days.

Planning for the Delegation

Now that you have determined what tasks to delegate and to whom, take a few moments to plan for the delegation. To do this, you need to answer the following questions:

- ♦ What is the overall goal or purpose of the task?
- ♦ What specific results do I expect?
- ♦ What does the task entail? What specific elements or skills are needed to successfully complete the task?
- ♦ What resources are available to the employee to get the task accomplished?
- ♦ What checkpoints or follow-up agreements need to be made?

Presenting the Delegation

After you have planned for the delegation, you should be clear on your expectations for getting the job done. These expectations must now be made clear to your employee. Keep in mind that your employee is likely to have some good ideas to offer, so plan on soliciting ideas from him or her as well. Below is a fail-safe process for ensuring delegation success. Be sure to follow each of the seven steps.

Step One: Explain the Overall Goal and Purpose

This critical first step lets the employee know the importance and value or relevancy of the task. Many supervisors make the mistake of skipping this step and starting by explaining the task. Specifically, they explain the how-to's of the task. You will find you get better results if you begin by explaining the big picture, the overall purpose of the task, prior to explaining any of the small details. When employees understand the overall goal, they make better decisions.

Step Two: Outline Expected Results

Once the employee understands the overall goal and importance of the task, he or she needs to know exactly what is expected. Do not get this important step confused with the next step, describing the task. The purpose here is to ensure that you and your employee see the same end result and agree on when that result will be in place.

Step Three: Describe the Task (optional)

This step is usually for inexperienced employees who have never done the task. You may need to provide some training here. If the task is a large or complex one, break it down into smaller, more manageable pieces for easier explanation. The purpose of this step is to ensure that the employee knows how to do the job. For experienced employees, let them decide. As long as they know the expected results, they can decide how to do the job. And guess what? Maybe they'll have a better way to do it!

Step Four: Discuss Resources

To do the job effectively, employees need to know what resources are available to them to get the task accomplished. Are they able to purchase equipment or supplies? Are they able to involve other employees? Are they able to enlist the help of other departments? If it takes working overtime, is overtime authorized? Be specific, so the employee is clear on what resources are and are not available.

Step Five: Confirm Understanding; Get Commitment

Here is where you make sure that you made yourself clear. Ask your employee to restate in his or her own words what is expected. You want to do this for two reasons: (1) it involves the employee and (2) you have confirmed knowledge as to whether the employee understands the task at hand. If you have ever delegated a task to an employee and then had the task completed incorrectly, you will understand the value of this point. Encourage the employee to ask any questions to confirm understanding. Last, ask the employee for his or her commitment in completing the task within the agreed-upon time frame. Without commitment, the task may not be done.

Step Six: Ask for Ideas

One of the best ways to empower and motivate your employees is to ask for their ideas. If you tell the employee how you have done the task in the past, make sure you ask him or her for ideas and suggestions on how to complete the task this time. When employees are given the opportunity to provide their own ideas, they take more responsibility for the completion of the task. When you ask for their ideas, be quiet and really listen. Very often a fresh perspective can provide great new ideas, especially if you have always done things the same way.

Step Seven: Establish Follow-Up Plan

Once the task has been clarified and confirmed and the employee's contributions have been solicited and valued, the next step is to establish some guidelines for working together. The supervisor always bears ultimate accountability for any delegated task. Remember, upper management assigns tasks to the supervisor, not to his or her employees. If the supervisor chooses to delegate, it is still ultimately the supervisor's responsibility.

Additionally, the supervisor is responsible for the quality standards and deadlines of any work coming through the unit. No supervisor can afford to turn an employee completely loose on a project. To ensure the fulfillment of supervisory responsibilities, a supervisor has to give adequate and proportionate attention to the people delegated the assignments. One method is to schedule follow-ups at certain completion steps throughout the task. Another more hands-off method is to check with the employee midway through, from the time you delegate the task to the task's completion. For this to be effective, you must make notes on your calendar so you do not forget. Be careful not to "micro-manage." Give the employee room to grow. When you think about it, that is why you can do these tasks so well. Someone gave *you* room to grow; you made some mistakes, and hopefully, you learned from the mistakes you made. The same process will prove equally valuable to your employees.

Problems You May Encounter When Delegating

Reverse Delegation

A common occurrence in supervisor-employee relations is what is often called reverse delegation, or upward delegation. It has also been described by William Oncken, Jr. and Donald L. Wass in the *Harvard Business Review* (November/ December, 1974 edition) as "ending up with the monkey back on your back." "Monkey jumping" works like this: You give one of your employees a task to complete. The employee stops you in the hall a few days later and states that he or she is stuck on the project and needs a decision from you. You reply that you are not sure and you will get back to the employee. Instead of having the employee take the responsibility and make the decision, you now have the project back on your desk. With enough of these monkeys, you find yourself working Saturdays while all your employees are enjoying a relaxing day off.

These are some of the reasons reverse delegation may take place:

1. *The employee wishes to avoid risk.* It is easier to ask the supervisor than to make a personal decision. To break this habit, refuse to decide for an employee. Simply ask, "What is your recommendation?" One supervisor solved this problem by placing a sign on her desk that said, "DBMP-BMA." The acronym stands for "Don't Bring Me Problems—Bring Me Answers."

2. *The employee is afraid of criticism.* If you are going to provide constructive feedback, do so privately and in a way that protects the employee's dignity.

3. *The employee lacks confidence.* Confidence can only be increased with experience and knowledge. You can help by providing support and encouragement.

4. *The employee perceives a lack of knowledge.* No responsibility should be delegated without the requisite information, knowledge, and authority. Provide whatever information and training is needed to set the employee up for success.

5. *The supervisor wants to "be needed."* The supervisor may feel that making decisions demonstrates indispensability. If you have this attitude, you will continue to find ways to get the "monkey" back on your back. You can serve your employees (and your organization) much better by helping them to grow.

6. *The supervisor fears being disliked by delegating or refusing to make a decision for an employee.* This is simply not the case. In a reported study by John Hemphill at Ohio State University, 500 groups of supervisors and managers were rated by their employees. The leaders who were rated "good" or "excellent" were the ones who made the greatest use of delegation. Conversely, leaders who scored "poor" were ineffective as delegators.

Accountability Factor

When you give a person responsibility and authority to carry out a job, you expect the person to meet the goals in the prescribed period of time. That expectation is what we mean by accountability. Another word for accountable is responsible.

Delegation consists of a set of responsibilities that the employee is expected to achieve. Supervisors must make sure that their employees are responsible. In other words, they do what they say they were going to do! It is your responsibility as the supervisor to hold your staff accountable for the commitments they make. Making sure that you and your employees demonstrate accountability is one of the most surefire ways to gain respect and credibility.

Why Delegation Works to Empower Employees

◆ *Delegating tasks to our employees shows that we trust them.* One of the fastest ways to build trust in a relationship is to take a risk with someone. Delegation is certainly a risk. As a supervisor, your reputation is on the line.

♦ *Most employees have a desire to work on their own.* When employees work on their own without constant over-the-shoulder supervision, they feel more pride and a greater sense of accomplishment.

♦ *By giving our employees more challenging tasks, they feel they play a significant role in the organization.* Delegation develops a sense of purpose, responsibility, belonging, and ownership within employees.

These three benefits alone are reason enough to delegate. Add to these the benefits stated at the beginning of the chapter and it is easy to see the value of delegation. Begin the delegation process now. Don't wait. Delegate!

Tips for Success: Delegation

1. To be successful as a supervisor or manager, you have to delegate.

2. Remember that effective delegation will not only expand productivity but will also serve as an employee development tool.

3. List your typical daily activities and determine what percentage are routine, fire-fighting, proactive, or employee-development. To be successful, spend more time in the proactive and employee-development categories.

4. Calculate the value of your time. Remember, if you delegate a task that only takes you 15 minutes a day, at the end of the year you will have gained 11 full 8-hour days.

5. Plan the delegation. The better your preparation, the better your employees will accomplish the delegated task.

6. When you delegate, present the overall goal and then outline the results you expect. Do not tell the employee *how* to do the task, unless he or she is learning for the first time.

7. Discuss what resources are available to get the delegated task completed.

8. Confirm understanding, ask for the employee's ideas, and ask for his or her commitment to get the task accomplished.

9. Establish methods of working together and following up.

10. After you have delegated the task, make sure that the employee has a feeling of ownership about the task.

Action Plan: Delegating to Succeed through Others

Three steps I can take to improve my delegation skills and when I will begin each step:

Action Step 1:
Target Date for Initiation:

Action Step 2:
Target Date for Initiation:

Action Step 3:
Target Date for Initiation:

Chapter

8

Coaching to Improve Performance

"The conventional definition of management is getting work done through people, but real management is developing people through work."

— *Aga Hasan Abedi*

Being a supervisor would be so easy if people just did what they were supposed to do! When we ask supervisors in our seminars the question, "Why don't employees do what they are supposed to do?" we receive these types of responses.

- ♦ The employee does not know how to do the task.
- ♦ The employee thinks the supervisor's way of doing it will not work.
- ♦ The employee is not motivated to do the task right.
- ♦ The employee does not know what he or she is supposed to do.
- ♦ The employee thinks his or her way is better.
- ♦ The employee thinks something else is more important.
- ♦ There are no positive consequences for correct behavior.
- ♦ There are no negative consequences for continuing wrong behavior.
- ♦ The employee is not capable of doing the task.
- ♦ The employee does not see the value in completing the task.
- ♦ There are obstacles that prevent the employee from completing the task.
- ♦ The employee has personal problems.

Now that we have a fairly complete list of reasons why employees do not do what they are supposed to do, the important question is this: "If you, as the supervisor, allow poor performance to continue because of these reasons, who is ultimately responsible for the poor performance?" Unfortunately (or fortunately), as the supervisor, *you are responsible*.

It is important to realize that almost all of these reasons for nonperformance are controlled by the supervisor or manager. Poor performance occurs because of poor supervision. If supervisors and managers took appropriate actions to make sure these reasons for poor performance are prevented or removed, the result would be satisfactory performance.

In this chapter, we will discuss how supervisors can effectively coach and counsel their employees for improved performance. We will also share a proven interactive management process supervisors can use to address most of the reasons why people do not do what they are supposed to do.

Why Should Supervisors Coach?

In Chapter 7, *Delegating to Succeed through Others*, we made reference to the fact that a manager or supervisor, by nature of the job, gives people things to do. Before you became a supervisor, your success was based solely on what you accomplished. Now that you are a supervisor, the rules have changed. Your success as a supervisor is no longer determined by what you accomplish, but rather by what your employees accomplish.

As a supervisor, your raises, promotions, demotions, and non-promotions are now based on the results your employees can generate. When your employees are successful, you will be viewed as a successful supervisor. In contrast, when your employees are failing, you will be viewed as an unsuccessful supervisor, no matter what you, personally, are accomplishing. The results of your staff are what determines your score.

To underscore the importance of what employees do, ask yourself this question: "Who needs whom more? Does the supervisor need the employees more, or vice versa?" Another way to put meaning to this question is to ask this: "If you did not show up for work tomorrow, what percentage of your department's workload would still be completed?" Usually, a supervisor's answer will be anywhere from 85% to 100% of the total workload. Now, let's reverse the question and ask: "If all your employees did not show up for work tomorrow, what percentage of the workload would be completed by you?" If you answered any higher than 15% of the total workload, you may be kidding yourself.

The bottom line is that you get paid for what your employees do, not for what you do. For this very reason, you need to do everything in your power to help your staff be as successful as possible. The more successful your staff is, the more successful you will be as a supervisor. We can even look at this point from the opposite direction—when your employees fail, you have failed also.

Why Supervisors Fail as Coaches

Supervisors complain that the employees who do not do what they are supposed to do are their biggest headaches. This headache is usually the source of built-up frustration from unsuccessful attempts to get the employee to change his or her behavior. Some supervisors have said they have tried for years to motivate an employee to change his or her behavior without achieving any significant results. There are several reasons why supervisors have difficulty in coaching.

1. *The supervisor has had no formal training in coaching.* Getting employees to change their behavior is not an easy task. Instead of getting each employee to understand that a problem exists and asking the employee for solutions, most supervisors do what they are comfortable doing: tell . . . Tell . . . YELL!

    The problem with telling someone they have to change is two-fold. First, you have no guarantee that the employee agrees there is a problem. And second, most employees become defensive when being told they are doing something wrong. In the coaching process explained in this chapter, we will learn that the best coaches *ask* questions, rather than *tell* answers.

2. *In frustration, the supervisor ceases to treat his or her employees with dignity and respect.* "I am only human," I heard one supervisor say as he yelled at one of his employees for making a mistake. When we have an employee who is not doing what he or she is supposed to do, we tend to respond in ways that aggravate, not help the situation. Some supervisors will attack an employee's personality: "You are not motivated," "You are not ambitious," or "You are careless." Some supervisors will bang doors, slam down phones, or even throw things.

    These same supervisors would never walk into the company president's office and exhibit these same aggressive behaviors. The reason why they do not exhibit these behaviors up the organizational ladder is because it would be self-destructive. They would be fired. Unfortunately, supervisors do not see that these behaviors are also self-destructive when used going down the organizational ladder. These behaviors usually achieve the exact opposite goal that the supervisor desires. They de-motivate, frustrate, and cause employees to increase undesirable behaviors.

3. *Supervisors fail to see employees as "true resources."* When supervisors encounter problems with machines, materials, facilities, or budgets, most figure out ways to make the most of what they have. For example, if you were the supervisor at a plant where a machine had stopped working, you would do everything in your power to get it up and running again. Most organizations do not have the luxury of replacing a machine every time it breaks down.

In contrast, when a *human* resource fails, supervisors are quick to explain the problem as "the employee's problem." By placing the blame on the employee, the supervisor absolves himself or herself of all responsibility to correct the "problem." The typical response to a human resource problem is to replace the person. It would almost sound funny to say, "It's the machine's fault . . . it's old . . . there's nothing I can do about it." In almost every area *except human resources*, supervisors are great at taking the responsibility to solve problems.

Most supervisors never calculate the cost of replacing one of their *human* resources. We recently heard an example of what it costs to replace an employee. A manager told us that it cost her nearly $50,000 to replace a $60,000-a-year employee. When you add up severance pay, advertising, interview time and expenses, agency fees, relocation expenses, reorientation, and training time, it is easy to see how these costs can quickly add up. For a highly specialized or technical employee, replacement costs can easily add up to several more thousands of dollars. Add to that the headache of trying to find a qualified employee in today's highly competitive labor market, and it makes sense to rethink the high cost of replacing an employee.

Managing all of your resources *except your human resources* goes against what you are paid to do as a supervisor. As a coach, your responsibility is to help develop *each* of your employees. As a supervisor, you must accept full responsibility for all your human resources, just as you always have with all of your non-human resources.

The Role of Employees

When the business you are presently involved in was started, someone exhibited certain behaviors that customers perceived as meaningful. Simply stated, someone satisfied a customer. As your organization satisfied more customers, it began to grow.

It is important to recognize that in any business there are no guarantees that it will be around forever. Statistics tell us that eight out of ten new businesses fail in their first three years. There are no guarantees that large businesses will be here forever either. In the last few years, companies such as Eastern Airlines, The Discovery Zone, The Broadway department stores, and The Incredible Universe have all "bitten the dust." A company will only survive as long as each individual in the company continues to do the things necessary for survival, as well as the things that customers consider important.

In many ways, a company is like a lifeboat. As long as all the people on the lifeboat do what they are supposed to do, we all have a chance to survive. Your department is also like a lifeboat. If every employee does what he or she is supposed to do, the department has a good chance of survival. If employees do not do what they are supposed to do, they are behaving in self-destructive ways.

When we hire an employee, what we are really hiring is the rental of their behaviors. This behavior might be a production behavior, a problem-solving behavior, a driving behavior, etc. Each job that must be done in your company is a collection of specific behaviors that, when done correctly, constitute a specific job. As the employer, it is our prerogative to decide which behaviors we want to rent. The behaviors we choose are usually the behaviors that will help the organization survive.

When an employee behaves in a way that does not support the job, that employee is acting contrary to the job. If the employee refuses to behave in those specific ways required of that specific job, they are showing self-destructive behavior. If the success of your unit depends on their behaviors to survive, their inappropriate behaviors are destructive to your unit as well. To turn a full circle, the survival of your lifeboat is at stake, and you, as the captain, are in equal danger of survival.

Attitude and the Coaching Process

"That employee has a rotten attitude" is a classic response supervisors use when they have problems getting an employee to do what he or she is supposed to do. What most supervisors assume is that any employee who does what he or she is supposed to do has a good attitude, and if the employee does not do what he or she is supposed to do, there's a bad attitude. However, relying on attitudes to determine your course of action isn't a good idea for two reasons:

First, it is difficult to truly know what an employee's attitude is. Attitudes are something internal and unique to every individual. If you think you know what an employee's attitude is, it is usually based on what your attitude is or would be in a similar situation.

We can even go so far as to say that we know what the employee's attitude is based on his or her actions. The problem with this line of thinking is that people at times do things in direct opposition to their true feelings. Haven't you ever communicated (using good manners and even kindness) with someone you did not like? We really do not know for certain what people's attitudes are. We only guess at what they are and then become trapped into believing our guesses are correct. As a rule, supervisors should stay clear of the mind-reading business.

Second, by placing blame on the employee's attitude, we absolve ourselves of responsibility for the problem. The real problem you need to deal with is not the employee's attitude, but the employee's behavior. If the employee is behaving in appropriate and productive ways, then it really does not matter what his or her attitude is.

For example, let's say a waiter hates his job. Normally, a waiter who hates his job sooner or later provides poor service. But if the waiter is exhibiting appropriate behaviors and the customers are happy, then you do not have a problem. If the waiter is giving poor service, then poor service is the problem you need to deal with, not the employee's bad attitude.

Attitude is not the issue when you are coaching an employee. Behavior is the only thing you can legitimately deal with. You can see it when it is bad, you can measure it, you can talk about it unemotionally, and you can acknowledge it when there is improvement. If you start trying to change behavior rather than trying to change people, you will no longer be faced with the resistance people naturally present because *they* do not want to be changed.

Ask Instead of Tell

Just because you are speaking to someone does not guarantee that you are communicating. Hearing is seldom the receiver's problem. The problem is usually related to the receiver's lack of concentration on the information the sender is sharing. Part of this problem is that the mind can think up to four times faster than we can speak. This means that while we are listening, we are also usually using the extra time to think of other things. The mind is typically reacting even before the message has been completed.

A good way to demonstrate this principle is to ask someone to say the first thing that comes to mind when you say the word "dog." If true communication is taking place, the person will simply repeat the word "dog." But because the mind is always thinking and reacting, people respond with words such as "cat," "puppy," or "friend." The receiver may not react to what you said, but he or she may think of something else because of what you said.

What does this mean to supervisors who are coaching employees? It means that as long as you are telling employees what they are doing wrong, the employee will be thinking of something else—usually the reasons why what you are saying is not correct. An example could work like this:

Supervisor: "Bill, you have been late three times this week. What can you do so you arrive to work on time?"

Bill: "Mary has been late also. Have you talked to her yet?"

For supervisors, one of the biggest mistakes they can make is telling a problem employee what they are doing wrong. As soon as you say the words, the employee will hear them, but think of something else, like "Look at Mary. She's late also."

Because the mind is primarily a reactive instrument, successful communication is a function of thought transmission, rather than information transmission. In coaching employees, thought transmission takes place by asking questions. In the previous example, the supervisor could have asked any one of the following questions:

Supervisor: "Bill, what happens when I need you first thing in the morning and you are not here?"

"Bill, when you are not here and your phone rings, other employees have to answer it for you. What impact does that have on their schedules?"

"Bill, if I allowed you to be late, what impact do you feel that might have on the other employees in our department?"

"Bill, when a customer needs you, and you are unavailable because you are late, what impact might that have on our customers?"

What is so interesting about this concept of thought transmission is that when the supervisor does not use it, the employee will. Think about a time when you ran into problems providing feedback to an employee. The chances are you felt frustrated because the more you told the employee, the more he or she seemed to find fault in what you were saying. The only way you can guarantee that the

109

employee understands there is a problem is to get the words to come out of his or her mouth through thought transmission. And the way a supervisor facilitates thought transmission is by asking the appropriate questions.

Preparing for a Coaching Discussion

Coaching is, in many ways, a negotiation. Just like a negotiation session, the better you prepare, the better your chances of obtaining a favorable outcome. Consider the following questions before you begin a coaching discussion. Your answers will provide a framework for a win/win interaction.

1. *What is the problem?* Identify the specific problem. Exactly what is happening that shouldn't be, or what should be happening that isn't? Some typical problems may include (a) coming in late, (b) excessive absences, (c) sales down, (d) customer complaints, or (e) incomplete reports. Make sure you define the problem in specific "behavioral" terms. Remember, a bad attitude is *not* a specific behavioral problem. However, ignoring customers or not providing follow-up within 24 hours is.

2. *What is the cause of the problem?* You may not know for sure what the cause of the problem is until you have the coaching discussion. However, you can begin to identify possible causes. For example, sales may be down because (a) the salesperson is no longer calling on new accounts or (b) maybe existing customers are not being asked about additional services that may be needed. Why are the reports incomplete? Is it because (a) the employee is not doing a thorough analysis, or could it be that (b) the employee is not getting the information he or she needs from someone else to complete the report? A clear understanding of the cause of the problem will speed up the problem-solving process and will allow for realistic and practical solutions.

3. *Does the problem warrant coaching?* If the problem is only an isolated incident or an issue that is not really important, it may not be worth your time or effort to have a coaching discussion. In addition, it could be harmful to the employee's motivation. An example would be the employee who stays late each night until the job is done and then comes in late one morning. If the supervisor were to talk to the employee about the one late arrival, there might be some resentment. The result of this kind of discussion might be two-fold: the loss of self-motivation and the loss of respect for the supervisor. Make sure the problem is in fact a problem before you have a coaching discussion.

4. *Is the employee capable?* Is the employee physically and mentally able to do the job? Does he or she have the skills, knowledge, and abilities to successfully complete the job or task? If the answer is "no," then education or training may be needed to properly prepare the employee.

   There is another aspect to this question. Does the employee have what he or she needs to complete the task? In other words, are the necessary resources available to the employee? Resources may include finances, other people, raw materials, equipment, and/or facilities. If the necessary resources are not available to the employee, they must be provided or the job expectations must change. Good managers set their employees up for success by making sure that they can do the job and that they have what they need to do a good job!

5. *Does the employee know right from wrong?* The most common reason employees do not know that they are doing something wrong is because they think they are doing it right. Some supervisors have a habit of only providing feedback in severe instances when the employee has demonstrated inappropriate behavior. The other times, when the employee is plodding along on the path of mediocrity, the supervisor says nothing. Many employees think that mediocre performance is good enough because no one has ever told them differently. If workers in any job believe they are doing what they are expected to do, why should it occur to them to do anything different? As a supervisor, your obligation is to have good communication with your employees so they know what is appropriate and inappropriate behavior.

6. *Are there rewards for non-performance or punishments for performance?* A classic example of how an employee might be punished for performance is when a worker in a production facility works faster than the rest of the employees, and as a consequence is given more work to do. The employees who take their time and work slowly are rewarded by having more work taken away from them. Supervisors experience this phenomenon every day. If you have problem employees, you seldom ask them to take on new tasks because you know it will be difficult to get them to agree to do the tasks. So, instead, you give the assignments to the employees you give all your tasks to because they are more willing to get things done. This is how supervisors can reward negative behavior.

   A supervisor at one company's facility brought in homemade cookies every time her workers complained. Within two months, she was bringing cookies three and four times a week. The employees know what works! Be careful that you are not actually rewarding someone for inappropriate behavior.

Suggestions for Dealing with Performance Problems

1. *Take immediate action.* The longer you wait to confront a negative behavior, the harder it will be to change. It does not take long before the inappropriate behavior becomes a habit—habits are very hard to break. Once you have determined that a negative pattern of behavior exists, take action.

2. *Give feedback privately.* Prior to beginning the discussion, you should make sure that you have a private room to meet in. Take steps to ward off any interruptions. If at all possible, hold the meeting one-on-one. Only in rare instances is a third party necessary. (If the employee is to be terminated or is unwilling to cooperate, you may need a third party, such as a union representative or a human resources representative.)

3. *Remain calm.* If you have ever driven home from work saying, "Now why did I say that?" chances are you may have regretted giving feedback to an employee when you were mad. If you are angry or emotional, postpone the discussion until you are feeling more in control. Remember, communication is permanent. Do not lose control of the discussion or say something that may later come back to haunt you.

4. *Be consistent.* Do what you say you are going to do. If you tell employees you are going to do something if their inappropriate behavior does not change, do what you say you are going to do. If employees do not feel you are going to take action, they may see no need to change.

5. *Correct behaviors selectively.* Do not use a correcting session to point out all the negative things that you have seen over time. If you coach properly, you should only be dealing with one or two inappropriate behaviors at a time. If you do not have ongoing communication with your employees, you may start to generate a laundry list of behaviors you want to discuss. The laundry list will have little impact and will likely get thrown out in the wash! Our general rule of thumb is, "If it's more than two, they think it's you!" This means that if you do bring out your long list of inappropriate behaviors, after about point five or six, the employee begins to think, "Why bother to even come to work? I must not be doing anything right. I never thought my boss liked me anyway. She's always picking on me!"

6. *Remain positive.* Keep your thoughts positive. Help the employee identify what is causing the problem, and what the employee will do to help resolve

the problem. Remember, the goal of this discussion is to make the employee more successful. Only in rare instances is an employee not willing to grow by changing negative behaviors.

Coaching Discussion Model

The purpose of the coaching discussion is to redirect the employee's behavior. You want the employee to stop inappropriate behavior and start demonstrating appropriate behavior. It is a two-way process, a *discussion*. The intended purpose is for the employee to be engaged in a discussion as well. In fact, the employee should be talking more than the supervisor or the manager. Use the following six steps of the Coaching Discussion Model to make your coaching discussions effective.

Step One: Help the Employee See the Existing Problem

This is the most important step of the entire coaching discussion. If the employee does not agree there is a problem, then the supervisor actually has two problems to deal with: (1) the inappropriate behavior and (2) the employee not thinking the inappropriate behavior is a problem.

Step One is a difficult area for supervisors. Many lack a feeling of competence in this area. Without preparation, this beginning can be difficult; therefore, many supervisors want to just skip over this step. But if the employee does not agree there is a problem, he or she will probably not have the motivation to improve behavior.

According to Ferdinand F. Fournies in *Coaching for Improved Performance*, there are only two reasons that will convince an employee that a problem exists: (1) if the employee understands the results or outcome of what he or she is doing wrong, or (2) if the employee perceives the negative consequences to himself or herself if there is no change in behavior. The results or outcome referred to in the first statement are the things that happen because of the employee's non-performance. The types of questions we could ask to gain agreement in this area include:

- ♦ "What is/are the result(s) of this behavior (non-performance)?"
- ♦ "What impact does this behavior have on other employees/departments?"
- ♦ "What would happen if all employees did this behavior?"
- ♦ "What would happen if I (the supervisor/manager) ignored this behavior indefinitely?"

- "Do you know how many times you have done this behavior in the last _____ ?"
- "What impact does this behavior have on our customers?"
- "What credibility do you feel I have with my boss when I allow this behavior to continue?"
- "I am puzzled as to why you don't perceive this as a problem, so can you elaborate?"

If the employee is still unwilling to admit that there is a problem by answering any of the above questions, you may need to move to the second stage of questioning.

- "What will happen if you continue with this behavior?"

When the employee responds with, "You could write me up or suspend me," you can then respond with, "You are right. And if you continued with this behavior after I documented this problem or suspended you, what else could I do?"

A second question you may try is, "Do you think I can decide to let you continue this behavior?"

If the employee states that allowing the negative behavior to continue is not your choice, you can respond with, "You are right! What do you think you can do differently so we no longer have this problem?"

If the employee states that you can decide to allow the behavior to continue indefinitely, you can respond with, "You are incorrect. As a supervisor, I am responsible for seeing that (the area of concern you are discussing) is not a problem in our department/company."

The employee's comments could activate some of the following responses:

- "You can suspend, demote, hold up my promotion, put something in my personnel file, fire me . . ." Your response could be, "You are right, because I need someone in that position who will do (describe the behavior) what needs to be done."
- "You can do anything you want, because you are the boss." Your response could be, "No, I cannot. Your choice of behavior limits my behavior."

Some of these questions and responses in this second round sound threatening. Well, you are right. If the consequences are realistic—that the employee could be suspended or fired—and if he or she is unwilling to change his or her behavior, it is important that the employee understands the consequences of his or her own behavior.

It may be difficult to get agreement that a problem exists. The following eight possibilities will help you evaluate the situation more thoroughly.

- ♦ You are not dealing with a behavior related to performance.
- ♦ What you are dealing with really is not that significant.
- ♦ It is important, but you have not correctly identified all of the negative consequences.
- ♦ You are trying to get the employee to acknowledge unrealistic or hypothetical consequences.
- ♦ You are not using thought transmission, but you are verbalizing the consequences instead of letting the employee verbalize the consequences.
- ♦ In the past relationship, you have never done what you said you were going to do and have limited credibility with the employee.
- ♦ There is a positive consequence for the employee to continue the negative behavior.
- ♦ The employee has psychological problems too severe to manage.

Step Two: Clarify the Cause of the Problem

Once the employee clearly sees that there is a problem, you can begin to ask "why." The employee may have an idea why the problem is occurring; the employee may know something you don't know. Do not assume that you already know the cause of the problem. Make sure you ask for input and ideas. It is more likely that the person doing the job will have an understanding of why the job is not being done right. This person is also more likely to have good solutions to the problem. As a supervisor, you just need to ask—and then listen.

Step Three: Mutually Discuss Alternative Solutions

Once you have gained agreement that a problem exists and you have clarified the cause of the problem, you are ready to move to solutions. You can say to the employee, "Now that we agree there is a problem, what do you think you can do differently to solve the problem?" Make sure to focus on the word *differently*, because if the employee keeps on doing the same behaviors, he or she will keep getting the same results. It is important that the supervisor lets the employee generate solutions. For example, if the inappropriate behavior is making errors in a document, then we would want to ask the employee what he or she thinks might be done *differently* to produce less typos. The employee might reply,

+ "I could proofread each page."
+ "I could have someone else proofread each page."
+ "I could run the document through Spell Check."

With each response, acknowledge the good ideas. Ask, "What else could you do?" Remember, you are trying to generate viable alternatives. If the employee cannot think of any ideas, you need to be prepared to ask questions to help steer him or her down the right path. For example, you could ask,

+ "Would it be beneficial to spend time proofreading each page?"
+ "Would it help you to have someone else proofread each page?"

Step Four: Mutually Select an Alternative(s)

Do not waste time in Step Three debating which alternative is feasible. If you criticize an alternative an employee shares, the employee will stop sharing. In Step Four, you are now ready to pick an alternative. Once again, the best way to select an alternative is to ask questions. Ask the employee which alternative he or she thinks will work best—and why. Let the employee think it through and let the employee pick the solution.

Step Five: Follow Up Completion of Appropriate Actions

Make sure to follow up with employees to see how they are doing. Many supervisors make the mistake of not following up to ensure that the agreed-upon action has been taken. The supervisor may be too busy to check or may trust that the employee is going to change his or her behavior. The employee will often change the behavior immediately after the performance improvement discussion. However, because there is no recognition for the improved performance, the employee slips back to inappropriate behaviors. Two months later, the supervisor sees the negative behavior again and assumes that there has been no change. If the employee has not modified his or her behavior, the new problem is that the employee did not do what he or she agreed to do.

Step Six: Recognize Achievement When It Occurs

This step can be a tough one. Let's say your employee has been performing at the 50% level, but satisfactory performance is at 90%. You provide coaching and during the next week the employee raises his or her performance to 60%. You think to yourself, "It is a little better, but he or she still has a long way to go." You do not want to say anything about the improvement for fear that the employee will feel that a little improvement is good enough.

If you want the improvement to continue, the key is to recognize it—no matter how small! Recognize the employee's progress. Then, ask the employee what can be done to bring the next round of improvement to an even higher level.

This model is successful in handling the majority of employee-related problems. If you adequately plan for the discussion, you will have positive results. In the rare instances where an employee is still not willing to improve the behavior— even after the discussion—the Corrective Action Feedback Model then becomes appropriate.

Corrective Action Feedback Model

Unlike the Coaching Discussion Model, the Correction Action Feedback Model is *not* a two-way discussion. It is the style most supervisors feel very comfortable with. In fact, in this model you actually ask employees to hold their comments and questions until you have finished presenting your information.

Step One: Specifically Describe the Problem Behavior

Example: "John, in the last month, you have been late to work 15 minutes or more at least five times."

Step Two: Express Feelings about the Behavior's Impact

Example: "John, I am disappointed that you continue to come to work late. We have discussed this matter several times. As your supervisor, I feel this is unfair to the other employees who get here on time. I also feel it wastes my time and the other employees' time. When we need you and you are not here, we have to come back again to look for you."

Step Three: Value the Employee

Example: "John, you have been in our department for two years. You know the operation well and I value the job that you do."

Step Four: Specify Desired Future Behavior

Example: "In the next three months, I am holding you responsible for getting to work on time every day."

Step Five: Project Positive and Negative Outcomes

Example: "John, if you are able to be at work on time each day for the next three months, here are the *positive* things that could happen:

First, I will get off your case about being late.

Second, I will put a letter in your employee file saying that you have improved.

Third, you will be eligible for a favorable performance review.

Fourth, you will once again be eligible for raises and promotions.

Fifth, you will keep your job."

Example: "John, if you continue to be late, here are the *negative* courses of action:

First, we will have this discussion once again, we will document it, and we will place a copy in your employee file.

The second time it happens, I will suspend you for two days without pay.

The third time you are late, you need to understand that I will fire you."

At this point, you must ask the employee if he (John) understands the consequences. If he says "yes," ask him to tell you what he understands. Take this step to make sure that he understands the major points.

There is no arguing that coaching is a tough supervisory skill. However, it is a skill that is critical to your success as a supervisor. No matter how accomplished your team, there will be times when you need to talk to a team member about changing some aspect of his or her performance. So, take time to prepare, envision yourself being successful, and confidently deal with the occasional coaching challenges that come your way. Remember, your ability to lead a great team and progress in your supervisory career will be in direct proportion to your ability to coach your team members.

Tips for Success: Coaching

1. Focus on behaviors, not on the employee's attitude.

2. *Ask* great questions; beware of *tell*.

3. Clearly define performance problems and understand consequences before you go into the performance improvement discussion.

4. Correct immediately. The longer you wait, the harder it gets to change negative behaviors.

5. Correct privately. One-on-one helps to maintain the employee's dignity and respect.

6. Help the employee understand that a problem exists, by asking questions.

7. Ask the employee for his or her suggestions about how to correct the problem.

8. If possible, allow the employee to select the solution.

9. If you choose to use the non-discussion model, make sure you clarify both the positive and negative outcomes for the employee.

10. Do what you say you are going to do. Ultimately, it will build trust and respect.

Action Plan: Coaching to Improve Performance

Three steps I can take to improve my coaching skills and when I will begin each step:

Action Step 1:
Target Date for Initiation:

Action Step 2:
Target Date for Initiation:

Action Step 3:
Target Date for Initiation:

Chapter 9

Conducting Valuable Performance Reviews

"Top performers in any field are
developed, not born."

—Joe Griffith

We were recently contacted by a small manufacturing firm that was interested in having us assist them with their performance appraisal system. Prior to our meeting with senior management, we assumed the company was interested in learning more about various performance review systems. Thinking this was the reason we were called, we came to the meeting prepared with a number of samples of different types of employee appraisal/review programs. Imagine our surprise when halfway through the meeting the CEO said, "We are not so much interested in changing the system we use, but in having someone from the outside conduct our performance reviews."

Collectively, the senior management in this organization had decided that having an outsider conduct reviews would be a better use of their supervisors' time and help keep the performance review and salary adjustment process more objective. We quickly explained that we did not think that conducting performance reviews from the outside would result in a positive outcome for anyone involved in the process—the employee, supervisor, or us, the consulting firm. We left the meeting more convinced than ever that the challenging process of conducting employee performance reviews is the least preferred supervisory activity, and the job nobody wants!

Despite the fact that supervisors typically look for every opportunity to move "conducting performance reviews" to the bottom of their daily "to do" list, effective performance review systems are vital to increasing employee effectiveness. Systems that incorporate a combination of on-the-job coaching, performance appraisals, counseling sessions, interviews, and performance improvement plans developed jointly by supervisor and subordinate can be extremely effective in raising employee performance. Many organizations that we work with have well-developed and clearly defined performance review systems in place. Yet on the whole, supervisors in these organizations still shy away from the process, and the system is feared and disliked by supervisor and employee alike.

In this chapter, our first goal is to help you become more familiar with the different aspects of a typical performance review system. Our second goal is to help raise your degree of confidence in your ability to conduct employee performance reviews that lead to greater rapport between you and the employees you supervise, and increased employee effectiveness.

Overview of the Performance Review Cycle

It is important to understand that the performance review does not just consist of going over the items listed on the review form with the employee on a yearly basis. The intent of any performance review process is to improve employee performance. In order to get improved employee performance, a continuous process is necessary. While it is true that the review interview is an extremely important part of the process, it alone cannot effect change in employee performance.

The review process begins when the supervisor clarifies what is expected of the employee. Typically, this is done by identifying significant job elements, or segments, and then developing standards of acceptable performance for each element. After the supervisor has had opportunities to observe the employee's performance, a performance review interview is conducted between the supervisor and employee. At the conclusion of the interview, a performance improvement plan can be developed jointly by the supervisor and employee. This plan details what the employee will be working on during the next review period.

The next step in the process is on-the-job coaching. The supervisor works closely with the employee to help raise the employee's level of performance. The first step in the process is then repeated at the end of the designated review cycle. To better understand the process, consider the following diagram:

Exhibit 9.1: Employee Performance Review Cycle

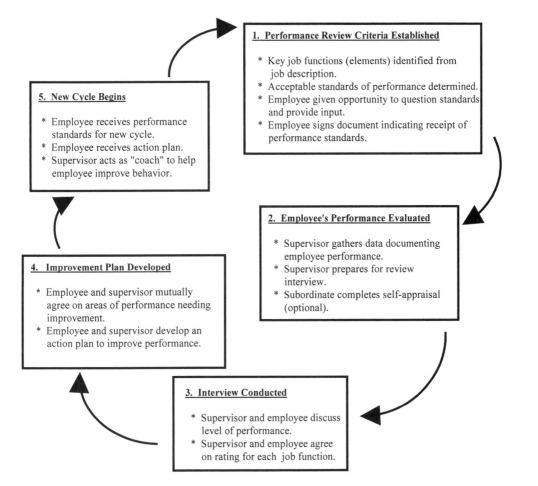

1. Performance Review Criteria Established

* Key job functions (elements) identified from job description.
* Acceptable standards of performance determined.
* Employee given opportunity to question standards and provide input.
* Employee signs document indicating receipt of performance standards.

5. New Cycle Begins

* Employee receives performance standards for new cycle.
* Employee receives action plan.
* Supervisor acts as "coach" to help employee improve behavior.

2. Employee's Performance Evaluated

* Supervisor gathers data documenting employee performance.
* Supervisor prepares for review interview.
* Subordinate completes self-appraisal (optional).

4. Improvement Plan Developed

* Employee and supervisor mutually agree on areas of performance needing improvement.
* Employee and supervisor develop an action plan to improve performance.

3. Interview Conducted

* Supervisor and employee discuss level of performance.
* Supervisor and employee agree on rating for each job function.

123

Developing a Performance Review System

Step One: Clarify Your Expectations

The first step in the review process is to select the significant job elements particular to the employee's position. Almost all organizations have job descriptions detailing the duties and responsibilities of a particular job. These descriptions can be an excellent source of information when selecting the basic job elements to use in the review process.

While job descriptions may have extensive details particular to the specific job, typically performance appraisals will only have five to seven categories, or elements. Within those categories, descriptions for acceptable performance are detailed. To be most effective, these job elements should be jointly reviewed and agreed upon by both the supervisor and the employee. In addition to understanding the specific elements of the job, the employee must also be familiar with the levels of expectation, or standards for performance, for each particular element. Standards of performance describe how the job will be done. It is important that the employee understands both the basic elements of the job and the expectations for acceptable performance. Knowledge of the standards for acceptable performance helps ensure employee success on the job. According to Duke Ellington, "It ain't what you do, it's the way you do it."

Step Two: Set Performance Standards

Job elements describe what must be done to accomplish the job. Performance standards describe how the job will be done. Together, they provide a guideline for the employee's performance and a basis for reviewing the employee's success on the job. When setting standards for performance, it is important that the employee be involved in the process. This helps ensure that the employee understands the standards and also helps motivate the employee to achieve or exceed the standard. When standards are being set, it is a good idea for both the supervisor and employee to initially set the standards independently. Then, after setting standards individually, the supervisor and employee should compare their standards and mutually agree upon acceptable standards. If many people are doing the same job, representatives of the group should initially set standards of performance for the job. Next, representatives should present their agreed-upon standards to the supervisor. Together, they mutually agree on the standards for acceptable performance.

What follows is an example of performance standards for the position of administrative assistant.

Job Description: Administrative Assistant

- ◆ Answer telephone calls and route calls to party requested.
- ◆ Take messages or route to voice mail when requested party is not present.
- ◆ Screen visitors.
- ◆ Schedule appointments.
- ◆ Use word processor for routine reports and letters.

♦ Receive and route incoming mail.
♦ Maintain filing system.
♦ Maintain department calendar.
♦ Maintain follow-up system for appointments, calls, and correspondence.

Exhibit 9.2: Performance Standards

Administrative Assistant

Job Elements	Performance Standards
Telephone	*Answers calls by the third ring. Takes messages or routes calls to correct voice mail.*
Greet visitors	*Welcomes visitors and requests they sign in. Gives visitor badge to each visitor. Notifies employee that he/she has a visitor.*
Maintain department calendar	*Keeps accurate, up-to-date master calendar for all department functions/deadlines. Notifies department employees of significant changes to calendar.*
Process incoming mail	*Opens correspondence unless marked "confidential." Routes all mail to correct department/employee the same day mail arrives.*
File correspondence	*All department correspondence filed within three working days of receipt.*
Type correspondence and reports	*All written correspondence completed by time requested and free of grammatical and spelling errors.*

Step Three: Determine the Rating Scale

Once the job elements have been set and acceptable standards for performance are mutually agreed upon, the next step involves determining a scale to allow the supervisor to differentiate between and among levels of performance. Organizations use a variety of rating standards to determine an employee's level of success. The following shows a simple system used to rate performance:

Job Elements	Performance Standard	Exceeds the Standard	Meets the Standard	Does Not Meet the Standard	Comments
1					
2					

Another system commonly used by organizations uses five rating standards:

Job Elements	Performance Standard	Consistently Exceeds Standard	Often Exceeds Standard	Meets Standard	Sometimes Meets Standard	Does Not Meet Standard	Comments
1							
2							

When determining a rating system, it is important to describe what each of the gradations used in the system means. For example:

Consistently Exceeds Standard: Employee's work consistently exceeds the levels of performance set for this standard.

Often Exceeds Standard: Employee's work usually exceeds the levels of performance set for this standard.

Meets Standard: Employee's work consistently meets the levels of performance set for this standard.

Sometimes Meets Standard: Employee's work is consistently below the levels of performance set for this standard.

Does Not Meet Standard: Employee's level of performance is unsatisfactory.

Here is another example of a performance review rating system:

Job Elements	Performance Standard	Above the Standard	Meets the Standard	Less than Standard	Needs to Improve
1					
2					

Above the Standard: Job performance that consistently and significantly surpasses the required job standards.

Meets the Standard: Regular and consistent work habits that fully meet the standard or requirements of the position.

Less than Standard: Occasional work that meets minimal requirements of standards; need for improved performance.

Needs to Improve: Work frequently completed at less than standard level; immediate improvement necessary.

Step Four: The Appraisal Process

During the rating period, the supervisor should be continuously gathering information about the employee's performance. Every attempt should be made to obtain information regarding the employee's performance at regular intervals throughout the rating period, not just the week before the appraisal interview. Evaluating an employee's performance continuously throughout the rating period helps ensure that the information gathered is fair, accurate, and representative of the employee's performance throughout the year.

When gathering information about an employee's performance, be aware of two pitfalls—the tendency to over-rate a favored employee or unfairly under-rate a difficult employee. In some cases, supervisors over-rate an employee whose actual performance does not truly measure up under close examination. For example, some people are awarded high ratings based on their past record, or because they get along well with the supervisor and other team members. Some are overrated because they may present themselves well, dress impressively, or are glib talkers. Some employees may have accomplished little of consequence throughout the year, but accomplish something outstanding two weeks before the review interview and are awarded a higher rating than they deserve.

On the other hand, some people may be rated lower than their actual performance on the job warrants, for a variety of reasons. Sometimes people receive lower ratings simply because they are different. For example, people who raise questions and are not afraid to disagree with the boss are often rated lower than employees who conform and accept the system. People whose personality traits differ significantly from their supervisor's may be unjustly rated lower. Just as some mediocre employees who perform an outstanding job the week before the review interview are awarded a higher rating than they deserve, some employees are unjustly awarded a lower rating simply because of a mistake occurring shortly before the annual review process concludes. Although the employee may have performed admirably throughout the year, the one mistake wipes out the employee's track record for performance and a lower rating is assigned.

Documentation

Unfortunately, conducting performance reviews is not the only task assigned to supervisors. Typically, because it is not a routine completed on a daily basis, we tend to put it towards the bottom of our daily "to do" list. In order to be objective, however, we cannot leave the data-gathering process until the day before we are scheduled to conduct the employee's annual review. It is important to periodically review the employee's job elements and performance standards and make notes throughout the year regarding the employee's level of performance. This can be as simple as occasionally jotting down a few quick lines noting evidence of either exceptional or unacceptable employee performance. Date the note and drop it into the employee's file. When it comes time to rate the employee, completing the performance appraisal form will require less time and effort because you have noted levels of performance periodically throughout the year. Further, adequate documentation collected at intervals throughout the year helps ensure that the supervisor remains objective and will not rate the employee based only on performance immediately prior to the end of the review cycle.

Of course, if you have concerns about an employee's performance, do not wait until the end of the performance review cycle to address the issue. Coaching and counseling throughout the cycle is far more effective than waiting until the end of the cycle and then presenting the employee with a list of concerns that you have had throughout the year. Remember, there should be no surprises during the performance review interview. If you have concerns about an employee's performance, the employee should already be aware of these issues.

Self-Appraisal

Some organizations encourage employees to be active participants in the appraisal process by evaluating and rating their own performance prior to the assessment interview with their supervisor. In such organizations, employees are reminded throughout the year to review their standards of performance and document areas where they feel they have exceeded the standard. Approximately one month before the employee's annual review, the employee is reminded to begin preparing for the review interview by completing the performance review form and rating him/herself as objectively as possible. Employees need to be cautioned about rating themselves higher or lower than they deserve. They must be advised to compare their performance against the standards of acceptable performance and not to a co-worker's on-the-job performance.

Organizations that promote self-appraisal as part of the annual review process cite increased productivity, higher morale, and greater rapport between supervisor and employee as benefits of the program. Employees who participate in the review process are more familiar with their standards of performance for their job and work harder to exceed the standards. Further, employees who complete the self-appraisal are better prepared to actively participate in the review interview. When a supervisor reviews the employee's self-appraisal, it communicates to the employee, "I value your input." The truth is, supervisors cannot be everywhere and see it all. Encouraging the employee to complete the self-appraisal process helps the supervisor by providing more documentation about the employee's performance. On the other hand, employees who have not participated in any part of the review process show up at the review interview ready to have their supervisor "pass judgment" on their performance. An employee who does not agree with the supervisor's appraisal of his or her performance may become defensive and argumentative.

Step Five: Getting Ready for the Interview

Performance reviews that make a difference and are of value to the employee require thorough preparation. Consider the following factors:

1. *Think about time and location.* Pick a time of day convenient to both parties and schedule the meeting in an area where the door can be closed and the conversation kept private. Make it known to others that unless there is a crisis, you do not want to be interrupted during the review interview with the employee. Conducting a productive annual review takes concentration and interruptions can distract both the supervisor and the employee. Consider

also the arrangement of the furniture. If possible, try sitting at a round table, or side-by-side with the employee. Sitting across from your supervisor who is seated behind the security of a desk can be intimidating for some employees. Sitting side-by-side helps equalize the situation and is more conductive to open communication between supervisor and employee.

2. *Complete all required paperwork in advance of the interview.* Make sure that you have reviewed all of your documentation and used it to complete the performance appraisal prior to beginning the interview. Have all the necessary forms ready and available so that you can conduct the entire interview without having to interrupt the process to find an additional form. If you are going to consider the employee's self-appraisal, leave the actual recording of the rating until you have given the employee time to provide input into the process.

3. *Determine your approach.* It is a good idea to determine, prior to the time the employee arrives, how you will conduct the interview. If the employee has competed a self-appraisal, ask for it now. The most straightforward method for proceeding with the interview is to start at the beginning and go through the job elements one at a time. The supervisor compares his or her rating with that of the employee for each element, and then mutual agreement is reached on the rating for that element. Another way of handling the review is to first look at areas where the employee has met or exceeded the performance standard and then progress to areas where the employee may need to improve. Whatever approach you decide on, make sure that you have thought through the process first and are thoroughly prepared when the employee arrives. Adequate planning will help you feel prepared and confident as you begin the interview with the employee.

4. *Plan your closing.* It is important to give thought as to how you will conclude the interview. Remember that what you say last sticks with the employee as he or she leaves and returns to the normal working environment. Plan to summarize the areas where the employee met or exceeded the standard. Offer praise and encouragement, if appropriate. Review areas of concern you may have with the employee's performance. End the interview by encouraging the employee to give some thought to areas where he or she did not meet or minimally met the standard. Suggest that the employee meet with you again in a week's time to complete a plan of action that will help the employee raise the level of performance in areas where acceptable standards were not met. Plan to end the interview on a positive note, perhaps by conveying to the employee your appreciation for his or her contributions to the company.

Tips for Conducting the Interview

1. *Create a positive climate.* To help the employee relax, it is a good idea to begin the interview with a few minutes of light, easy conversation. Perhaps start with a comment about a recent event at work, a sporting event, or something in the news. Beginning this way helps build rapport with the employee and may help the employee overcome his or her initial nervousness. As stated previously, sitting at a round table or side-by-side further equalizes the situation and enhances rapport with the employee.

2. *Ask questions and listen.* In order for the review to be effective and be of value, you must encourage the employee to talk. Many employees are hesitant about participating in an annual review, feeling that it is their supervisor's job to determine their ratings, and their job to accept the ratings without question. Open-ended questions such as, "Will you tell me about occasions when you have exceeded this element?" will provide you with further documentation and convey to the employee that the review is a two-way process involving both the boss and the employee.

   In order to build rapport with the employee, supervisors must not only ask for employee input, but truly *listen.* By that, we mean listen without interrupting and listen with an open mind. While we may have already decided an employee's rating, the employee may well be able to present information that will change our perception about his or her performance in a particular area. Listening with an open mind tells the employee, "I value your input," and helps build rapport with the employee.

3. *Focus on performance.* In order to remain objective, avoid such descriptions as "attitude," "not professional," and "unreliable" when describing an employee's performance. These terms are vague, mean something different to everyone, and are hard to measure. Further, employees understandably become defensive when a supervisor tells them they have a "bad attitude" or are "not professional." They immediately begin searching for exceptions to convince you otherwise.

   Instead, focus specifically on the job elements and the performance standards. Measure the employee's level of performance against the performance standards indicated in the performance review document. People are more receptive to negative feedback when it deals specifically with the standards indicated in the review document. They do not accept negative feedback when it attacks them personally. Under no circumstances should an employee's performance be compared with the performance of another employee. Comparing employee performance builds resentment between employees and never achieves the outcome you desire.

4. *Avoid confrontation.* When discussing an employee's level of performance in comparison with the performance standards indicated in the review, avoid confrontation and argument. It is true that there may be a disagreement between how you have rated the employee and how he or she has rated him/herself. To get further information, ask questions and listen. Arguing will destroy the rapport you are trying to build with the employee and limit the two-way communication you are trying to establish. The truth is, you are the boss, and both you and the employee know this. You have the authority and the power of your position. You have the right to determine the employee's rating. However, arguing and using your power to override the employee will not create the effect for which you are striving. The employee should leave the performance review with a clear picture of his or her level of performance and an understanding of how that performance could be improved in the future. Ensuring that communication remains two way helps guarantee that the performance interview will meet the needs of both the supervisor and the employee and result in a "win-win" situation for both people.

5. *Emphasize an employee's strengths.* It is normal to be preoccupied with thoughts about performance areas where you would like to see the employee improve. Do not overlook the employee's strengths, though. Acknowledge what the employee does well and build on these strengths. For example, a supervisor might be concerned with the number of errors in letters typed by an administrative support employee. However, the same employee routinely handles a large volume of incoming calls efficiently, greets customers warmly, schedules appointments without conflicts, and generally demonstrates a high level of performance in all areas of responsibility other than written correspondence. The supervisor conducting the assistant's performance review should recognize areas of performance that meet or exceed the standard and offer praise, if appropriate. This helps strengthen the relationship between the employee and supervisor. It also increases the employee's degree of confidence in his or her own ability to perform the job responsibilities. Further, the employee does not leave the performance review interview thinking that you are dissatisfied with his or her performance in general.

6. *Identify areas for improvement.* Discuss areas of concern you have with the employee's performance relative to a particular job standard. It is impor-

tant to acknowledge specifically the performance that does not meet the standard. For example, you may note that the employee averages two to three errors per written page of correspondence. It is important to have samples of the correspondence to demonstrate why you are concerned about the performance. The acceptable level of performance indicated in the employee's job standards is "written correspondence is grammatically correct and error-free."

Other than acknowledging the samples of errors on the correspondence, do not dwell on the past. Instead, focus on future employee performance. For example, you might ask the employee, "What can you do differently in the future to avoid these errors that make us look less than the professionals we are?" Generally, the employee will be able to come up with suggestions for improvement. If not, be ready to make suggestions or provide tips as to how the performance can be improved. It is always more effective, however, for the employee to generate his or her own ideas about how to improve performance. Many employees resent being told how to change their behavior. If, however, they are permitted to come up with their own solutions, they are more committed to making changes in their behavior that will result in increased levels of performance.

7. *End the performance review interview positively*. It is important to review the employee's strengths before the conclusion of the interview and end on a positive note. Of course, you are concerned about the employee's need to improve in some areas. However, you do not want the employee to leave thinking that the purpose of the meeting was only to address areas of concern. Acknowledging acceptable areas of performance helps ensure that the employee will continue to make an effort to meet or exceed the standards. Focusing only on the negative aspects of the employee's performance, or ending the interview on a negative note, will increase the likelihood that the employee will leave thinking, "Why bother? You don't think I'm making a real effort anyway. In the future, you'll get just enough from me so that I can collect my paycheck!"

Step Six: The Performance Improvement Plan

Often, the employee leaves the review interview with a good idea about areas of his or her performance that are going well, and a vague-to-general idea of areas where improvement is needed in performance. Typically, the supervisor breathes a sigh of relief after the interview and thinks, "Whew, I don't have to worry about that for another year!" It has been our experience that this is where the performance review process ends in most organizations. In order to be truly effective, though, it is necessary to go one step further. Either at the conclusion of the review interview or, ideally, at a later date, the employee and supervisor need to mutually develop a performance improvement plan.

A performance improvement plan describes a course of action taken by both the supervisor and employee that will lead to improved employee performance on the job. During the review interview, job elements in which the employee was not meeting minimum acceptable levels of performance were discussed. The first step in developing an improvement plan is to pick one, or possibly two, job elements to be worked on. Typically, if there is more than one job element requiring improved performance, the most critical one should be chosen first for the plan.

When considering the element to pick, think about the payoffs in terms of increased productivity, greater teamwork, and more profitability for your organization. Also, consider the degree of difficulty the employee will experience as he or she strives to improve performance. You may wish to select a relatively easy job element first. Targeting an easy element for improvement first will give them a feeling of success. This will undoubtedly generate a positive feeling of confidence and help the employee rise to the challenge of assuming more responsibility and working on even more difficult goals.

Remember, if you initially select too many job elements for inclusion in the performance improvement plan, the whole process may seem overwhelming to the employee. Employees can tackle one or possibly two areas that are targeted for improvement at the same time. More than that may lead to a feeling of despair and the thought that "It's just too much to change. I'm not doing anything right!"

Tips for Creating the Performance Improvement Plan

1. *Make the plan simple, practical, and easy to understand.* Target one or two areas in which the employee needs to improve performance. Provide examples of how the work will improve. Here is an example: "The employee will correctly file all correspondence, using standardized office procedures, within three working days of receipt of the correspondence." When the employee is unsure about where to file the correspondence, he or she will ask a supervisor for specific directions regarding filing the document.

2. *Include specific timelines for targeted behaviors.* To ensure that both you and the employee have a clear understanding of when and how the behavior will be improved, include specifics regarding time. For example, "The employee will answer all incoming calls before the fourth ring. The employee

will correctly route all incoming calls within five seconds. If a caller is placed on hold, the employee will verify every thirty seconds that the caller wishes to remain on hold and not leave a message or be connected to voice mail."

3. *Identify training.* Be specific about training that will help the employee improve performance. For example, you may wish to write in the employee's performance improvement plan, "Attend a class on Effective Telephone Techniques during the month of April." "Spend four hours with a customer service supervisor reviewing effective techniques for receiving/routing telephone calls before the end of May." In addition, be specific about whose responsibility it is to arrange the training for the employee.

4. *Demonstrate a positive attitude.* If you initiate an employee performance improvement plan thinking that it probably will not make much of a difference in the employee's behavior, that outcome is exactly what you will get! If, however, you are committed to helping the employee identify areas of concern and then create a plan that will help the employee develop, you will most likely see an improvement in both the employee's behavior and attitude. We are convinced that when supervisors demonstrate a genuine interest in employee development and keep a positive attitude about the employee's ability to improve performance, employees will be motivated to make changes in behavior.

Remember, making changes is tough, and it is tougher for some employees than others. If an employee is going to improve, there must be a support system in place. The employee may need additional coaching from the supervisor. Additional training may be required. Encouragement (more than anything else) is needed during a time of change so that the employee will have the confidence to experiment with new ways of doing things. Acknowledge signs of increased levels of performance, particularly in the beginning when the employee is making the first few tentative steps towards improvement. As the employee continues to make progress meeting the goals listed in the performance improvement action plan, recognize the growth with praise, encouragement, increased responsibility (demonstrating the supervisor's confidence in the employee), and, if appropriate, monetary rewards.

In conclusion, the most important aspect of any performance review process is obviously not the format or technique utilized, but the underlying attitude by which both the employee and supervisor view the entire process. If supervisors lack confidence in their ability to review employee performance, dread conducting reviews, and see reviews as a waste of time (and generally go out of their way to avoid the process), whatever evaluation system is in place will be a failure. However, when supervisors view performance evaluation as part of an ongoing process that can positively lead to improved employee performance, there are far-reaching benefits not only for the individual, but also the organization as a whole. Supervisors with that perspective no longer view conducting performance reviews as "the job that nobody wants!"

Exhibit 9.3: My Personal Improvement Plan

My Personal Improvement Plan
Review Date: _____

1.   My areas of strength during the last review cycle:

      _____
      _____
      _____
      _____

2.   The job elements where I need to improve my performance:

      _____
      _____
      _____

3.   My goals for improving my performance:

      _____
      _____
      _____
      _____

4.   Action steps needed for me to accomplish my goals:

Action	Who Is Responsible?	When
_____	_____	_____
_____	_____	_____
_____	_____	_____
_____	_____	_____

_____   _____
Employee Signature   Supervisor Signature

_____   _____
Date   Date

Tips for Success: Performance Reviews

1. Gather examples of performance, both positive and negative, throughout the year—not just the two weeks before the performance appraisal is due.

2. Be positive. Remember to include documentation showing where the employee is doing a great job—not just for areas where there is room for improvement.

3. Make sure you are familiar with all the performance standards and rating criteria for the job before conducting the review process with the employee.

4. Plan your schedule so that you will not be interrupted when giving feedback to the employee. Doing so demonstrates respect for the employee and the process.

5. Pick a quiet, private location and give consideration to the seating arrangements. When possible, come out from behind your desk.

6. Ask for employee input. Listen. Listening shows that you care and value the employee's insights.

7. Focus on behavior. Remember, people cannot change their personalities, but can change their behavior.

8. Be specific about what improved performance looks like. Use examples.

9. Remember to look for positive changes in employee behavior and recognize the employee's success.

10. Put a date on your calendar to remind yourself to check back with the employee who is working on an improvement plan.

Action Plan: Conducting Valuable Performance Reviews

Three steps I can take to improve my employee performance reviews and when I will begin each step:

Action Step 1:
Target Date for Initiation:

Action Step 2:
Target Date for Initiation:

Action Step 3:
Target Date for Initiation:

Chapter 10

Building a High-Performing Team

> "A house divided against itself cannot stand. There are only two options regarding the commitment to teamwork. You're either In or you're Out. There is no such thing as life in-between."
>
> —*Pat Riley, Coach of Miami Heat*

One of the challenges every supervisor and manager faces is the task of bringing people together to function as a team. In today's competitive environment, supervisors need to decide what will enable their work group to provide the highest level of quality, customer service, or task accomplishment. Although there are rare exceptions, in most situations the ability to respond to quality and customer service is much stronger when people operate as a team. Organizations as diverse as Ford, Motorola, 3M, General Electric, and Burlington Northern and nonprofit organizations such as charities and schools have all been able to adapt to a rapidly changing economy and environment by utilizing the advantage of teams.

Why Are Teams Successful?

1. *They bring collective skills and experiences together that exceed those of any individual team member.* Although we would like to think that we can do things better and faster as individuals, it is well-documented that high-performing teams consistently outperform the contributions of an individual.

2. *Teams have a common goal.* When all team members have a common vision or goal and are committed to turning the goal into a reality, there is an energy or force that is created that cannot be duplicated by any one individual team member.

3. *The future of business is in teams.* One of our staff members phoned an insurance agency to get some information on an automobile policy. Since the agent assigned to the policy was on vacation, the receptionist stated that it would be approximately ten days before the agent would be available to respond with the information. In today's competitive environment, is ten days an acceptable amount of time to wait for insurance information? It is not! A team approach would have enabled this firm to provide information in a more timely manner.

    If competition and consumer demands are not sufficient reasons for teams, consider that employees also value the feeling of being part of a team. Most employees, if given the opportunity, will leave organizations where they feel isolated or they do not feel their contributions are valued.

4. *Teams can be fun.* Although most people can cite significant individual accomplishments, if you did not share that accomplishment with anyone, it is hard to describe the accomplishment as "fun." In contrast, when you think about accomplishing something great when you were a part of a team, most times you can look back and say, "Not only did we do a great job, we had fun doing it!"

Teamwork Defined

"A team is a small group of people (typically fewer than twenty) with complementary skills who are committed to a common purpose and a set of specific performance goals. Its members are committed to working with each other to achieve the team's purpose and hold each other fully and jointly accountable for the team's results," according to *The Wisdom of Teams*. It is important to recognize that just because you are a supervisor with a specific group of people assigned to complete a specific organizational task, that does not necessarily mean you are leading a team. A team is not just any group working together. Groups do not become teams just because someone labels them a team. If any significant piece of the preceding definition is lacking, then what you have is a group of people who work together.

Building a Team Is a Challenge

Most supervisors and managers will agree that there have been times in their careers when they have not been able to build a team. For whatever reason, the team just did not come together. Supervisors and managers are quick to rationalize why the group did not perform as a team. Some of the responses we have heard include:

- ◆ Team members lacked commitment.
- ◆ The long-term employees are more comfortable working independently.
- ◆ Some people refuse to change and work with others.
- ◆ The employees and/or the organization have tried teaming before and it did not work.
- ◆ Upper management sends a message that they encourage teams, but their non-supportive actions speak louder than words.
- ◆ The team is composed of at least one person (perhaps more) that others do not want to work with. It takes more time to accomplish something as a team than it does working independently.
- ◆ No one on the team was accountable.
- ◆ The team had politically-based membership, rather than performance-based membership.
- ◆ The team had low goals or expectations.

What Makes a Great Team?

In our consulting practice and research, we have uncovered five characteristics that are common among all great teams.

1. *Great teams have a common, shared goal.* Team members are equally committed to a common purpose and goals, as well as a working approach for which they hold themselves mutually accountable. As a supervisor or manager, you have the opportunity to set the goals for your team. This technique is used by the majority of supervisors. The supervisor tells the team what needs to be accomplished and how to accomplish the task, whether on this shift or during a specific period of time. People need to know what needs to be accomplished.

   What we also know is that if the team does not buy into the goal and make a commitment to accomplish the task, the task will probably not be completed or not be completed correctly. As a supervisor, there are many times when management or a customer dictates a goal to you—i.e., we need 200 units shipped by Friday. In this case, as the extended arm of management, you do not have a choice. The task has to be completed. But you are better off asking the team if this is something it thinks it can accomplish by Friday. If team members say "No," the appropriate question would be, "What would we have to do, or do differently, to accomplish this goal?" In this particular example, a team member responded that if he could get the products from another internal department one-half day earlier, it would be tough but the team would be able to accomplish the task. The supervisor was able to get the other department to provide the products a half-day earlier and the shared goal was accomplished on time.

As the supervisor, you are better off asking and finding out what objections or concerns team players have about the goal than to assume that it is a shared goal just because you told the group what needed to be accomplished.

2. *The team has a positive vision of what the team is trying to accomplish.* The term "vision" can be clarified as a clear mental picture of a desired future outcome. Someone on the team (either the supervisor, leader, or other team member) is able to convey a positive vision of the team's results. On a consulting project with a manufacturing company, a cross-departmental group of people came together to improve the level of quality in one of the organization's new products. It was evident at the first meeting that three members of the team really believed that management had empowered them to solve the problems. Although there was some cynicism from two team members, the strong belief from the three members that this team really could have a positive impact was enough to overcome the cynics and get all team members to pull together to solve the problems.

As a supervisor, whether you have a positive or negative vision of the future, you will be influential. For example, if you as the team leader *do not* have a positive vision of your team's ability to accomplish the goal, and no one on your team does either, there is a strong chance you will all be right!

3. *Great teams are driven by performance challenges.* It is the challenge that energizes a team to greatness, regardless of its location in the organization. A common set of demanding performance goals, or a significant accomplishment that needs to be completed, or a large problem that is having a negative impact on both people and the organization most of the time will lead to the creation of a strong hign-performing team. Teams thrive on performance challenges; they produce mediocre results without them.

Lack of performance challenges that are meaningful to the team members involved is one of the largest reasons why teams have failed. Almost every large organization can share horror stories about how teams have orchestrated one type of team disaster or another. In many of these situations, team members did not understand why teams were being formed. When there is a question of "why," you can guarantee that a challenging goal or accomplishment is also nonexistent. As a supervisor or manager, you need to ensure that your team is working on a challenging goal that is meaningful to each member of the team.

4. *Great teams value and respect the contributions of each member.* Team members need to recognize that each individual brings a unique gift or contribution to the team. Also, it is important that each team member recognizes that it would be harder to accomplish the task without each individual's unique contribution. When we talk about value and respect, we have observed instances where value and respect for others do not transcend outside the team setting. For example, a supervisor stated to us that his most valuable technician was not someone he respected off the job. He went on to add, "But when it comes to producing high-quality parts and solving big problems, this person is the best!"

5. *Great teams win.* It does not matter whether you are on a sports team or in a business environment, great teams accomplish their goals or tasks. It is your challenge as a supervisor or manager to build a winning team. Anyone can win with ten ideal or perfect employees to do the job. The problem is that in real life this never happens.

143

In reality, most times you are given a mixture of people. A few may fall into the ideal/perfect category. The majority will fall into the "middle-of-the-road" type. They are not ideal/perfect, but they are not problems, either. Last, you will most likely have one or two difficult employees. These are the people who are *so challenging* that you find yourself lying awake at 3:00 A.M. asking the question, "Why do they have to report to me?" When employees challenge you, you will find many times that your value and respect for these people decreases.

However, it is important to understand that these difficult employees are not bad. *They are the people who help you to strengthen your leadership skills.* As you navigate your way through the challenges, do not take your eye off the individual's value and the contribution he or she can make to the team. When difficult employees buy into the vision and common goal, they have the ability to become middle-of-the-road or even ideal employees.

Supervisors and managers need to develop the ability to take this blending of people and talents and formulate a positive vision, set a challenging, shared goal, and build value and respect for each team member's contribution. When this happens, you will find that your team's chances of winning increases tremendously.

Stages of Team Development

Stage One: Formation

In this first stage, it is actually safe to say that you have a group of people who work together, rather than a true team. People in this stage will gather together to share information or to decide what actions will help individuals better fulfill their specific job functions, but there is not a committed focus toward a common goal. Some of the key characteristics of groups in this stage include:

- ◆ Lack of honest communication
- ◆ Members are watchful and guarded
- ◆ Minimal group goal accomplishment
- ◆ Learning new jobs and roles
- ◆ Hesitant participation
- ◆ Uncommitted people
- ◆ Unspoken concerns
- ◆ Unclear roles and responsibilities

If you were the team leader observing these characteristics on your team, the question becomes, "What can I do to help move the team forward?" The following five suggestions will help move a team through the team development process.

1. *Meet often.* When new teams come together, team members feel a lack of "belonging" to the team. Because of this lack of "belonging" and uncertain relationships and unclear roles and responsibilities, it is sometimes easier for individuals not to meet at all. Everyone will go on doing their own jobs without feeling a need to come together as a team. By meeting more often in the beginning of team development, the members get to know and trust one another earlier in the process.

2. *Conduct introductions.* If people do not know each other well, it will be helpful to have people introduce themselves. As the leader, it is your responsibility to give people an opportunity to know one another.

3. *Give a proper orientation to the team.* Any time a new member joins a team, this addition has the potential to send the team back to the forming stage. It is helpful to give new members the proper history and background of your team.

4. *Clarify goals of the team.* We know that one of the key characteristics of a great team is having a challenging goal. It is important that all team members be involved in the goal setting and clarification process.

5. *Ask for commitment.* When teams are new, we do not know who is really committed to the team's goals and who is not. You will find it helpful to directly ask people for the commitment to helping the team be successful. You may also find it helpful to ask each team member what he or she would like to personally achieve as a member of the team.

Stage Two: Conflict

As members get accustomed to working with each other, conflict or feelings of hopelessness or helplessness may arise. We have listed some of the outward characteristics of this stage of team development:

- ◆ Blaming
- ◆ Competition
- ◆ Lack of trust
- ◆ Infighting
- ◆ Whining
- ◆ Feeling stuck
- ◆ Polarization (i.e., day shift vs. night shift)
- ◆ Minimal work accomplishment

These characteristics are not bad, but rather a natural course of direction in the team-building process. As the supervisor or manager, it is part of your job to know what you can do to help move the team forward. The following six suggestions provide specific guidance.

1. *Address team members in conflict.* The worst thing you can do when conflict arises on your team is to ignore it. You may ask two team members to sit down and resolve their conflict, or you may sit down and play the role of a mediator in resolving the conflict. Either way, you are addressing the conflict, rather than ignoring it.

2. *Maintain conversations in the aim frame.* We advise supervisors in our seminars to be "aim frame thinkers" vs. "blame frame thinkers." Aim frame thinkers ask two questions: "Where do we want to be?" and "How do we get there?" These two questions keep all conversations healthy and productive. Blame frame thinkers also address two questions: "What's wrong?" and "Who can we blame?" With these last two questions we only have two guarantees—nothing will be accomplished and it will divide the group.

3. *Meet often.* Groups in conflict will actually stop meeting because members would rather avoid one another than discuss the conflict. Force the group to meet and discuss the sensitive issues. If you stick to the aim frame, it will go well.

4. *Focus on results.* This is the stage when many managers spin their wheels trying to make the relationships "right." You may find it more productive to focus your energy on the results the team produces. When the team members are totally focused on results and are held accountable for the results, many of the relationship problems will be resolved by the individuals involved.

5. *Eat together.* The last thing that people in conflict want to do is eat lunch together. This suggestion works because when people eat, they tend to talk about personal things rather than work. People begin to learn about each other as individuals, rather than "the guy from XYZ department."

6. *Ask participants to sit in different seats.* Groups in conflict have set seat assignments that many times they will refuse to change because it might mean they would have to sit next to someone they do not like. Prior to each meeting, tell people they must sit in a different seat next to someone new. In fact, you might even lead by example. It works!

Stage Three: Functional Work Group

The best way to define this stage is to say that this is when teams get their jobs done. There is not a lot of conflict, but then again, there is not a lot of excitement either. Teams come together each day, do their assigned duties, and then leave. Some of the key characteristics of this stage include:

- Getting organized
- Establishing procedures
- Displaying team cohesiveness
- Using interactive dialogue
- Confiding in each other
- Confronting issues as a team

You may ask the question, "If the team is not broken, why try to fix it?" The reason is because a team in this stage is capable of much more. With a few adjustments, you can help to improve the level of commitment, the level of productivity, and the amount of fun and satisfaction individuals gain by being a part of the team. Some actions to help the team move forward include:

1. *Set new goals.* If members are comfortable where they are, see if the team can come up with any new challenges. It is during the times when we are challenged that we succeed and do our very best.
2. *Provide training.* In the functional work group stage, people may begin to feel like they have stopped growing. Find out what people would like to learn and help them promote their personal and professional growth.
3. *Encourage innovation.* This is the stage when you will hear the line, "But we have always done it that way—why change?" Change creates growth in individuals and teams, and growth helps to increase satisfaction.
4. *Recognize what is right.* In this stage, supervisors tend to become involved when something is not right. This means that people only hear from you when something is wrong. Recognize those things that are also right.

Stage Four: A High-Performing Team

This is the stage where the definition of teamwork, listed at the beginning of this chapter, fully develops. You will begin to see some of the key characteristics of a high-performing team:

- Members care about one another
- High energy
- Aim frame discussions
- Closeness
- Common vision and purpose
- Fun as a team
- Creative problem solving
- High trust among team members
- Continuous improvement

This time, the discussion is not centered around what can you do to move the team forward, but rather what can you do to help keep the team performing at high levels. Some ideas include:

Ideas for Sustaining High Performance

1. *Celebrate successes.* In watching great teams perform, we have observed that they will find a reason to celebrate every success. Part of their motivation is knowing they will recognize the superior accomplishments of the team. For example, a human resources department recently completed the design of their employee orientation program. It was a huge project where everyone was involved. At its implementation, the department had a pizza party, complete with balloons! Team members had so much fun that the party carried over into a local restaurant after work hours.
2. *Do a team audit.* When things are going great, most people will feel comfortable addressing the question, "What could we have done even better?"
3. *Change your role to facilitator.* High-performing teams will operate whether the leader is present or not. Become a facilitator, rather than the "supervisor." High-performing teams know what needs to be done.
4. *Set new goals and vision.* If the group is not continually setting new challenging goals, the team will lose its drive and motivation. People want to be a part of a team that is accomplishing something great.
5. *Have fun.* There is no greater reward than being a part of a fun team!

Assessing Your Skills as a Team Leader

The following checklist provides you with a quick assessment of your current ability as a team leader. The 16 items outline some key abilities required for leading a team.

Exhibit 10.1: Team Leader Assessment Checklist for Team Leadership Skills

Read each statement and then place a check on the line after the appropriate number to indicate your current ability. Ratings run from 1 (low) to 10 (high). Respond as you think a consensus of your team members would score your abilities.

		Low									High
1.	I set measurable goals.	1__ 2__ 3__ 4__ 5__ 6__ 7__ 8__ 9__ 10__
2.	I really listen to others.	1__ 2__ 3__ 4__ 5__ 6__ 7__ 8__ 9__ 10__
3.	I give clear directions.	1__ 2__ 3__ 4__ 5__ 6__ 7__ 8__ 9__ 10__
4.	I develop trust with and among others.	1__ 2__ 3__ 4__ 5__ 6__ 7__ 8__ 9__ 10__
5.	I inspire positive team performance.	1__ 2__ 3__ 4__ 5__ 6__ 7__ 8__ 9__ 10__
6.	I confront conflict in a positive manner.	1__ 2__ 3__ 4__ 5__ 6__ 7__ 8__ 9__ 10__
7.	I remain objective when someone disagrees with me.	1__ 2__ 3__ 4__ 5__ 6__ 7__ 8__ 9__ 10__
8.	I keep meetings on topic.	1__ 2__ 3__ 4__ 5__ 6__ 7__ 8__ 9__ 10__
9.	I effectively manage time in a meeting.	1__ 2__ 3__ 4__ 5__ 6__ 7__ 8__ 9__ 10__
10.	I provide a clear vision to team members.	1__ 2__ 3__ 4__ 5__ 6__ 7__ 8__ 9__ 10__
11.	I effectively delegate work to others.	1__ 2__ 3__ 4__ 5__ 6__ 7__ 8__ 9__ 10__
12.	I establish positive relationships with key employees and customers.	1__ 2__ 3__ 4__ 5__ 6__ 7__ 8__ 9__ 10__
13.	I am able to influence upper management.	1__ 2__ 3__ 4__ 5__ 6__ 7__ 8__ 9__ 10__
14.	I am patient with people who are slow or who challenge me.	1__ 2__ 3__ 4__ 5__ 6__ 7__ 8__ 9__ 10__
15.	I recognize the stages of team development and am able to move the team through the stages.	1__ 2__ 3__ 4__ 5__ 6__ 7__ 8__ 9__ 10__
16.	I have an ability to _____.	1__ 2__ 3__ 4__ 5__ 6__ 7__ 8__ 9__ 10__

Effective team leaders must realize that they don't know all the answers, and that they cannot succeed without other members of the team. Work on improving any "Low" ratings and maintain or even reinforce the skills of "High" ratings.

Leading Your Team Out of a Crisis

From time to time, every supervisor or manager finds themselves in charge of a team in crisis. Crises come in many shapes and sizes. A few we have seen supervisors struggle with include: team members who do not get along, company financial problems, morale or motivation at an all-time low, quality problems, customer service problems, departments at war with each other, and top management not supportive of a team or department.

The deeper the crisis, the more challenging it is for supervisors and managers to figure out how to solve the problems and put the team back on track. Many times, supervisors and managers do not know what action they should take. Many possible actions seem to have the potential to send the team into an even deeper crisis. Because of this lack of definite action, the supervisor or manager "hopes" that the situation will get better on its own. We can say that very seldom does the team come out of crisis on its own when the supervisor or manager is using the action of "hope." The following ten action steps will help you lead your team out of a crisis:

1. *Face reality.* When a crisis hits and supervisors/managers are not sure what to do, the first inclination is to deny that the problem is as big as it really is. The analogy that comes to mind is that of the ostrich. We think that if *we* bury our heads in the sand, the problem will not seem as large as it really is. But just like the ostrich, when we stick our head in the sand, we leave other parts of our body exposed. Face reality—the problem most likely will not go away unless you do something to solve the crisis.

2. *Take action.* If you wait until your boss steps in to solve the problem or other team members decide to help solve the problem, you may wait forever. What is worse is that supervisors and managers who do not take action to solve team problems are not doing their jobs. Be empowered. You have the ability to take responsibility for decisions and actions that will lead the team from crisis. If you are not empowered to do this, then there is a good chance your team is going to remain in crisis.

3. *Prioritize.* When teams fall into a crisis, there are usually many problems impacting the team. You cannot fix all the problems at once, so it is in your best interest to get the team involved and prioritize the actions that need to

be taken. If the team is unwilling to prioritize actions, then you will have to decide which problems to solve and in what order.

4. *Focus on results.* When teams are in crisis, there is a tendency to focus on trying to fix the relationships that have broken down. While the thought or attempt is good, we have found it much more productive for floundering teams to focus on results. When everyone is focused on the purpose of the team and the results it must produce, many of the relationship problems will resolve on their own. If the team is not productive, there will always be relationship struggles.

5. *Recruit the cream of the crop.* When teams go into crisis, it is usually the very best team members who leave. They join other departments or find new jobs in other companies. Unfortunately, the most difficult team members never seem to leave. They would much rather tell everyone how bad things are than to do anything to change the situation. In a crisis, analyze your people assets and spend time asking the top performers to band with you and help solve the problems. Most people will stay in a bad situation if they know they can help improve the crisis and if they feel valued and have a positive vision that tomorrow will be better than today.

6. *Praise and recognize your people often.* The reason we emphasize this as a specific point is because when a team goes into crisis mode and you are the leader of this team, you tend to focus your energy on what is going wrong instead of recognizing all the things that are going right. When people do not feel valued and the team or organization is in a crisis, you start to hear team members say, "I don't get paid enough to put up with this garbage." One way we can minimize this feeling in our team members is to value their contributions and recognize them for doing things right.

7. *Tighten discipline.* When teams go into crisis, there are usually many things happening that are not conducive to good teamwork. For example, we might find members coming to work late, people coming to meetings late or not coming at all, work being completed with inferior quality, internal customer service lacking between departments, and last, people not taking responsibility to solve problems. When a crisis occurs, it is in your best interest as a supervisor or manager to tighten, not loosen, discipline. This means you need to hold people accountable for coming to work on time or producing quality parts. Without tightening the boundaries or setting detail standards, you send out messages to all team members that negative behaviors are acceptable.

151

8. *Identify who is responsible and what role that individual will play.* In a moment of crisis, it is critical that you clarify who is responsible and what role that individual will play in leading the team from crisis. The point is to keep focusing on the results. When a team is in crisis, you will usually find that team members are clear on what is wrong and who is to blame, but they are not clear on what needs to be done and who is responsible. As the supervisor, you can assign roles and responsibilities.

9. *Overcommunicate.* When a supervisor or manager is in over his or her head with team problems, there is a tendency to focus energy on operational rather than leadership tasks. You begin to utter these words: "All I do around here is put out fires." As a supervisor, your primary role is to support others. Increase your frequency of communication with team members—both information provided by you and information given to you from the team. Most of the time, your team has what is needed to solve the problems if you utilize them as a resource. Increase your communication in a crisis and it will lessen the negative impact of the crisis.

10. *Maintain a positive mental attitude.* If you throw in the towel because you feel the situation is hopeless, then most likely your team members will view the situation as hopeless also. Not having a positive mental attitude can have a negative impact on a supervisor's or manager's career. If you have no hope of the situation getting better but someone else does, either on the team or in the organization, your team members will begin to follow someone else. A supervisor or manager with no followers is not a leader.

We are the first to agree . . . teams are not for everyone or every situation. Nonetheless, teams usually outperform other groups or individuals, but they can also help individuals perfect their strengths and overcome their weaknesses.

Tips for Success: Team Performance

1. Great teams have clear missions and visions, and great goals. Make sure your team has a common, challenging goal that makes team members stretch to reach.

2. Create an environment where the contributions of all team members are recognized and valued, not just the "stars."

3. Don't oil the squeaky wheel. Value creativity. Recognize and reward those that challenge "the way we always do things around here."

4. Confront conflict. If you stick your head in the sand, remember what part of you is exposed!

5. At every opportunity, try switching from being a directive leader to a team facilitator.

6. Promote cross-training to multiply the number of "experts" on your team.

7. Set goals with specific deadlines. Goals without deadlines are only "hope."

8. People need to feel they belong. Praise and recognize your people frequently.

9. Success is not permanent. Focus on recruiting the "cream of the crop" as you anticipate the need for new team members.

10. Celebrate success!

Action Plan: Shaping a High-Performing Team

Three steps I can take to develop my team-building skills and when I will begin each step:

Action Step 1:

Target Date for Initiation:

Action Step 2:

Target Date for Initiation:

Action Step 3:

Target Date for Initiation:

Chapter 11

Selecting and Hiring Winners

"The world is full of willing people; some willing to work, the rest willing to let them."

— *Robert Frost*

One manager recently confided to us, "I don't know much about wrongful terminations, but I sure have made some wrongful hires in my time!" In the previous chapters, we have discussed the skills needed to effectively manage employees once they are on the job. In this chapter, we will review the skills needed to hire the right people. When the right person is in the right job, it makes all the other skills we have discussed in this book much easier to practice.

Hiring the wrong people is also very costly to an organization. These costs include (1) high turnover rates, (2) decreased productivity, (3) poor morale, (4) potential damage to the company's reputation, and (5) costs associated with recruiting, hiring, and training a replacement for a terminated employee. Your hiring decisions will be among the most expensive and long-lasting decisions you will make for your organization. To ensure that you will be making the best hiring decisions, become familiar with the six key elements of the hiring and selection process.

1. Understanding the hiring process
2. Preparing for the interview
3. Conducting the interview
4. Questioning the applicant
5. Ensuring fair and legal interviews
6. Making the hiring decision

Assessing Your Interviewing Skills

As preparation for this subject, try the assessment tool in Exhibit 11.1, which consists of some questions that will help you assess the current strength of your interviewing skills.

Exhibit 11.1: Self-Assessment of Interviewing Skills

There is no grading scale for this assessment. If you circle a high number of "Yes" responses, the greater will be your need to learn and practice effective interviewing skills.

Yes	No	1.	Have you ever hired a person who did not have the skills you thought they had?
Yes	No	2.	After the interview, have you ever thought of something you wish you had told the candidate?
Yes	No	3.	When the interview is complete, are you still confused about the candidate's qualifications?
Yes	No	4.	Of the five people you have most recently hired, have any left for employment elsewhere?
Yes	No	5.	Have you ever asked a question of a candidate and then later found out that the question was not legal to ask?
Yes	No	6.	Do you ever find that you do not have time to adequately prepare for the interview?
Yes	No	7.	Do you tend to do more talking than the candidate?
Yes	No	8.	Have you ever found that you did not hear the candidate's response because you were thinking of what question to ask next?
Yes	No	9.	After the interview, have you ever thought of something you wish you had asked the candidate?
Yes	No	10.	Have you ever protected your nervousness by sitting behind your desk or some other comfort zone of authority to conduct the interview?

Understanding the Hiring Process

1. *Determine the need to hire.* The hiring process begins with an identified need. This need is apparent when there is a void somewhere in the organization. Voids may occur when new tasks, responsibilities, or projects are assumed;

when someone gets promoted, quits, or gets fired; or when the current number of people available is no longer enough to keep up with the demand.

2. *Establish the job opening.* Once the need is clear, a job opening is formally established. This entails completing the discussions and/or paperwork your company requires. The Human Resources department needs to begin the recruitment efforts within the guidelines and budgetary constraints set by your company.

3. *Write or clarify the job description.* When the job opening is established, the next step is to finalize a clear job description. If the job description is vague or unclear, it will be difficult to hire the right candidate. Without a clearly defined job description, a number of candidates could be theoretically qualified. Some specific questions should be addressed in the job description. Ideally, job descriptions should be reviewed each time the position becomes vacant.

   a. What are the primary responsibilities of the position?
   b. What specific duties will be performed on the job?
   c. What skills or training are required to do the job?
   d. What additional skills would be a valuable addition but are not absolutely necessary?
   e. Is travel required in the position? If so, how much?
   f. Are there any additional comments you feel are pertinent to the job?

4. *Generate a list of candidates and analyze their resumes.* Once you are clear about which skills you are looking for, the next step is to generate a list of possible candidates. Candidates may come from either inside the organization or outside. Internally, candidates should come from (a) promotion from within your department, (b) job posting on the company bulletin board, (c) transfer from inside the company, or (d) employee referral program. Externally, candidates should come from (a) advertising resources, (b) former employees, (c) technical schools, colleges, or universities, (d) trade shows or meetings, (e) government or community agencies, (f) agencies or search firms, or (g) the Internet.

   Here are some general questions to ask yourself in trying to choose which candidates to select for interviews:

   ♦ "What previous jobs has the applicant held that are related to this one?"
   ♦ "Does the applicant have the specific education or formal training needed for this job?"

♦ "Why is the applicant interested in leaving his or her present position?"
♦ "Are there any gaps in the applicant's employment record?"

5. *Plan the interview schedule.* Once you have selected the candidates you are going to interview, the next step is to plan for each interview. Jot down individualized notes for each candidate on how you will guide the specific interview. You will also want to record any additional information you think you need to make an effective choice. (There will be more information on preparing for the interview in the preparation section.)

6. *Conduct the interview.* Always review the three primary purposes for the hiring interview.

   a. To get information. The interview may be your only real opportunity to get as much information as possible from the candidate. This information is critical for you to make the best possible "educated guess" in predicting the future success of an applicant.

   b. To give information. A secondary purpose is to share with the candidate the specifics of the job, as well as background information on your company. It also includes "selling" the position to the top candidate(s). Giving information is one of the most abused interviewing skills. Interviewers tend to say too much too early or not enough at the appropriate time.

   c. To promote good public relations. A third purpose of the interview is that it fulfills an important organizational goal. Since you will be offering jobs to only a small percentage of the candidates you interview, it is important that you use the interview to promote goodwill for your organization. All applicants should leave the interview feeling that they have had an opportunity to be heard and that they were treated fairly. Applicants who do not end up coming to work for you are likely to go to work for a competitor of yours or even become a customer. They should leave the interview thinking well of you and your organization.

7. *Select the best candidate.* Once you have interviewed candidates and agreed upon your first choice, you are ready to make an offer to an applicant. Be sure to provide the applicant with enough information so the person can decide whether or not this job will be a good fit for his or her talents. This is also where you will be "selling" the job and your company. You will want to point out specific advantages and benefits of coming to work for your organization. Other specific issues that need to be addressed include (a) the starting salary or hourly wage, (b) benefits, (c) hours or schedule,

(d) salary increases, (e) vacation and holidays, and (f) opportunities and qualifications for promotions.

Preparing for the Interview

In preparing for the interview, it is helpful to be aware of some of the most common errors that interviewers frequently make.

1. *Talking too much.* Studies indicate that most interviewers talk 50% or more of the time during an interview. An interview that is dominated by the interviewer fails to accomplish the most crucial purpose of the interview—to get information from the applicant. An effective interviewer will conduct the interview so that he or she spends only about 20% of the time talking and the applicant spends 80% of the time talking.

2. *Telegraphing the desired response.* Interviewers often lead or help the candidate get the "right answer" by telegraphing the answer that they want to hear. For example, the interviewer says, "How do you feel about working on teams? We have a very strong work ethic around here that values teamwork." Now, what would you say to this? "No, I think teams are a lousy idea!" Make sure that your questions are straightforward and do not telegraph the desired response.

3. *Failing to know job requirements.* You cannot conduct an effective interview without first knowing the specific job requirements. This is where effective preparation pays off. Too many interviewers do not have a complete understanding of the job or what it entails. These interviewers are at a significant disadvantage in not being able to select the person with the right qualifications. Take the time to conduct a thorough job analysis that will clarify specific job duties, responsibilities, skills, knowledge, and abilities.

4. *Jumping to conclusions.* Interviewers often make the mistake of making quick judgments and jumping to conclusions before they have enough information to make a sound decision. If the applicant says one thing that does not fit with what you are looking for, it does not mean that he or she is not the right person for the job. On the other hand, if an applicant says something that you are very impressed with, this should not be the single contributor to your decision to offer the job.

5. *Reacting to the "halo" effect.* This common mistake is made when the interviewer happens to really "like" the applicant. Sometimes you will just hit it off with someone. A quick rapport is established and you seem to get

along very well. You can almost build a friendship within the interview because the chemistry just seems to fit. This is when an interviewer may make the hasty judgment that this applicant would be "perfect" for the job. Beware! You may be under the *halo effect*. You have put a "halo" over the head of the applicant. He or she can do no wrong—even though he or she may be *wrong* for the job.

6. *Being disorganized.* Interviewers who do not take a systematic approach to the interview will be disorganized and may lose valuable time getting the information they need. Effective interviewers take an organized approach and plan out the interview sequence. This pre-planned structure ensures that the interviewer will be able to cover what is needed to make the best possible selection.

Now that you are aware of some of the most common errors made by interviewers, you are ready to prepare for the interview. The key steps in preparation include (1) conduct a job analysis to determine job requirements, (2) review the resumes and applications, and (3) plan the interviews.

1. *Conduct a job analysis to determine job requirements.* One of the most critical aspects of preparing for the interview is to define the requirements of the job. During the interview, you will be determining whether there is a good match between the candidate's experience and the job requirements. Many interviewers rely on job descriptions and general assumptions to get their information about the job. Most job descriptions provide a general summary of the job duties and responsibilities. They do not usually go far enough in describing specific skills and abilities needed to do the job.

To get a more thorough grasp of the true job requirements, outline your responses as you read through the following questions:

♦ What skills, knowledge, and abilities are absolutely essential to do the job?
♦ What specific education or training is required to do the job?
♦ What are the specific duties and responsibilities of the position?
♦ Describe key involvement with others (management, employees, customers, vendors, or peers).
♦ What are the potential sources of satisfaction or the pluses of the job?
♦ What are the potential sources of dissatisfaction or the negatives in the job?

- ◆ Is there a career path available? If so, what is it?
- ◆ What other job or career opportunities might be available to a person in this position?
- ◆ What specific behaviors or personal characteristics are important for this position? (Be specific in describing these behaviors. For example, if the position requires creativity, what specifically would be expected? To initiate new ideas for product development? To present a variety of approaches or solutions to problems?)
- ◆ What specific situational or environmental factors are required for the position? (Include things like long hours, overtime, shift work, weekend travel, relocation, physical requirements, office space, or work environment.)

2. *Review the resumes and applications.* Once you have done a thorough job analysis, you are now ready to review the individual applicant's resume, application, and any other pertinent background information. Note any unusual aspects of the person's work history or education. As you review the information, write out questions you can ask during the interview to get more data or to clarify information. Also, note areas where you can ask for specific examples. For instance, if the resume indicates that the person has headed up a number of problem-solving teams, you can ask for specific examples of how he or she led the team, what problems or roadblocks were encountered, and what was ultimately achieved by the team.

   The reason for taking the time to review the applicant's information is not only to give you more data about the applicant, but also to help you prepare for the interview. A careful review of the applicant's material will assist you in formulating pertinent questions to maximize your time in the interview.

3. *Plan the interviews.* At this point, you should have a thorough understanding of the job requirements, a good sense of the individual applicants, and specific questions ready to ask in the interview. The last part of preparation before conducting the interview is to plan the interview schedule and arrange the appropriate physical setting.

   In planning the interview schedule, you need to determine how much time you will spend in the interview. The average recommended time for an initial interview, after screening the resume and the application, is 30 to 45 minutes. For highly technical or very involved positions, the interview may go on for one hour or more.

   Once you have decided how much time you want to devote to the interview, you need to design a structure that will allow you to get to all the questions

161

you want to ask. If you are going to plan for a 45-minute interview, determine how much time you want to spend in each area. For example, you may want to spend the majority of time on specific types of work experience to ensure that the applicant has a certain level of proficiency in a particular technical skill.

Plan ahead regarding how much time you will spend in each area and stick to your plan. If you alter your plan, you may find that your interview time is up and you haven't even gotten to the most important questions! (In the next section on conducting the interview, you will see an interview structure that will help you plan your time accordingly.)

The second part of planning for the interview includes planning for the appropriate physical setting. The most important aspect of the physical setting is that it be comfortable and relaxing. Remember, both you and the applicant will be a little—if not a lot—nervous. Creating a comfortable environment will ease the situation.

Furniture should be placed for easy conversation. If you are using an office with a desk, pull your chair around so you are not behind the desk. Make certain that there will be no interruptions during the interview. Have whatever materials you will need available, including the candidate's resume, application, and your notes. Make sure that you are ready to conduct the interview. This means that you should clear your mind—and desk—of all other distractions. Plan on devoting your full attention to the applicant. This short interview may be the only time you have to make one of the most important business decisions you will ever have to make. It deserves your full attention.

Conducting the Interview

When conducting the interview, an organized approach must be followed if you want to get all the information you need in the allotted time. One way to achieve this is to follow an organized structure or format. The following organizational format will ensure that you get to the most critical questions. You will need to determine how much time you plan to devote to each of the elements of the interview structure.

1. *Welcome/greeting*. The purpose is to welcome the applicant and put him or her at ease. Welcome the applicant with a smile and a handshake. Introduce yourself and your title or position. Offer coffee, water, or other refreshment and guide the applicant to the interview location. Once you are both seated

and ready to begin the interview, start the conversation with "small talk" to get the applicant to talk, "break the ice," and "open up." This could include, "How was the traffic coming in this morning?" or any other non-controversial area of general interest.

2. *Interview structure preview.* The purpose is to let the applicant know what to expect and reduce anxiety about the interview process. The preview allows you to transition from the welcome to the actual interview. It tells the applicant what you have planned for the time that you are together. It should include the general areas you plan to cover and how much time you have planned for the interview.

The preview could go something like this: "Well, because we don't have much time today, I'd like to get started on the interview. Let me tell you what I have planned. I'd like to start with your work experience and then talk about your education. After that, I'll ask you to give me a self-assessment of your strengths and development needs. Then, I'll take some time to answer your questions and to give you more information about the position and our company."

3. *Work experience.* The purpose is to get specific information, examples, and illustrations of the applicant's work experience, job skills, and knowledge. Most interviewers will begin with the most recent work experience and work backwards. However, another approach argues for beginning with the earliest work experience and moving forward. This approach will allow you to see the career path that was taken and to follow the applicant's thinking and line of reasoning in making his or her career decisions.

Ask questions to get details about what type of work was done, how it was done, and what results were achieved. Ask follow-up and probing questions to get more details. For example, if the applicant says that one of his or her duties included training, a series of follow-up questions might include:

- ♦ "How did you go about determining the content for the training?"
- ♦ "Give me an example of one of the key training points and how you presented it."
- ♦ "What kind of results did you achieve with the training?"
- ♦ "How did you measure your success?"
- ♦ "What might you do differently if you had the chance to do it over again?"

4. *Education.* The purpose is to understand the applicant's specific education and training and to see how that education relates to the necessary job requirements. You can use the same basic process to cover education as you

163

did for work experience. By working chronologically, you are asking the applicant to "tell the story" of his or her educational background.

5. *Self-Assessment.* The purpose is to get the applicant's perspective of his or her own strengths and development needs. Ask the applicant to give you his or her perspective of what he or she considers to be personal strengths and the areas needing improvement. Most applicants are generally prepared for this question. However, if you ask good follow-up questions, you will be able to get some very valuable data.

6. *Present information and answer questions.* The primary purpose of this segment is to "sell" the employee on the job. At this point, you will have a good idea whether this seems to be the right person for the job. If this is a top candidate, discuss the benefits of the job and how it will meet his or her needs. If you will not be seriously considering the applicant, you will not need to spend much time in this area. However, you do need to complete this section to ensure a fair interview and to promote good public relations.

    Answer the candidate's questions and elaborate on information that will satisfy any concerns. Tailor the information that you have to present to the candidate's needs. Include information that is particularly important to the candidate.

7. *Close the interview.* The purpose is to determine the applicant's level of interest in the job, explain next steps, and end the interview on a positive note. Determine if the applicant is interested in the position by asking directly, "What is your level of interest in the position?" Explore any doubts or reservations the applicant may have about the position or the company.

    Explain the next steps. This could include identifying another person you would like the applicant to interview with, when they will be notified about the next interview, or when the hiring decision will be made.

    End the interview on a positive note by thanking the applicant for taking the time to speak with you. Clarify what the applicant can expect next. Do not make an offer or a rejection statement at this time. You will need some time to analyze your interview notes and to think through the process.

Questioning the Applicant

As we stated earlier, the goal of the interview is to get the best information possible so the interviewer can make a good selection. The primary tool for getting good information is to ask good questions. There are two different types of questions: the close-ended question and the open-ended question.

1. *Close-ended questions.* Close-ended questions are questions that can be answered with a *yes* or *no*. For example, if you asked an applicant if he or she likes his or her present job, the answer could simply be *yes* or *no*. The disadvantage of using close-ended questions in an interview is they do not produce the maximum amount of possible information. Close-ended question begin with words like "Is," "Can," "Do," "Did," "Will," and "Are."

2. *Open-ended questions.* Open-ended questions are questions that need expansion to be answered. They usually start with words like "What," "Where," "When," "Why," "How," "Tell me," "Explain," and "Describe." The advantage of using open-ended questions is that you will receive more information rather than less. For example, if I ask, "What do you really like about your present job?" I am going to receive much more information than I did in the close-ended example.

The following examples illustrate how you can change close-ended questions (CL) to open-ended questions (OP).

CL Do you have good communication skills?
OP What do you feel your key strengths are in the area of communication?

CL Were you attracted to work here because of our benefits?
OP What attracted you to seek employment with our company?

CL Did you make any major mistakes in your last job?
OP Can you describe a major learning point from your previous jobs?

CL Have you ever had a personality clash with a boss?
OP Tell me what you have liked and disliked about previous bosses.

CL We have a very fast-paced environment here. Are you motivated?
OP What type of business environment do you enjoy best?

There are many other useful open-ended questions for interviewing purposes.
- How would you describe your past job in detail?
- Tell me how you spend a typical day on the job.
- Why do you want to leave your present job?
- What are your greatest strengths?

- What are your biggest weaknesses?
- What are you doing to overcome them?
- On your past jobs, what significant contributions did you make?
- What specific tasks do you enjoy most? Why?
- What specific tasks do you like least? Why?
- Tell me about the most challenging project you have ever had to tackle.

Open-ended questions are powerful questions because they do not lead the applicant down a specific direction. If you asked the question, "Do you enjoy working on computers?" what candidate would disqualify himself or herself by saying *no*? However, if you asked an open-ended question like, "What did you dislike about your last job?" and the applicant responds that he or she disliked working on the computer all day, you have a pretty sound indication that this may not be the best applicant for a position that requires extensive computer work.

Ensuring Fair and Legal Interviews

Effective interviewers are well aware of the legal issues that are in place to ensure fair interviews. Exhibit 11.2 provides guidelines on questions you can and cannot ask during an interview.

Exhibit 11.2: Interviewing Guidelines

Subject Matter	Acceptable	Unacceptable
Name	*"Have you ever used another name?" "Is any additional information relative to change of name, use of an assumed name, or nickname necessary if we need to do a complete check on your work and education record? If yes, please explain."*	*"What was your maiden name?"*
Residence	*Place of residence.*	*"Do you own or rent your home?"*

Exhibit 11.2: Interviewing Guidelines *(continued)*

Subject Matter	Acceptable	Unacceptable
Age	*Statement that hire is subject to verification that applicant meets legal age requirements. "If I hire you, can you show proof of age?" "Are you over eighteen years of age?" "If under eighteen, can you, after hire, submit a work permit?"*	*Age. Birth date. Dates of attendance or completion of elementary or high school. Questions that tend to identify applicants over age 40.*
Birthplace, Citizenship	*"Can you, after hire, submit verification of your legal right to work in the United States?" Statement that such proof may be required after a decision is made to hire the candidate.*	*Birthplace of applicant, applicant's parents, spouse, or other relatives. "Are you a U.S. citizen?" Citizenship of applicant, applicant's parents, spouse, or other relatives. Requirements that applicant produce naturalization, first papers, or alien card prior to a decision to hire.*
National Origin	*Languages applicant reads, speaks, or writes, if use of a language other than English is relevant to the job for which applicant is applying.*	*Questions as to nationality, lineage, ancestry, national origin, descent, or parentage of applicant, applicant's parents, or spouse. "What is your mother tongue?" Language commonly used by applicant. How applicant acquired ability to read, write, or speak a foreign language.*

167

Exhibit 11.2: Interviewing Guidelines *(continued)*

Subject Matter	Acceptable	Unacceptable
Sex, Marital Status, Family	*Name and address of parent or guardian if applicant is a minor. Statement of company policy regarding work assignment of employees who are related.*	*Questions that indicate applicant's sex. Questions that indicate applicant's marital status. Number and/or ages of children. Provisions for child care. Questions regarding pregnancy, child bearing, or birth control. Name and address of relative, spouse, or children of adult applicant. "With whom do you reside?" "Do you live with your parents?"*
Race, Color	*No acceptable questions.*	*Questions as to applicant's race or color. Questions regarding applicant's complexion or color of skin, eyes, hair.*
Credit Report	*No acceptable questions.*	*Any report that would indicate information that is otherwise illegal to ask, e.g., marital status, age, residency, etc.*
Physical Description, Photograph	*Statement that photograph may be required after employment.*	*Questions as to applicant's height and weight. Require applicant to affix a photograph to application. Request applicant, at his or her option, to submit a photograph. Require a photograph after interview but before hire. Videotaping interviews.*

Exhibit 11.2: Interviewing Guidelines *(continued)*

Subject Matter	Acceptable	Unacceptable
Physical or Mental Disability	*Statement by employer that offer be made contingent on applicant passing a job-related physical examination. "Can you perform (specific task)?"*	*Questions regarding applicant's general medical condition, state of health, or illnesses. Questions regarding receipt of Workers' Compensation. "Do you have any physical or mental disabilities or handicaps?"*
Religion	*Statement by employer of regular days, hours, and shifts to be worked.*	*Questions regarding applicant's religion. Religious days observed. "Does your religion prevent you from working weekends or holidays?"*
Arrest, Criminal Record	*Job-related questions about convictions, except those convictions that have been sealed, expunged, or statutorily eradicated.*	*Arrest record. "Have you ever been arrested?"*
Military Service	*Questions regarding relevant skills acquired during applicant's U.S. military service.*	*General questions regarding military service, such as dates and type of discharge. Questions regarding service in a foreign military.*

Exhibit 11.2: Interviewing Guidelines *(continued)*

Subject Matter	Acceptable	Unacceptable
Organizations, Activities	*"Please list job-related organizations, clubs, professional societies, or other associations to which you belong—you may omit those that indicate your race, religious creed, color, disability, marital status, national origin, ancestry, sex, or age."*	*"List all organizations, clubs, societies, and lodges to which you belong."*
References	*"By whom were you referred for a position here?"* Names of persons willing to provide professional and/or character references for applicant.	Questions of applicant's former employers or acquaintances that elicit information specifying the applicant's race, color, religious creed, national origin, ancestry, physical or mental disability, medical condition, marital status, age, or sex.
Notice in Case of Emergency	Name and address of person to be notified in case of accident or emergency.	Name, address and relationship of relative to be notified in case of accident or emergency.

Note: Any inquiry, even though neutral on its face, that has an adverse impact upon persons on a basis enumerated in the Fair Employment and Housing Act (race, sex, national origin, etc.), is permissible only if it is sufficiently related to an essential job function to warrant its use.

Department of Fair Employment and Housing, DFEH-161, State of California, Rev. 5/97.

Making the Hiring Decision

Now that you have taken the time to plan the process and conducted a thorough interview process, you are ready to make the selection decision. Because you have carefully analyzed the job, you will be able to quickly screen out unqualified applicants and select from the most qualified candidates.

Even with the extensive data you have, you may find it difficult to decide among the top two or three candidates. You may want to go through a rating and ranking process, assigning numerical measurements so you can "add up" the qualifications of each candidate and select the candidate with the highest rating.

1. *Ask some additional questions to make the final decision.*
   - *Accomplishments.* What was really accomplished on previous jobs?
   - *Responsibilities.* Is this level of responsibility right, too high, or too low?
   - *Skills and knowledge.* Does the candidate have what it takes to do the job?
   - *Strengths.* Are the key strengths present? Will these strengths add to the position?
   - *Weaknesses.* Does each specific limitation impact the job? Is it offset by a necessary strength? Can this weakness be remedied through a brief orientation, learning on the job, or other training?
   - *Stability.* Is this an important factor or not?
   - *Compatibility.* Will this candidate be compatible with others in your department? Others in the organization?
   - *Past behavior.* Is there repeated evidence or a pattern of successful performance?

2. *Plan new employee orientation.* Now that you have hired a new employee, it is important that you get the employee off to a good start. Make sure that you will be available to give your undivided attention to the new employee for the first few hours of his or her first day. If the new employee is forced to sit around doing nothing until the supervisor can find the time to get him or her started, you will not be providing a very warm welcome. Do not have a new employee report until you know you will have the time to properly prepare and introduce the employee to his or her work assignment.

   The following checklist will help to ensure that employees are properly oriented to a new company and job.

Welcome the new employee.

- Introduce the new employee to co-workers
- Explain the function of each person you introduce
- Give the employee a tour of company, department, and plant
- Explain where restrooms, coffee areas, and parking facilities are located

Introduce the new employee to the job.

- Make certain that the new employee's working area, equipment, tools, and supplies are prepared and available
- Explain the levels of supervision within the department
- Provide the new employee with necessary training
- Explain use of phone, copy machines, company vehicles, mail procedures, and/or supply procedures
- Explain hours of work
- Give new employee department telephone numbers
- Review location of first aid equipment

Coordinate with Human Resources Department.

(If HR does not cover these responsibilities, they should be covered by the supervisor.)

- Time cards/sheet guidelines
- Payroll procedures
- Probationary period
- Performance evaluations
- Holidays and time off
- Employee handbook
- Company ID card
- Security guards or security measures

Tips for Success: Selection Process

1. Take time to understand your organization's hiring process.
2. Remember, the three primary purposes of the hiring interview are (1) get information, (2) give information, and (3) promote good public relations.
3. Let the job applicant talk. Plan on spending 80% of the time listening and 20% talking.
4. Do not give away the answers you expect.
5. Conduct a job analysis—know the job requirements.

6. Get the whole picture. Avoid jumping to conclusions.

7. Take time to plan the interview.

8. Use open-ended questions to get complete and thorough answers.

9. Know the law and make certain that you conduct fair and legal interviews.

10. Start your new employee off on a positive note by providing a warm welcome and thorough orientation.

Action Plan: Selecting and Hiring Winners

Three steps I can take to improve my interviewing skills and when I will begin each step:

Action Step 1:
Target Date for Initiation:

Action Step 2:
Target Date for Initiation:

Action Step 3:
Target Date for Initiation:

Chapter 12

Facilitating Productive Meetings

"Meetings do not need to be punishment. After all, gatherings to discuss a subject of common interest are what parties are all about."

— *Philip B. Crosby*

Ask any group of managers and supervisors to list their top three most time-consuming activities and "unproductive meetings" always surfaces on their lists. These same managers and supervisors regretfully admit that about half their time in meetings is wasted. Unfortunately, we never know ahead of time which half of the meeting is going to be the productive half. If it were known, we could plan accordingly and better manage our time!

One manager recently complained, "The biggest waste of time in our company is our management meeting on Monday mornings. The meetings are aimless and accomplish little." In today's hectic work environment, this manager isn't alone in his dislike for meetings that don't value an employee's time. Meetings that start late, don't accomplish much, and run late aggravate those in attendance and contribute little to the organization. In this chapter, we will talk about critical components for planning and leading a successful meeting. After reading this chapter and practicing these skills, you will find your confidence as a group leader growing as you successfully plan and conduct productive meetings.

To Meet or Not to Meet?

The first step in planning a successful meeting is to make an important decision. The decision is whether or not to even hold a meeting. Many meetings should *not* occur at all. Meetings that are called because a manager is unable or unwilling to make a decision are examples of meetings that should not take place. Another inappropriate reason is to call a meeting simply for the sake of meeting. In today's world of information overload, to meet without a specific purpose is inexcusable.

Informational Meetings

Legitimate reasons for calling a meeting fall into two broad categories. The first category is for the exchange of information. Informational meetings are held for the purposes of coordinating activities, exchanging information, building morale, or selling a concept or idea. There are a number of reasons to hold an informational meeting:

- ♦ To inform employees about a change in production quotas
- ♦ To explain to employees how to read their revised earnings statement
- ♦ To introduce an organization's vision and values statements

The number in attendance at an information meeting is determined by how many employees need to know this information. Generally, in informational meetings the communication flow is one way—from the leader to the participants. In meetings of this type, the emphasis is on presenting the information the group needs to know. Leaders conducting information meetings need to be thoroughly prepared, but usually will not be interacting with the audience. Their goal is to share the knowledge they have about a particular topic with their audience. Their success is determined by how well they deliver the information to the participants.

Decision-Making Meetings

The second reason for calling a meeting is to involve those in attendance in problem-solving, decision-making, or goal-setting processes. Here are a number of reasons to hold a decision-making meeting:

- ♦ Gather input to help the organization resolve a budget deficit
- ♦ Discuss revising the shift schedule to equal workload
- ♦ Plan department realignment for higher productivity and profitability

As these meetings involve the participants, the number in attendance needs to be limited to those members of the organization who are knowledgeable and will contribute to the decision-making process. Ideally, attendance at these meetings is limited so that participants all have the opportunity to contribute to the group process. Leaders of groups tasked with making decisions must know how to encourage those in attendance to express themselves and be creative in proposing solutions. Leaders must know how to generate participation, but also how to steer the group back when they stray from the task. Further, leaders of decision-making meetings must know what to do when emotions sidetrack participants or when a decision seems blocked.

Planning a Productive Meeting

Step One: Creating the Agenda

After determining whether a meeting needs to be held (and if it does, what type), the next step is to begin the planning. Every meeting should have an agenda. An agenda sends participants the message that you value their time enough to do prior planning. It lets participants know ahead of time what they will be doing during the meeting. Agendas don't always need to be typed up ahead of time. They can be written on a flip chart or handwritten, copied, and distributed at the meeting. If the meeting involves participant input, we recommend getting an agenda out to the participants ahead of time. Participants then have an opportunity to prepare themselves for the meeting. They can make sure that they have all the data needed to make an informed contribution to the meeting.

An agenda should include the following:

1. *Start time.* Establish a start time and then begin right on time. Starting on time rewards those who are prompt and ready to start at the announced time. When you have a reputation for starting on time, people attending your meetings will show up on time!

2. *Topics.* The topics to be covered at the meeting should be listed next, in the sequence in which they will be discussed during the meeting. Be brief here, and include only enough information for participants to be able to identify the subject.

3. *Break time.* If a meeting is scheduled to run more than ninety minutes, schedule in a short break. When participants start their break, be very specific about the time you will resume. Start again promptly at the announced time. People will get the message that you value their time and intend to keep the meeting moving productively.

4. *Summary.* End every meeting with a short summary of the topics covered and the outcome. Although this activity doesn't take long, it helps participants focus on the content of the meeting and reminds them that the meeting accomplished something.

5. *Follow-up.* After the summary, review participants' future responsibilities. Whatever participants have agreed to contribute—whether it be assuming responsibility for a task or gathering more information for a future meeting—should be reviewed before the meeting adjourns.

6. *Adjournment time.* Having been held captive in too many meetings that ran long past schedule, we suggest honoring the adjournment time. Stick to your agenda. Work hard to keep the meeting progressing towards the established goals. End on time. If consensus on an issue is close, or if you know that the remaining agenda items can be covered quickly, ask the group's permission to extend the adjournment time by a few minutes. Otherwise, end the meeting as scheduled and plan another meeting to come to closure on the items that still remain an issue. As with starting on time, ending meetings on time will quickly build your reputation for being an organized leader with respect for others' time.

Step Two: Selecting the Participants

Generally, when deciding who should participate, the smallest number of appropriate people is the best guideline to follow. Consider the type of meeting you will be conducting. If it is to be an informational meeting, the participants will include all those who need the information. On the other hand, if the meeting will have a problem-solving format, then you should consider the following criteria when you select participants. Participants attending problem-solving meetings should have:

1. *Expertise in the problem.* Select participants who have knowledge or technical expertise in the area that will be considered during the meeting.

2. *Commitment.* Participants should have a mutual interest in solving the problem so they will be committed to the problem-solving process.

3. *Diversity.* When selecting participants, consider team members who have different facts, opinions, and feelings. They will contribute more creative solutions to complex problems.

4. *Open-mindedness.* Participants attending the meeting will have diverse opinions. However, they need to be able to listen to one another and openly consider solutions presented by others.

Step Three: Arranging the Facility

Adequate prior planning in selecting and setting up a meeting room will contribute significantly to conducting a productive meeting. Consider the size of the room in relation to the number of participants. Will there be enough room to comfortably accommodate participants and any required furnishings and audio-visual aids? Check also to see that the heating/cooling, lighting, and ventilation are adequate for the size of your group and the activities you have planned during the meeting.

Determining what type of meeting you will be conducting (informational or decision-making) will dictate the arrangement of the furniture. Generally speaking, participants attending informational meetings can be seated facing forward so that they can maintain eye contact with the group leader. They may not need tables. Participants attending decision-making meetings should be seated so that they face one another. If participants are not all familiar with one another, have name tents for team members.

The Role of the Leader

As a leader of a group, you are responsible for creating an environment in which people can and do contribute to discussions that lead to recommendations. You are in charge of creating and maintaining a climate in which people feel free to contribute and in which arguments are minimized and focus remains on the objective. Throughout the meeting, you are tasked with monitoring progress and providing the direction needed to keep participants on track. You will be continually analyzing the group's progress and refocusing the direction, if necessary, to make certain that the group moves forward to meet its objective.

With practice, you can conduct a productive meeting and do it well. First, be prepared to lead. Make sure that you have the agenda ready and the room arrangements made, and that you are knowledgeable about the items that will be discussed during the meeting. Determine whether your meeting will have an informational or decision-making format. Second, make sure that you are familiar with the meeting process and your role as a leader. Third, believe in yourself. Management would not have assigned you the role of group leader if they did not believe that you could handle the situation. They respect your ability.

Next, view the role of group leader as an opportunity to take additional responsibility within your organization. Being a leader takes more preparation than being a participant. Welcome the required extra effort as an opportunity to excel and do whatever it takes to prepare yourself to lead the group.

Finally, aim for excellence. Set high standards. Expect excellent contributions from the members of your team. Lead by example. Your team members will respect you, recognize your effort, and contribute more to your meetings.

Rational Decision-Making Process

Your role as a leader in a decision-making or problem-solving meeting will require that you have an understanding of the Rational Decision-Making Process. This process provides a structured order and keeps participants' attention focused on the problem.

Step One: Analyze the Problem

First, spend time leading the group while members analyze the problem. During this time, participants will contribute their perspectives about the problem or situation that has brought the group together. This is not a time for participants to suggest solutions. Make certain that all participants have the opportunity to share their views about the problem. This is important because people from different sections of the organization may view the problem from entirely different perspectives.

Step Two: Define the Problem

After all participants have had the opportunity to share their perspectives relating to the problem, define the problem. Lead the group to consensus on a clear definition of the problem. Once the problem is clearly defined, you are ready to start the process that will move the group forward to a solution or recommendation.

Step Three: State the Desired Outcome

At this point in the meeting, participants have discussed and defined the problem. It is now time to state the objective or the end result the participants want to achieve. For example, a group of supervisors may be trying to determine an equitable system for scheduling. After discussing concerns raised by employees regarding the schedule, the group determines that its objective will be to develop a schedule that gives employees an equal number of weekends and holidays off.

Step Four: Generate Alternative Solutions

There are a number of ways that alternatives can be generated. Typically, the most common is by open discussion. Two more structured procedures that will produce more alternatives and encourage greater creativity are the Brainstorming Process and Nominal Group Technique, as described on the pages that follow.

Step Five: Use Consensus to Reach Agreement

Both the Brainstorming process and the Nominal Group Technique are processes that help groups reach agreement on a decision or resolution of a problem. Both techniques help a group generate alternative solutions and reach consensus, or agreement, on a solution. There are several reasons why leading a group to consensus is more advantageous than voting on a decision. Although voting is appropriate for larger groups, it generally should not be used in smaller groups, particularly when participants work with one another on a day-to-day basis. Voting creates winners and losers. Although both groups will continue working together after the decision is made, the losers may have a tougher time accepting the solution reached by the group. This is understandable, because their solution wasn't the one picked. Reaching agreement by consensus, however, maximizes the support of the decision by group participants. Although participants may not be in total agreement, reaching agreement by consensus leads to a decision that participants can support with a high degree of commitment.

When leading a group to consensus, make sure that all participants have time to present their positions and are not interrupted. Encourage members to listen carefully and consider all proposed solutions. If a group seems to be deadlocked and unable to reach consensus, encourage it to look for the next most acceptable alternative.

Remember that differences of opinion are normal and to be expected. When a group has trouble reaching a decision, it is because the participants have a commitment to the outcome. If they didn't care, they would reach consensus quickly and not waste their time arguing their position. Your task as a leader is to help them go through the process of generating possible solutions, sharing their opinions, and reaching a decision that is acceptable to the group.

While the final decision reached may not be the most optimal one in some participants' minds, it should be one that they can support. Do not end the meeting without checking with those participants who raised differing viewpoints during the discussion. For example, ask John, "John, is this a decision that you can support?" If the participant says "No," then ask, "What would need to be different in order to gain your support?" Continue the process until you are confident that the decision reached is one that will be supported by the group. While reaching consensus is a more time-consuming process than voting, it is a process that builds group cohesiveness and commitment to reaching a workable solution.

Brainstorming Process

Step One: List All Ideas Generated by the Group

Encourage group members to contribute their ideas, even if they think that they may not be workable solutions to the problem. To ensure that everyone is heard, only one person speaks at a time.

Step Two: Welcome Creativity

"Off-the-wall" suggestions and comments may seem completely off target, but may provide other participants with the stimulus for generating a workable solution. Off-the-wall suggestions are often the jumping off point for devising novel solutions to complex problems.

Step Three: Make No Evaluation

Participants must not dismiss, criticize, evaluate, or judge team members' contributions during this phase of the brainstorming process.

Step Four: Limit Discussion

The intent of the brainstorming process is to generate ideas. Do not discuss ideas at this point, as it slows down and limits the brainstorming process. Discussion should only occur when another participant needs clarification on a particular idea.

Step Five: Encourage Contributions

The more ideas participants contribute, the more likely it is that a workable solution will be devised. Continue to list participants' ideas, even though they may be repetitious. Duplicates can be deleted later. If the group needs stimulus to continue generating ideas, think of the five W's and the H—Who, What, When, Where, Why, and How?

Step Six: Record Ideas

Designate a recorder to write down all ideas generated, preferably on a flip chart or chalkboard so that participants can easily see all suggested solutions.

Step Seven: Rest on Decision and Incubation

Once consensus is reached and a decision made, take some time to sleep on the decision. What seems like a novel solution to a complex problem today may not meet the needs of all concerned tomorrow. It is best to take some time so that participants and others affected by the decision have the opportunity to think through the aspects of the proposed solution.

Nominal Group Technique

Another type of decision making is Nominal Group Technique. A variety of alternative solutions are suggested by group members. Next, participants using this form of decision making rate alternatives using agreed-upon criteria such as cost, availability, and feasibility. Each alternative generated by the group is rated using a numerical system or a scale of low, moderate, or high. Participants usually first rate the alternatives individually. Then, the group rates the alternatives by consensus or by adding the individual ratings.

Step One: Write Individual Responses

Each participant individually writes out ideas/solutions in response to the question/problem posed. Make sure that participants have enough time to consider solutions and pose their responses.

Step Two: Record Group Responses

Ask each individual to report his or her solutions. This can be done with the entire group or in smaller groups to speed up the process. Record the responses as they are reported to the group.

Step Three: Rate the Responses

The entire group (or the smaller groups) then rates the responses against the agreed-upon criteria. The ratings are reported for each alternative and then added together. Sometimes it is helpful to use colored dots to have individuals or groups rate their responses. For example, looking at a list of proposed solutions, a green dot might be placed next to the most favorable solution, a blue next to the second most favorable, and a yellow next to the third. Dot voting is a quick way to rank alternatives.

Step Four: Drop Low-Rated Responses

Alternatives with low ratings are dropped from the list.

Step Five: Rate Remaining Alternatives

The remaining alternatives are again discussed, rated, and summarized. Then, those receiving the lowest ratings are dropped from this list.

Step Six: Repeat Process

This process of discussion, summarizing, and rating continues until a final choice is agreed upon by the group. This becomes a process of elimination to the final choice.

Tips for Generating or Stimulating Discussion

When a group is trying to reach consensus on a solution, it is important that all the participants engage in discussion. Participants must feel comfortable and confident that their contributions will be heard. Facilitating a meeting in which participants have the confidence to contribute is challenging. Understanding the following ten techniques will help you lead the group in an atmosphere of free exchange and will maximize participant discussion.

1. *Pick the right type of question.* There are three general types of questions: general, specific, and direct. Each will elicit a particular type of response.

   General questions are broad and non-specific. They are addressed to the group in general. They will elicit a wide range of general responses. Because of their non-threatening nature, general questions are best used to start off the discussion in a meeting.

   Specific questions require answers that are focused and limited. It is best not to ask specific questions until participants in the group are comfortable and the discussion is flowing freely.

   Direct questions are asked of a particular individual. Like specific questions, it is best not to ask direct questions until you are assured that the individuals within the group are feeling confident enough to respond. Many people still remember back to their school days when they feared not having the right answer when the teacher called on them. They may freeze when called on directly. Until participants reach a point when they feel that their contribution to the group will not be a threatening experience, do not use direct questions.

2. *Ask participants what they think.* One particularly effective technique used to generate discussions is to ask members of the group to share their feelings or opinions about a particular topic. Questions such as, "What is your

thinking on . . . ?" or "What made you come to that conclusion . . . ?" or "Would you tell me more about your thinking on . . . ?" all will get participants involved in the discussion.

3. *Ask for more explanation.* When you don't understand a participant's contribution or you realize that members of the group aren't clear on an issue, ask for clarification. For example, "John, I'm not sure I fully understood your last comment. Could you explain it again for us?" or "Joan, this looks like it's confusing you. Would it help if Mike explained it again?"

4. *Paraphrase participants' contributions.* When your goal is understanding, paraphrase participants' responses. Questions such as, "If I understand it correctly, are you saying that . . . ?" or "Mary, could you restate what you just said so that we can make sure we understand?" or "John is suggesting . . ." all will help the group focus on what is being said.

5. *Ask for a review of progress made.* When many ideas have been presented, it is a good idea for you to summarize the information that has been presented, or ask a member of the group to do so. For example, "We've heard a lot of good ideas in the past hour. Would someone volunteer to summarize what we have come to agreement on?" or "Jack, you don't seem to be in agreement on this point. Would you please summarize your major objections?"

6. *Support and encourage participants.* When it becomes apparent that someone is not contributing, you might say, "Let's give Mary a chance to tell us her thinking on . . ." or "We understand your suggestions, Dale. Now, let's ask for Tom's thoughts on . . ." or "Before we go to the next point, I'd like to get Betty's opinion on this."

7. *Refocus the group's attention.* When the group seems to be straying off task, to help them refocus, ask, "Are we on the right track here?" or "Is this one of the goals we identified?" or "Are we limiting our thinking? Are their other ways to get this done?"

8. *Encourage examples.* When the group is having trouble understanding a concept, ask for an example. Examples will help clarify issues and help members gain mutual understanding. "Maria, could you give us an example to help us understand?" or "Michael, I'm not sure that I'm understanding what you're proposing. Could you give me an example?"

9. *Address differences of opinions.* When it becomes apparent that a group member is not in agreement, address the participant specifically. Failure to acknowledge disagreement now may cause problems in the future. "Paul, I'm sensing that you are not in agreement with this proposed solution.

185

Could you tell us why you don't agree?" "Elaine, I think you have a differing opinion. Please tell us your thoughts on this topic."

10. *Check for group consensus.* Checking for group consensus can be done periodically throughout the meeting. This helps the group come to closure on items already discussed and focus on items still under discussion. "We've covered five items this morning. Let's check to see if we're in agreement on . . ." "Before we take our break, let's check to see if we agree on . . ." "Is this solution one that we can all accept?"

Handling Difficult Behaviors

Occasionally, no matter how carefully prepared you are for a meeting, you will run into a challenging situation. Whenever you call a group of people together to make a decision, there is always the possibility that you will witness some interaction problems among group members. Be aware of typical distracting behaviors and use the techniques for correcting them to keep your meeting on track and productive.

1. *The Experts.* These participants are "know-it-alls" and they are only too willing to vociferously share their expertise with other members of the group. They frequently offer their opinion, regardless of whether or not it has been solicited. Their expertise can threaten other group members. Further, experts tend to alienate other group members who may tune out and quit contributing to the group process. One way to handle experts is to acknowledge their viewpoint or opinion and then solicit input from other group members. "Peggy, we appreciate your thoughts on the proposed schedule change. Joe, do you have any other thoughts about the proposed changes?" Never argue with an expert. Acknowledge that you see the situation differently and ask that they remain open-minded during the problem-solving process. Suggest that they may wish to talk with you privately during the break to give you more information.

2. *The Attackers.* Participants of this type argue, ask questions continually, and may challenge the group leader's expertise. Their tone of voice may be threatening or belligerent. They may have a meeting agenda of their own, and it most likely will not complement your agenda. The best way to deal with attackers is to acknowledge their disagreements. Arguing with them will only make them dig their heels in further and offer more resistance. Try saying, "Mike, I hear what you are saying and I commend you for having the courage to oppose this process. Could you give us more information about why you feel so strongly about this particular issue?" If the attackers

continue, like the experts, you may ask them to talk to you further about their position either at the break or after the meeting.

3. *The Distractors.* Some distractors ask too many questions. Their questions may not be related to the topic being discussed and sidetrack the group's progress. One way to handle a distractor who repeatedly asks questions is to use discretion when calling on participants. Call on other participants. If distractors continue to interrupt the group process with unrelated questions, acknowledge them and indicate that most likely their questions will be answered as the group works through the problem-solving process. Sometimes leaders and group members are distracted by people whispering. To alert whisperers that their activity is distracting, stop talking yourself. Usually, when there is no talking, whisperers get the message that they need to join the group. Another tactic is to physically stand near the whisperers. Again, this signals them that their personal conversation is distracting the group. You can also call on the whisperers directly and ask them to share their thoughts with the group.

4. *The Complainers.* Sometimes group members come to the meeting with a negative mental outlook, more commonly known as a bad attitude! Rather than looking for solutions, they seem to find fault with everything. This can be intimidating for group leaders, but it also creates a negative meeting environment. Instead of arguing with them and trying to persuade them to change their outlook, acknowledge their concern. "Joseph, I am hearing that the possible solutions we've discussed are not acceptable to you. I am asking that you remain open as the group continues their discussion. If you still have concerns, let's get together at the end of the meeting." Acknowledge their concerns, but don't let their negative attitude become infectious and impede the group's progress.

5. *The Non-Participants.* Group participants sometimes "tune out" the group. These participants may miss steps in directions, ask questions that have already been answered, or physically withdraw from the group. The best way to get non-participants back in the loop is to call on them directly. Ask them specific questions or solicit their opinion about the topic under consideration. Maintaining eye contact with them is another technique that will help ensure that they stay focused.

6. *The Loudmouths.* Participants who are bad listeners or monopolize the conversation by talking too long or interrupt frequently are loudmouths. Like attackers and distractors, they can be challenging for other group members. One way to handle loudmouths is to try thwarting them by calling on others. If they persist, try summarizing their responses and moving

on. For example, "Connie, you feel that the best approach for us would be
. . ." or "Mark, what are your thoughts on this subject?"

In closing, remember that individuals who can lead others to agreement on a
common goal are effective managers and assets to their organization. Upper
management will recognize your ability to lead people and reward you with
more responsibility. Increased responsibilities will enhance your opportunities
for advancement within your organization. Like the acquisition of any skill, leading effective meetings takes practice. Using the techniques covered in this chapter, you will, with practice, be able to motivate participants to contribute,
facilitate the group's progress as they reach agreement, and effectively lead a
meeting in which participants leave saying, "That was a great meeting! We really
accomplished our goal!"

Exhibit 12.1: Meeting Evaluation for Participants

At the close of a meeting, distribute this evaluation form to participants.

MEETING EVALUATION

Based on your observations, how would you rate the meeting today?

1. To what extent did the meeting follow the agenda?
    Not at all   1   2   3   4   5   6   7   8   9   10   Completely
2. To what extent did the meeting accomplish the stated objectives?
    Not at all   1   2   3   4   5   6   7   8   9   10   Completely
3. To what extent was the knowledge of the participants used?
    Not at all   1   2   3   4   5   6   7   8   9   10   Completely
4. To what extent was decision making shared by all participants?
    Not at all   1   2   3   4   5   6   7   8   9   10   Completely
5. To what extent did participants work together as a team?
    Not at all   1   2   3   4   5   6   7   8   9   10   Completely
6. When decisions were reached, to what extent was the follow-up action
    clearly stated?
    Not at all   1   2   3   4   5   6   7   8   9   10   Completely
7. Comments:_____

_____

_____

Exhibit 12.2: Meeting Planning Checklist

When preparing for a meeting, review the specific tasks and then check each one off as it is completed.

Specific Task	Completed
Determine whether or not a meeting needs to be held.	
Decide what type of meeting is appropriate (information/decision).	
Decide who should attend the meeting.	
Select a meeting time.	
Select a meeting place.	
Develop an agenda.	
Notify participants of the meeting.	
If participants require preparation time, send agenda beforehand.	
Arrive early to check room arrangement.	
Check to see that all A.V. equipment is operational.	
Start meeting on time.	
Review agenda with participants.	
State objective/outcome for meeting.	
Encourage participation.	
Keep group discussion focused on topic.	
Lead group to consensus.	
Summarize group progress.	
Decide what follow-up action is required.	
After meeting, write up minutes and distribute to participants.	

Tips for Success: Meeting Facilitation

1. Before you plan to call a meeting, ask yourself this important question, "Do we need to meet, or is there a more efficient way to accomplish our goal?"

2. If a meeting is worth calling, an agenda is a must. The agenda signifies the importance of the meeting and lends structure and organization throughout the meeting.

3. Get the agenda out to participants prior to the meeting, allowing them enough time to focus their thoughts and do any advance preparation prior to the meeting.

4. Arrange the facility according to the type of meeting. If discussion is required, plan to have participants facing one another.

5. Begin and end meetings on time. Doing so says that you value the participants' time and intend to use it efficiently. Nothing is more frustrating for a prompt person than showing up for a meeting at the announced start time and then wasting twenty minutes waiting for other participants before the meeting begins.

6. In your opening statements, clearly state the desired outcome for the meeting.

7. Encourage participation. If you sense that there may be disagreement, even if nothing is said, have the confidence to call directly on individuals. For example, "Susan, I am feeling that you have some thoughts about this issue. Would you share them with us?"

8. Keep the discussion focused. If needed, remind participants about the goal for the meeting and redirect comments that do not relate to the current discussion.

9. Make every effort to come to agreement by consensus, not by voting. Periodically check in with participants to see if they can support decisions under consideration.

10. Summarize progress and review responsibilities at the end of the meeting. Don't end until participants are sure about the next steps and their individual responsibilities.

Action Plan: Facilitating Productive Meetings

Three steps I can take to develop my planning and facilitating skills and when I will begin each step:

Action Step 1:

Target Date for Initiation:

Action Step 2:

Target Date for Initiation:

Action Step 3:

Target Date for Initiation:

Chapter 13

Developing Consensus

"The fastest way to learn is to discover a person or group which reaches totally different conclusions than your own when looking at the same reality.""

—*Robert Theobald*

We recently developed a training program for a manufacturing client that supplies products for the defense industry. The company was interested in training because its biggest customer had just told them, "You've got some problems with quality that you need to fix. Don't just make this a management fix. Get your people involved. They know firsthand where to make the changes. Listen to them. If you can't make these changes, you may be dropped from our list of vendors." This was the first time we had specifically heard a customer dictate how a problem would be solved within a company! All of a sudden, our client had a real interest in learning how to use consensus to creatively solve problems.

Global competition, mergers, acquisitions, changes in governmental regulations, and increased customer demands all spell constant change for organizations. Selling change to employees at all levels within the organization is easier when employees are involved and feel ownership related to the change. Getting input and recommendations from employees requires a supervisor who is able to achieve group consensus.

Historically, if we look back to the 1950s, employees did not expect to be involved in management decisions. In fact, many employees did not want to be asked to provide their opinions on decisions that affected the company. That was management's job. As one old-timer stated to us in an interview, "You'll have to pay me more money if you want me to do management's job. That's why they make the big bucks." In today's workforce, an employee who does not want to be involved in the decision-making process is in the minority. Based on the authors' experience in conducting employee opinion surveys, it is almost guaranteed that when employees are not involved in the decision-making process, the organization's level of morale and motivation will decline.

It is critical that today's managers and supervisors be responsive to the rapidly changing events going on around them—within their organization, the economy, and the environment. Leaders must be effective at creating a dynamic system comprised of networked teams of knowledgeable workers. To be effective in today's workplace, today's managers must shift their focus from making decisions to empowering others to make decisions.

Consensus Defined

Consensus is a state of mutual agreement among members of a group where all legitimate concerns of individuals have been addressed to the satisfaction of the group. Consensus requires that everyone be heard and understood. There is a common misconception that consensus management means that all decisions, no matter how significant, must be made by the group coming to consensus. This is not the case. There will always be times when it is appropriate to make decisions without getting others on the team involved. One example of a decision that would be more appropriately made by the manager working independently is deciding whether a team member should be coached or terminated. A second example where independent decision would be more effective is when there is a short window of time available to execute the decision. Consensus building takes time.

Often when we discuss consensus with managers they tell us they reach consensus with their team by taking a vote. Consensus is not about taking a vote. Consensus means that all members on the team have discussed their concerns, are heard, and feel strongly that they can live with the outcome of the decision and can publicly support the decision. If consensus is taken to its extreme, it means one member of the team can veto the decision. Consensus works best when all members of the team are clear on the team's mission and vision, and are able to put personal interests aside to enable the team to accomplish team goals.

Benefits of Consensus Building and Shared Decision Making

There are many benefits to consensus building and shared decision making. Some of the benefits and advantages of consensus building and shared decision making include:

- *Greater diversity of opinion.* When team members are involved in the decision-making process, there is opportunity to hear different viewpoints. Different viewpoints are critical to a manager's success. If everyone thinks just like the manager, the decision process is easier, but there is a good chance of being blind-sided by something that was never considered because there was no avenue to generate differing viewpoints. With differing viewpoints and critical examination of the decision, the manager increases his or her chances of making a good decision.

- *Shared responsibility.* When the time is taken to involve team members in the decision-making process, team members feel a greater level of responsibility in creating a successful outcome. One of the classic employee lines when a decision fails is, "Well, it sure wasn't my idea. If they'd asked me, I could have told them it would never work." By working through team members' concerns and objections, there is a higher level of team member commitment to make the decision a success.

- *Builds teamwork.* Although consensus building at times can be messy, if leaders will follow through with the process, consensus building can ultimately lead to a stronger team. People who have listened to differing viewpoints, feel their viewpoint has been legitimately heard, and have been involved in determining the course of action usually feel a stronger bond to the team.

- *Greater understanding.* One of the great questions employees love to ask is, "Why are we doing this?" or "Who was the genius who made this decision?" What they are really saying is, "I don't understand why this decision was made and why I need to change in order to turn this decision into a reality." When employees are involved in the decision-making process, there is a greater understanding of the "why" behind every decision.

- *Faster implementation.* Although consensus building takes longer to make the decision, it is always faster to implement once the decision has finally been made. To leave the group out of the decision-making process, we can make decisions as rapidly as we can think. The problem with making individual decisions is that if team members are needed to execute the decision, it always takes longer to successfully turn the decision into action because the people who are needed to implement the decision do not feel ownership for the decision's success.

- *Greater long-term success.* When employees feel they have been involved in determining the course of action, the chances for success are bound to increase. One specific area where we see a higher chance of success is when employees run into a roadblock or a problem. When team members have

195

been involved in determining the course of action, they will usually find an appropriate solution when they encounter a problem. If team members have not been involved in the decision, they may have decided that the decision will not work, sometimes even before the implementation process begins.

Advantages of Individual Decision Making

As we mentioned earlier, not all decisions should be reached by consensus. Individual decision making also has advantages. Some of the advantages include:

- *Decisions can be made quickly.* The best part about making an individual decision without input from others is that we can make decisions quickly. When time is of the essence, we can make three decisions in under a minute and do it all while we are driving to work. The only thing left to do is tell people what needs to be done. Although individual decisions are quick to make, they almost always take longer to implement if the actions of others are needed to successfully implement the decision.

- *Decisions are confidential.* There are times when decisions have to be made confidentially. If a team member needs to be terminated, it is not in the team's best interest to bring a group of people together to make the decision. Discussing one employee's inadequacies is inappropriate in a group setting.

- *Decisions are critical to the organization's success.* If decisions are critical to the organization's success and the leader feels that the right decision has to be made immediately, then it may be more appropriate to make an individual decision. Some decisions that may be more appropriately made by an individual or select group include: clarifying the organization's vision, setting standards, making choices when others are unwilling to take a risk, and determining a course of action when values conflict.

- *Decisions involve individual responsibility.* If no one else needs to be involved in turning the decision into a success, then it is far more beneficial to leave the group out of the decision-making process. We recently interviewed a sales person who stated he had made the decision to get each client proposal out to the client within three days of the request. In this case, the sales person put together his own sales proposals. No one else needed to be involved in creating a successful outcome.

Leading a Diverse Group to Consensus

As consultants, we are frequently retained to help build teamwork within groups of people who do not work well as a team or who have a difficult time making

196

group decisions. The skill we most frequently use to enhance teamwork is building consensus. Often when there is disagreement among team members, it is centered around small pieces of large issues. Recently we worked with a bank that had a major disagreement at the senior management level over who their "real" customer is. In its mission, the bank stated that it is a commercial bank—its primary customers are businesses. Several members of the senior management team were not happy with the mission statement because various branches of the bank serve a large number of individual customers, rather than the business clients as described in the mission. When the mission statement was re-worked, the group was able to come to consensus by changing the mission statement to:

"We are a locally based commercial bank providing creative financial solutions and exceptional service to the businesses and individuals in the communities we serve. For every challenge, a solution."

The four critical factors in leading a diverse group to consensus are:

1. *Create a compelling positive vision of the outcome.* When we use the word *vision*, it is just a fancy word for a clear mental picture of the outcome. A great analogy of a clear picture of the outcome is the box top of a jigsaw puzzle. When you build a jigsaw puzzle, you always know exactly what you are trying to build because you have a clear mental picture of the outcome. Without the box top, it would make jigsaw puzzle building very frustrating. As the manager, if you cannot see how to bring the group to consensus, how can you expect a fellow team member to create a positive outcome? By interviewing members of the team and collecting different viewpoints, a manager will begin to see the common denominators among team members that will enable the group to reach a consensus decision. The critical factor is that the manager or supervisor must visualize the positive outcome much earlier than the rest of the team sees its own ability to come to a consensus decision.

2. *Have a high level of confidence that you can make a positive difference.* To be successful in building consensus, you have to have a deep-seated belief that you can lead the group to consensus. As Mark Twain stated, "Whether you think you can or think you can't, you are right." If you do not have a positive vision, and you do not believe you are the person who can lead the group to consensus, others on the team will read your lack of confidence and it will undermine your ability to create a successful group process. One manager recently asked us, "What happens when you feel you don't have the confidence to lead the group to consensus?" In a situation where the

manager lacks confidence, we recommend meeting with individual team members one-on-one until you truly understand each team member's "real" concerns. Once you have interviewed each team member, create a graph of where agreements and disagreements exist. Where you find disagreements, generate solutions that can help facilitate the consensus building session.

3. *Develop the ability to communicate with empathy.* The ability to communicate to all team members with empathy is one of the most critical success factors in leading a group to consensus. By definition, empathy implies that the listener has the ability to understand what message the communicator is sending. Empathy is different from sympathy. Sympathy implies that you acknowledge a person's emotion. For example, "I am sorry to hear that your car was stolen." Empathy implies that I care and I want to understand. For example, "I am sorry to hear that your car was stolen. It's a real hassle to be without wheels. I know how you must feel." To be effective in leading a group to consensus, you do not need to be able to feel what each team member is feeling. However, you do need the ability to understand what each team member is communicating.

   One of the authors recently conducted a seminar where a participant stated that he was not concerned that his teenager was experimenting with drugs. When the author asked the participant why he was not concerned or doing anything to stop the teenager from taking drugs, the participant replied, "I did it when I was a teen-ager and I turned out all right." Although it was difficult for the author to condone a parent who allows his or her children to take drugs, it is easier to understand where this participant was coming from when he communicated his perspective. It is important to remember that each team member comes to the table with his or her own personal experiences and, in some cases, "baggage." If team members believe that you have the capacity to understand their perspective or empathize—even if you do not agree—you will find it easier to bring the group to consensus.

4. *Focus on the aim frame.* When groups disagree, many times members slip into a discussion of what is wrong with the current situation or the proposed topic of conversation. Sometimes it can even get nasty, with some team members blaming others for the situation. When groups have a difficult problem to resolve and are trying to come to a consensus, it is helpful for the manager to focus the group in the aim frame. Focusing on the aim frame asks the group two questions. First, where does the group want to be with the decision or what is the ideal outcome? The second aim frame question is: How do we get there? If groups are steered by the manager or facil-

itator into the aim frame, even some of the most difficult topics to discuss will remain in a positive focus.

Preparing for the Consensus Building Session

Conduct a comprehensive assessment of the situation. Before leading a team meeting where consensus on an issue is to be attained, it is important for the manager or facilitator to have a full understanding of where all team members are coming from regarding the topic. One of the challenges for managers is that after they work with team members for a period of time, they believe they know what each team member thinks on the issue to be discussed. This "knowing" where team members stand will lead to getting blindsided in meetings and not being able to bring the group to consensus. Part of the inability to lead the team to consensus stems from the team member's belief that the manager or facilitator does not understand his or her perspective. The underlying purpose of conducting a formal or informal interview with each team member, prior to the consensus building session, is to gain an accurate understanding of the team's reality. Here are some guidelines:

- ◆ *Interview each member of the team when possible.* When the number of people is too large to interview everyone, we recommend gathering the widest range of opinions possible. To make certain that you have a full understanding of the issues, ask the people you interview if there are other team members you should also talk to to ensure mutual understanding. If others are selecting who you should talk to, be aware that you may be receiving only one side or perspective. Understanding the range of issues enables the manager to facilitate many different points of view.
- ◆ *Make certain that both informal and formal leaders are included in the assessment process.* Just because someone on the team does not have a formal title does not mean that they are not an informal leader. When it comes to building consensus, everyone on the team has a stake in reaching a mutually agreeable decision and should be held responsible for the successful implementation of the decision. Do not leave team members out of the process.
- ◆ *Get the toughest people involved up-front; ask for their commitment/help in the interview.* Everyone has worked with a really difficult employee at least once. With really difficult people, there is a tendency to leave them out of the decision-making process until the last possible moment because they are so hard to involve in the process. To leave difficult people out of the decision-making process is a big mistake when it comes to building consensus. In fact, to be successful, it is helpful to get them involved first, rather

than last. Go to the difficult people and interview them, and in the interview tell them that you need their help in bringing the group to a mutually agreeable decision.

The authors recently interviewed a school union site representative who had a reputation throughout the entire school district of being incredibly difficult to work with. In the interview, we stated that we did not think we could come to consensus without his support and asked him what it would take for him to be supportive of the process. The site representative stated two concerns that were relatively easy to assimilate into the consensus building process. The site representative was supportive and the consensus building process was a success.

♦ *Determine what questions to ask in the interview process.* What follows are several questions we have found useful to ask when conducting an assessment and gaining the background information needed to build consensus:
   ♦ How would you describe the current situation the team is facing?
   ♦ What are your concerns as we move through the decision-making process?
   ♦ What do you see as the opportunities or possible solutions in bringing the group to consensus?
   ♦ From your perspective, what would be the ideal outcome? If not ideal, what could you live with and also publicly and actively support in regard to this decision?
   ♦ What are the group's "undiscussables"? (These are the types of concerns that group members will talk about one-on-one but will not publicly bring up to discuss as a team.)
   ♦ If you were in my shoes, what would you do to bring this group to a consensus decision?
   ♦ If we were to resolve this one issue, would you then be able to support the rest of the group's decision? (Ask this question if there are specific points of disagreement.)
   ♦ If this solution is not acceptable or agreeable, then what do you suggest?
   ♦ If we do not come to agreement, what happens?
   ♦ Is there anyone else you would suggest I speak with to ensure that I have a full understanding of the issues?

Develop the Agenda

To lead a consensus building meeting, it is helpful for the leader to formulate an agenda. An agenda produced in advance will help to keep the team focused and on track. Invariably there are always some team members who toss out tangents that are designed to take the group off track. A well-formulated agenda allows the leader to maintain control and focus on the purpose of the discussion.

Assign Responsibilities

To successfully facilitate a group to consensus, four distinct roles need to be assigned or played by members of the group. One person might be able to handle all four roles, although this is difficult and unlikely.

A. *Facilitator*. The facilitator plays the role of the observer. The group sets the agenda and turns it over to the facilitator for execution. The facilitator's job is to hold the group to the contract it made when it set the agenda and assigned times to the items.

B. *Minutes-Taker*. The minutes-taker records the exact wording of proposals, ideas, and any modifications that come up. The facilitator relies on the minutes-taker to remind the group of precisely what it has agreed to. It is easy for group members to leave meetings with different ideas about the decisions that were made. Keeping precise records of the meeting ensures that the group's consensus will be accurately reflected.

C. *Timekeeper*. The timekeeper works with the facilitator to hold the group to the specified times for agenda items, and to pace the group through that time. Also, this person may remind the group of the amount of time left for the agenda item.

D. *Monitor*. The monitor observes the emotional flow of the meeting. While the facilitator focuses on the content and the agreed-upon process of the meeting, the monitor focuses on the people and their interaction. He or she has the ability to intervene at times. A monitor may state, "Cheryl, it looks like you do not agree with what is being said. Why don't you tell the group what you are thinking?" The facilitator may have overlooked this specific individual, because the facilitator focuses on calling on the people who raise their hands because they want to actively participate in the group.

Meeting Procedures for Reaching Consensus

You have conducted an assessment of the situation. You think you understand the issues and concerns. You have a positive vision that you can lead the group to consensus. Now all you have to do is hold the meeting. These suggestions will assist you in assigning roles and setting up the meeting room for optimum success.

♦ *Arrange seating to facilitate face-to-face interaction.* Each member of the group needs to be in a position where he or she can see all other members of the team, and vice versa. As the facilitator, set up the room so the chairs

201

are in place prior to the group's arrival. Make certain that no one is seated with his or her back to the facilitator. When the facilitator cannot see the eyes of all participants, it is much more difficult to lead the group to consensus. Usually, the most difficult people will try to sit with their backs to the facilitator. Do not let this happen! If people sit down in places where face-to-face interaction is not possible, it is appropriate to ask them to move.

♦ *Review the team's purpose for the meeting.* It only takes a few minutes, but these minutes may save the group hours. Clarify agenda topics, priorities, and time limits. Review the purpose of the meeting so all members are focused on the goal.

♦ *Make sure all people know each other.* It is easy to assume that all members of the group know one another. Make sure that everyone in the group is properly introduced.

♦ *Select members for the facilitator, minutes-taker, timekeeper, and monitor.* You may think that it would be easiest to assign the roles to team members prior to the start of the meeting. However, this is not a good idea; some members of the group will think that the outcome of the meeting has been orchestrated from behind the scenes. Usually, the facilitator has been assigned. Allow team members to select who will fulfill the other three roles.

♦ *Set standards for interpersonal behavior.* The group should agree on certain standards of behavior. Listening with the intent of understanding another person's perspective is the key to collective decision making. Group leaders foster the consensus process by valuing and encouraging individual differences, which can reduce and perhaps avoid arguments, competition, and judgments.

Once the "nuts and bolts" have been taken care of and participants are familiar with the consensus decision-making process, it's time for you to take the lead. The following tips will help ensure your success.

♦ *Start off on a positive note.* One of the authors starts off each consensus building session by asking team members, "What is going well or right since the last time the team met?" Her reason for starting off with the question is that it helps pave the way for a positive consensus building discussion. Even in teams where there is a lot of disagreement and controversy, there are always things that are going well, and it helps the consensus building process to recognize what is going right.

- *Let the group generate issues/concerns that members feel need to be discussed.* As the manager or facilitator, you have brought the topic to the table for discussion. It is important that the manager and facilitator ask team members what the issues are surrounding the topic that they would like to see discussed. If the manager tries to control the discussion, it will be impossible to reach consensus. Generate a list of the issues, and then help the team to isolate the common themes.

- *Isolate the specific areas of disagreement.* What is fun about consensus building is that you usually find out that the specific areas of disagreement are small, rather than large. Before the consensus discussion commences, the issues of disagreement are always large because people speak in generalities. Once people start really listening to each other and exploring the common ground, the issues of disagreement usually turn out to be small, not large.

- *Deal with only one issue at a time.* Because of the diversity of opinions, consensus building can easily throw an on-target discussion off track. As the manager or facilitator, it is critical that you deal with only one issue at a time or you will hopelessly wander from topic to topic and never reach consensus.

- *Create an action plan.* Once consensus is reached, it is critical that an action plan be created. The actions need to be clarified so team members understand (a) what the action is, (b) when it needs to be accomplished, and (c) who is responsible for the accomplishment of the action item.

- *Set future time and date to meet.* A follow-up meeting needs to be set to track progress of the decision or there will be a tendency for the group to slip back to old habits that were in place prior to the consensus building session.

Although the ability to successfully bring a group to consensus is one of the most difficult skills we have presented in this book, we are confident that, like all skills, it can be mastered with practice. As organizations continue to ask employees to do a lot more with a lot less, the need for a leader who can build consensus will continue to grow. Practice the skill. It will be well worth your time.

Tips for Success: Consensus and Decision Making

1. Begin with a clear vision of the outcome you desire.

2. When the group isn't able to come to agreement, focus on the "aim frame." Refer back to the vision and ask, "Where do we ultimately want to be?" or "How are we going to get there?"

3. Before leading the group, do your homework. Interview a cross-representative sample of participants before bringing the group together. This will prevent you from being "blindsided."

4. Remember to include negative thinkers. Get them involved from the outset. There is a much greater chance of them buying into the solution if they are involved.

5. Prepare an agenda.

6. Consider the room arrangement. When possible, seat participants so they can see other group members.

7. Keep the discussion focused. Deal with only one issue at a time.

8. When stuck, try to isolate specific areas of disagreement.

9. If the group generates ideas that do not pertain to the current discussion, "park" them on a flip chart to be dealt with later, or at another time.

10. Remain positive. It is critical that you have a deep-seated belief that you will be successful at leading the group to success.

Action Plan: Developing Consensus

Three steps I can take to develop my consensus/decision-making skills and when I will begin each step:

Action Step 1:

Target Date for Initiation:

Action Step 2:

Target Date for Initiation:

Action Step 3:

Target Date for Initiation:

Chapter 14

Managing Conflict

"The pure and simple truth is rarely pure and never simple."

— *Oscar Wilde*

Understand that as a supervisor or manager, no matter how carefully you plan, periodically you will have to deal with conflict. Whether it be conflict between employees, with a vendor, or with a customer, conflict has a way of uniquely appearing, demanding that we acknowledge and deal with the challenge. Just as you would not ignore poorly-produced products or inferior job performance, you can't afford to ignore conflict. While it is unrealistic to think that you can create a conflict-free environment, you can learn more about how to resolve issues so that conflict doesn't overwhelm you and impact your company's productivity. The intent of this chapter is to give you the tools that you need to understand what causes conflict, how to deal with conflict, and how to keep conflict under control in your organization. With practice, you will become confident in your ability to resolve conflicts that typically arise in the day-to-day operations of an organization.

Defining Conflict

First of all, understand that conflict is a fact of life and is here to stay! Wherever you have groups of people working together, you are going to experience conflict. Know that this is a normal occurrence and that the better you understand conflict, the better you will be able to effectively deal with the challenges inherent in supervising people.

Many relatively successful supervisors and managers have a fear of conflict. Much of their fear stems from misconceptions about the subject of conflict. One way of diffusing that fear is to explore and shatter some misconceptions that are commonly associated with the subject of conflict. Learning more about dealing with conflict will help reduce your fear of conflict and enhance your business, family, and social contacts.

Common Misconceptions about Conflict

1. *If you ignore conflict, it will take care of itself.* In most cases, nothing could be further from the truth. While it may be true that in some cases you can choose to ignore conflict, recognize that this is a coping strategy, not a solution to conflict. For example, if you continue to accept sub-standard products from a vendor without trying to resolve the quality problem, you avoid conflict. If, however, the sub-standard products delay your production or result in an inferior final product, you may have avoided conflict but cost your organization in the long run. Most often, when conflicts are ignored, things usually get worse. Generally speaking, it is best to develop a plan to deal with challenging situations and not assume that conflict will resolve itself.

2. *Conflict results from poor management.* As stated earlier, conflict happens! Relationships in the workplace are diverse and subject to periods of disharmony. The effective supervisor or manager acknowledges conflict as a challenge and deals with it when it presents itself. Confident supervisors know that some tension in the workplace is normal; they have a positive attitude about their ability to resolve conflict. For example, relationships are sometimes stretched when employees perceive that others are not working as hard as they are. If one employee consistently takes longer breaks than is permitted, as a supervisor, you must deal with this. If you choose to ignore it, the conflict will escalate and other employees will become resentful. If, however, you address and correct the problem with the employee abusing the break time, you will gain the respect of your other employees. Taking the opportunity to coach and counsel employees regarding inappropriate behavior increases your effectiveness as a manager and helps reduce potential conflict.

3. *Anger is a destructive emotion.* Anger, like other human emotions, exists and is neither positive nor negative. Anger in the workplace does not have to be thought of as a bad thing. Anger only exists where there are strong emotions. If people have no commitment and do not care about an issue, they will not exhibit anger. However, if anger is vented appropriately, it can help people move forward and resolve their conflict.

Recently, a supervisor angrily confronted an employee who repeatedly started work two minutes later than other employees. The employee was genuinely surprised because he knew that the company had a two-minute grace period for starting work, and he didn't abuse that. Once the supervisor explained to the employee that it was important for the morale of his co-workers that he start work on time, the employee began getting to work on time. In this case, the supervisor was angry about what he perceived as an employee violating the company's lenient grace period for starting work. The employee's perception of starting time obviously conflicted with his supervisor's. The supervisor's anger precipitated a confrontation with the employee, and the conflict was resolved.

4. *All conflict must be resolved immediately.* In some cases, a rush towards resolution of conflict may actually limit your success. Some conflict is best managed by a series of interventions, not a quick fix. It is important to maintain a vision of the big picture and not try to find a solution for every conflict. For example, when your staff complains about their workload, it is best to thoroughly explore their concerns. You will find it helpful to involve the group in a problem-solving session where you can discuss their feelings and explore alternatives. To deny the problem by refusing to discuss it will only make the conflict worse.

5. *Conflict indicates low regard for the organization.* Actually, just the opposite is true. If people didn't care about their organizations, they would not expend the energy. Generally, conflict occurs in areas where people have a deep concern. Conflict can help clarify emotions and serve as a tool for helping to determine an organization's core values. It is not uncommon for conflict to occur between departments within an organization. Employees dealing directly with customers may have difficulty relating to employees in other departments, such as accounting. Both departments accuse the other of missing the "big picture" or not really caring about the company. In reality, employees in both departments care deeply about the organization. Bringing both sides together to discuss their concerns will help the two departments resolve their differences and will actually make the organization stronger.

Stages of Conflict

We find it helpful to view conflict in three different stages. By viewing conflict in stages, you will find it easier to determine the severity of the conflict and its impact on the organization. Once the level of conflict is determined, it becomes easier to determine a plan of action and work towards a realistic solution.

209

Exhibit 14.1: Conflict Stages

Stages	Characteristics of Conflict Stages
One	1. Individuals agree to meet and discuss the facts. 2. Both sides believe they can resolve the conflict. 3. Individuals can discuss the problem without involving personalities. 4. Parties involved stick to the facts and work toward a solution. 5. Individuals agree on a solution and implement it positively.
Two	1. A sense of competition exists between both sides. 2. Parties focus on "winners" and "losers." 3. The facts become obscured by personalities. 4. The language used is emotional and general. (Phrases such as "They always," "She never," and "They are such" obscure facts and intensify emotional responses to the conflict.) 5. Parties are more willing to continue the conflict for the sake of making themselves look good than they are willing to attempt to resolve the conflict.
Three	1. Parties are obsessed with "winning." 2. Attempts are being made to "get rid" of others. 3. Sides become polarized; each side attempts to attract followers. 4. Leaders or spokespersons for each side emerge. 5. Corporate good becomes secondary to the goal of each side winning. 6. There appears to be no common ground, issues have escalated to only black and white options, solutions seem unattainable.

Stage One Conflict

Conflict at Stage One is real, but often not intense. Typically, people working together will have different goals, values, and unique individual needs. In Stage One conflicts, people feel discomfort and possibly anger, but do not get very emotional about the conflict. Once the problem has surfaced, facts and opinions are shared openly and the parties involved generally feel a sense of optimism about their ability to resolve the problem. In Stage One conflict, communication is typically specific and clear because the people and the problem are not intertwined. Brainstorming activities will work well at this level, because people are willing to discuss the problem specifically and leave out the personalities.

Tips to help managers and supervisors resolve Stage One conflicts:

♦ *Get all employees involved to carefully examine the conflict.* Get both sides talking and make sure that they both listen to one another.

- *Make sure that employees stick to the issues.* Don't let either party bring up emotional issues from previous conflicts. Deal only with the facts relating to this particular conflict. Ask whether their reaction is in proportion to the problem.
- *Help employees identify points of agreement first.* Working from the points of agreement, try to identify and resolve the points of disagreement. Help employees see the big picture and get beyond their issues of conflict.

Stage Two Conflict

Conflict at the Stage Two level becomes characterized by a win/lose attitude. The wins and losses characteristic of Stage Two conflict seem greater because the people involved are emotionally tied to the problem. How one looks in the eyes of others is suddenly very important. At this level of conflict, people keep track of their verbal victories, witnesses take sides, and sides begin to keep track of their wins and losses. Whereas conflict can be handled at Stage One with various avoidance or coping strategies, these strategies will not work when dealing with Stage Two conflict.

Tips to help diffuse conflict at the Stage Two level:

- *Interview for accuracy.* Interview all parties individually or independently so you know the issues prior to bringing together the people who are in conflict. When you accurately know all the issues and perceptions, you will be in a better position to resolve or mediate the conflict.
- *Create a neutral atmosphere.* Create a safe, neutral atmosphere in which to discuss the conflict. Seat participants in a circle, not across from one another. Seating participants close to one another, without the security of a table or desk between them, helps set the right tone for conflict resolution.
- *Create an agenda.* Have an agenda and be responsible for keeping participants focused on its contents.
- *Keep the group focused in the aim frame.* Groups focused in the aim frame ask two questions: "Where do we want to be?" and "How do we get there?" Focusing the group on these questions will reduce finger pointing and blaming.
- *Focus on the facts.* Take whatever time it takes to make sure that you have all the details. Make sure that you clarify any generalizations. Ask participants to clarify who *they* is and how many times *always* means.
- *Encourage teamwork.* Each participant is equally responsible for finding an acceptable alternative to resolve the conflict.
- *Focus on points of agreement and look for middle ground.* At this point, do not suggest compromise. Typically, people involved in Stage Two conflict are

emotional. To them, a compromise may mean giving up and may feel like a loss. Keep exploring alternatives until both parties can agree on a solution.

♦ *Recognize that helping people resolve conflict takes time.* Allow enough time for each party to express all their concerns regarding the conflict. Take what time is needed to find a solution to the conflict that is agreeable to all parties. Rushing or forcing a resolution may create a quick fix, but not a lasting solution to the conflict.

Stage Three Conflict

When conflict escalates to Stage Three, being right and wanting to punish wrong become increasingly important. Sides are drawn and people rally around their cause. The conflict becomes all-consuming and parties involved make it the center focus, expending a large amount of their effort and energy in their commitment to their cause. In true Stage Three conflict, issues are intense and there is little middle ground. Sides polarize and insiders try to persuade outsiders to join their cause. Both sides enlist support by promoting their cause as being what is best for the organization. In truth, as the conflict escalates, both sides become increasingly more committed to winning and frequently lose sight of what damage their conflict is inflicting on the organization.

When Stage Three conflict reaches the point that it severely impacts organizational morale and productivity, outside intervention is needed. If the conflict is limited to one area of the organization, a neutral party from another area within the organization can be called in to mediate the dispute. If, however, the conflict permeates the entire organization, it is best to call in mediators from outside the organization. Regardless of where the mediating team comes from, they must be seen as neutral by all parties involved in the conflict.

Mediators will be required to sift through many layers of emotion to get down to the underlying facts. Facts surrounding the incidents that initially started the conflict may have become clouded and obscure as the conflict escalated. Mediators should first interview representatives of each side privately. Once the mediator has the facts, both sides will be brought together and the mediator will attempt to get agreement on the facts. Working with both sides, the mediator will then seek consensus on an acceptable alternative to end the conflict.

In the event that mediation attempts are not successful, the next formal step in conflict resolution is arbitration. In arbitration, each side presents its argument before a neutral arbitrator. The arbitrator listens objectively and decides for one side or the other. The benefit of this process is that one side clearly wins. The disadvantage, obviously, is that one side loses. In the interests of organizational morale and productivity, arbitration should be the last step in the conflict resolution process. All other methods of negotiating and mediating conflict should be exhausted first before arbitration is considered.

Tips for dealing with conflict at the Stage Three level:

- *Make a commitment to get all the details.* This will require time, but the outside intervention team must commit to interviewing as many people as necessary to ensure that they get the facts right. This will require sifting through a great deal of information clouded by emotion, but is a critical step and should not be overlooked.
- *Recognize and understand the intensity of individual commitment to a cause.* From an outsider's point of view, you can logically think through the conflict. Know that to those personally involved in the conflict at this level, logic and reason will not necessarily persuade them to think differently. Concentrate on getting agreement on the facts and mediating a solution that is acceptable to both sides.
- *Once the conflict is resolved, concentrate on corporate goals.* Conflict at this level is intense and a period of healing will be required after it has been resolved. Make sure that both sides understand the need to commit to their organization's goals. As a manager or supervisor, recognize the skills of your employees and the contributions they make for the benefit of the organization. Redirect energies away from the conflict that polarized sides and impacted negatively on the organization. Focus on the future and what all employees can contribute towards common organizational goals.

213

Conflict Management Styles

Different types of controversies call for different types of conflict management styles. We will briefly discuss five main management styles for dealing with conflict. Once you have a basic understanding of these different styles, you can select the one most appropriate for the specific conflict.

Management Style One: Withdrawing

In the withdrawing or avoiding style of conflict resolution, little value is placed on either self or others. A manager using this style will withdraw and may pretend that conflict isn't happening. Sometimes, though, this can be an appropriate style to use. If more time is needed to study a conflict, or if the issue is relatively unimportant, this style works well. If, however, a manager uses this style as a response to all types of conflict, tense situations may escalate and the manager will quickly gain a reputation for doing nothing when conflict divides parties. Two departments, for example, may be in conflict with one another for what they perceive to be budgetary inequalities. The vice president responsible

Exhibit 14.2: Methods for Resolving Conflict

Methods	Results	Appropriate, if . . .	Inappropriate, if . . .
Withdrawing	Person tries to solve problem by denying its existence. Results in win/lose.	Issue is relatively unimportant. Timing is wrong. Cooling off period is needed. Short-term use.	Issue is important and will not disappear.
Smoothing	Emphasizes area of agreement. Differences are played down. Surface harmony exists. Results in win/lose and in variations of resentment and defensiveness.	Same as above. Also when preservation of relationship is important.	Reluctance to deal with conflict leads to evasion of an important issue when others are ready and willing to deal with issue.
Forcing	One's authority or position, majority rule, or a persuasive minority settles the conflict. Results in win/lose if the dominated party sees no hope for self.	When power comes with position of authority. When this method has been agreed upon.	Losers have no way to express needs. Could result in future disruptions.
Compromising	Each party gives up something in order to meet midway. Results in lose/lose if "middle-of-the-road" position ignores the real diversity of the issue.	Both parties have enough leeway to give. Resources are limited. When win/lose stance is undesirable.	Original position is unrealistic. Solution is too watered down to be effective. Commitment is doubted by parties involved.
Collaborating	Win/win. Abilities, values, and expertise are recognized. Each person's position is clear and emphasis is on joint solution.	Time is available to complete the process. Parties are committed and trained in use of process.	Not enough time or abilities and commitment is not present.

for both departments chooses to ignore comments she hears from each department about the other. Rather than diminish, the feelings of mistrust and resentment continue to grow between the departments until lack of internal support between the departments begins to impact negatively on the entire organization.

Management Style Two: Smoothing

Parties may decide to use a smoothing style of conflict management when it is important to maintain a positive relationship. Smoothing places a high value on the wants and needs of others and a lesser value on self-gratification. This strategy places less emphasis on differences between parties involved in the conflict and greater value on reaching common ground. One party may decide to oblige the other in order not to "rock the boat." The obliging party may decide that attempting to confront the issue may cause damage to the relationship and that the outcome would not be worth jeopardizing the relationship. The obliging style results in a win/loss outcome. In this case, one party has decided that obliging the other party is worth the loss in order to maintain the relationship. Taking this calculated loss is fine as long as one party does not build resentment against the other. For example, a small start-up company may put up with a rude customer because it needs the business. Eventually, though, as the business grows, employees at the firm will resent having to continue the relationship with the rude customer.

215

Management Style Three: Forcing

The forcing or dominating style of conflict management is just the opposite of the smoothing or obliging style and results in a win/lose outcome. Parties using this style place a high value on self and a low value on others. This style is appropriate to use when the issues are minor or a quick decision is needed. This strategy may also be employed by someone having greater expertise or authority in an area than the other side. In this case, simply put, one side dictates the outcome for the other side. Although this method quickly resolves conflict, care must be taken to ensure that the losers do not feel bullied. In other words, just because one party can mandate a solution, it may not be the best approach because the losers will build resentment and harbor hostility. The dominating style of conflict resolution, used repeatedly over time, does nothing to foster cooperation and may actually escalate conflict in an organization. A manager, for example, repeatedly handles all scheduling conflicts relating to job assignments by dictating who will do what. Over a period of time, this leads to resentment and a feeling that, if given the chance, employees could themselves do a better job of examining job assignments and resolving the conflict equitably.

Management Style Four: Compromising

This style of managing conflict is a middle-of-the-road solution. Parties involved in compromising tactics place neither high nor low value on self or concern for others. Often, this approach is used when other methods have failed, yet both parties are still desirous of a positive outcome. At this point in the conflict, both sides have reached the point where they are willing to give up something in order to resolve the problem. I suggest you say "lose-lose and win-win" outcome, because both parties come away with something, though certainly not as much as they wished. Compromise results in a lose/lose outcome. Compromising tactics work best when issues are complex or when there is an equal balance of power between the parties involved. For example, a vice president responsible for two departments arguing over a budget would call representatives from both departments together. Each side would then present their facts, feelings, and suggestions for change. Working with the representatives, a compromise is devised that more equitably distributes resources. Although neither department gets all that they wanted, both departments would support the compromise solution.

Management Style Five: Collaborating

This style is best used to solve problems when issues are complex. Parties using this style of conflict resolution have a high regard for both themselves and others. In other words, both parties are committed to a win/win outcome and are willing to work together to derive that outcome. When using the collaborating style to resolve conflict, both sides must be willing to examine their differences factually and reach a solution that is acceptable to all. Parties using this style work hard to think creatively and come up with an acceptable solution. Their goal is to gather as much factual information as needed to generate a solution acceptable to all parties. This style takes time and will only work if both parties are committed to the outcome. For example, over a period of time workers in a small office have become divided. Each side feels that the other is not working as hard and not contributing its fair share to the organization. Under the leadership of the manager, both sides sit down to talk about their feelings and examine solutions. Objectively, they look at various job responsibilities, realign some responsibilities, and commit their support to a united team effort.

Handling Conflict Positively

One of the challenges of dealing with conflict is to help people maintain healthy relationships during and after periods of conflict. Simply resolving the problem is not enough. The people involved must be satisfied with the outcome and attention must be given to their emotional well-being. If these two areas are not addressed, chances are that other problems will surface in time. The following tips will help you maintain healthy relationships during periods of conflict.

♦ *Acknowledge conflict.* Workplace conflict happens. Effective supervisors acknowledge conflict and take steps to help employees resolve conflict.

♦ *Encourage participation.* As conflict escalates, the people involved become consumed with their cause and the good of the organization becomes secondary. Managers and supervisors can help people overcome problems that split groups by encouraging participation. Getting parties involved to admit ownership of the problem and work towards resolution helps build commitment to the good of the organization.

♦ *Create a safe environment.* Creating a neutral environment in which both parties can present their facts, discuss the problem, and suggest ideas for resolving the conflict is one way to support and encourage participation leading to conflict resolution.

♦ *Encourage commitment.* Reminding people that collectively "we" own the problems and collectively "we" have the power to resolve them is a good technique for encouraging commitment to ending the conflict.

♦ *Question to determine the facts.* Conflict, by nature, gets emotional. Although people may not intentionally lie, their perspective colors their perception of the facts. As a leader during conflict resolution, keep listening and questioning to make sure that you have the facts straight. As people passionately present their case, this will be a challenge.

♦ *Listen, listen, listen.* During periods of conflict, listening skills are critical. It costs you nothing to listen and gives you a much better perspective on the problems surrounding the conflict. As managers and supervisors, we are used to doing the talking. We feel confident when we are in charge of the conversation. As leaders dealing with conflict, however, we need to stop talking and start listening.

♦ *Listen objectively.* In order to support people during conflict, don't argue with their facts. Instead, keep questioning, making sure that all parties have an opportunity to be heard before any decisions are made. Typically, when the facts are separated from the opinions, it becomes easier to think creatively and propose alternative solutions leading to an acceptable solution to the conflict being discussed.

♦ *Focus on the problem, not the people.* This is a challenge, because in Stages Two and Three, the people and the problem are intertwined. Personalities align with one another and the details surrounding the facts or situation that originally started the conflict become obscured. As a leader, you must

217

work hard to keep the people issues separate from the facts. Insist that parties focus on the facts. If emotions flare and parties begin attacking one another personally, steer the discussion back to the facts. Insist that parties listen to one another as they present their facts. Get agreement from both parties on the facts. Sticking to the facts downplays emotional responses and enhances the problem-solving process.

♦ *Take more time to reach a decision, if necessary.* Although we are not recommending avoidance as a problem-solving technique, declaring a "time-out" at some point in the conflict resolution process may be helpful. Occasionally people become so passionate about their cause that they lose their perspective. Sometimes the facts needed to resolve a problem are not available. Leaders must communicate why they are delaying the decision so that the parties involved maintain their confidence in their leadership.

♦ *Follow-up.* Initially, after conflict has been addressed and resolved, it is usual for things to appear to be going more smoothly. Don't assume this will last. Periodically check back with both parties to ask how things are going. If issues emerge, get both parties together again and address the concerns before the situation escalates.

Finally, recognize that despite all that you do to keep your leadership positive and focused on organizational goals, conflict in the workplace will be inevitable! If we worked only with machines, conflict would not be a challenge. As we work with people, though, it can be expected that relationships will be stretched from time-to-time and we will be faced with the task of helping people resolve stressful situations. Use what you have learned in this chapter to confidently counsel, mediate, and lead during a time of organizational conflict. Your ability to help others deal rationally with conflict will identify you as a valuable team player within your organization. Remember that conflict does not have to be feared, and it does not necessarily spell disaster for a team. Knowing what you now do about conflict resolution, recognize it as an opportunity to practice and further enhance another one of your supervisory skills!

Conclusion

The following seven-step format will help you deal effectively with conflict in the workplace:

1. Recognize that a conflict exists.
2. Define the area of disagreement.
3. State desired outcomes.
4. Identify benefits of reaching agreement vs. consequences of not.

5. Generate alternatives.
6. Select the best alternative.
7. Implement and follow up.

Tips for Success: Conflict Resolution

1. *Don't ignore conflict* Chances are if the conflict is left alone, it will escalate—not go away.

2. *If you work with people, there is potential for conflict* This is no reflection on your ability as a supervisor or manager. What will distinguish you is your ability to confidently deal with workplace conflict.

3. *Before attempting to resolve issues, make sure you know the facts* The best way is to talk with employees one-on-one to learn firsthand about their perceptions regarding the conflict.

4. *Remember to listen more than you speak when resolving conflict* As a manager or supervisor, we are accomplished problem-solvers. When the conflict revolves around people and feelings, it is critical that you listen, listen, and then listen some more!

5. *Make every attempt to remain objective and neutral* Your team is looking to you as a role model. They will be influenced by how you resolve conflict. If you are calm, objective, and solution oriented, you are demonstrating positive techniques for resolving conflict.

6. *To help you remain objective, focus on the problem, not the people involved with the problem* Doing this helps you stay detached from the emotion surrounding the conflict and helps you better focus on positive outcomes.

7. *During periods of conflict, help employees refocus their attention on your team's goals* When you emphasize goals and outcomes, it demonstrates your commitment to resolving the conflict and focuses energy back on the reason we are in business.

8. *If you reach a stalemate when attempting to resolve conflict, declare a time out* Giving those involved a time to cool off may help all parties better focus on solutions.

9. *When resolving conflict, attempt to utilize the collaboration method, which strives to achieve a solution that is mutually acceptable to all parties* Using the collaboration style helps ensure that neither party in the conflict feels like the "loser."

10. *Once the conflict is resolved, periodically check back with the participants to make sure that there are no further issues*

219

Action Plan: Managing Conflict

Three steps I can take to manage conflict within my department and when I will begin each step:

Action Step 1:
Target Date for Initiation:

Action Step 2:
Target Date for Initiation:

Action Step 3:
Target Date for Initiation:

Chapter

15

Negotiating for Win/Win Results

"In life, you do not get what you deserve, you get what you negotiate!"

— *Dr. Chester Karrass*

Managers and supervisors frequently face these kinds of situations requiring negotiation skills: agreeing on appropriate schedules and deadlines for projects, solving problems with clients, setting the salaries of employees, obtaining more personnel for the department, and maintaining high customer service standards with staff. Utilizing effective negotiation skills is the only realistic and successful approach to meet the challenges of today's rapidly changing environment. In this chapter you will learn what negotiation is and become acquainted with the supervisory skills you need to be a great negotiator.

What Is Negotiation?

What do you think of when you hear the word "negotiation"? Microsoft and the U.S. Department of Justice locked in a heated argument about monopolies? The U.S. president and Indian political figures debating the ethics of nuclear testing? Sports figures threatening to switch allegiances unless they get their specified millions? Labor and management locked in an 11th-hour contract struggle for a 4% raise? Buyer and seller haggling over the price of a house or a car? Most of us think of negotiation in terms of a win/lose type of scenario.

At a San Diego State University-sponsored seminar on negotiation, the following question was posed to participants: "How often do you negotiate?" The choice of answers included "Often," "Seldom," or "Never." Surprisingly, over 36% of the respondents answered "Seldom" or "Never." Unfortunately, this was a trick question! The correct answer is "Always." Everything in life is negotiated, under all conditions, at all times—from asking your significant other to take out the morning garbage to merging into a freeway lane in rush hour traffic; from deciding with an employee what time frame to schedule the completion of a project to deciding which 11:00 P.M. news program to watch with your family. Every aspect of your life is spent in some form of negotiation.

Gerard I. Nierenberg, the author of the first book on the formalized process of negotiation and the president of the New York City-based Negotiation Institute, Inc., explains the concept: "Whenever people exchange ideas with the intention of changing relationships, whenever they confer for agreement, then they are negotiating." Dr. Israel Unterman, a deceased professor of management at San Diego State University, expanded Nierenberg's definition slightly: "Negotiation is conducted neither to widen nor to breach the relationship, but to form a new or different configuration."

In short, most of us are constantly involved in negotiations to one degree or another for a good part of any given day. Negotiation should be considered as a positive way of structuring the communication process.

Typical Negotiated Transactions

The following list of some typical transactions demonstrates where you can improve your position by negotiating.

- Defining the price, terms, and accessory items on any purchased item.
- Prioritizing the workload and job assignments with employees.
- Raising the performance standard of a difficult employee.
- Gaining cooperation from another department.
- Determining a delivery schedule with a client.
- Deciding the starting date for a new employee.
- Discussing what your salary will be with your boss.
- Providing performance reviews and salary increases to your employees.
- Visualizing what level of quality your employees will provide.
- Establishing a time to meet or determining the length of a meeting.

Try the exercise in Exhibit 15.1 to see if you currently have what it takes to be a good negotiator.

Exhibit 15.1: Negotiation Assessment

How Good a Negotiator Are You?

Like any management skill, negotiation can be learned, practiced, and mastered. This questionnaire focuses on the personal characteristics necessary to be a great negotiator. Circle the number that best reflects where you fall on the scale. The higher the number, the more the characteristic describes you.

1. I enjoy dealing with other people and I am committed to creating a win/win outcome.

    1   2   3   4   5   6   7   8   9   10

2. I enjoy solving problems and coming up with creative solutions.

    1   2   3   4   5   6   7   8   9   10

3. I am willing to ask questions to get needed information in order to make the best decision.

    1   2   3   4   5   6   7   8   9   10

4. I do not take my counterpart's strategies, tactics, and comments personally.

    1   2   3   4   5   6   7   8   9   10

5. I like to uncover the needs, wants, and motivations of my counterpart.

    1   2   3   4   5   6   7   8   9   10

6. I am able to think clearly under pressure.

    1   2   3   4   5   6   7   8   9   10

7. I have good self-esteem and tend to have a high level of aspiration and expectation.

    1   2   3   4   5   6   7   8   9   10

8. I recognize the power of strategies and tactics and use them frequently.

    1   2   3   4   5   6   7   8   9   10

9. I am willing to compromise to solve problems when necessary.

    1   2   3   4   5   6   7   8   9   10

10. I am a good listener.

    1   2   3   4   5   6   7   8   9   10

Grand total: _____

Scoring:

90+: You have the characteristics of a great negotiator. You recognize what negotiation requires and you are willing to apply yourself accordingly.

80–89: You should do well as a negotiator, but you have some areas that need improvement.

70–79: You have an understanding of negotiation but some important areas need improvement.

0–70: Go over the questions again. You may have been hard on yourself, or you may have identified some key areas that you will need to concentrate on when you negotiate.

Negotiation's Possible Outcomes

A negotiation will end in one of four possible outcomes. The outcome will be one of lose/lose, win/lose, lose/win, or win/win. In most situations, our goal should be to achieve a win/win outcome.

Outcome One: Lose/Lose

Lose/lose is the outcome when neither party achieves its needs or wants and is reluctant to negotiate with the same counterpart again. In 1987, I tried to negotiate a $30,000 printing contract with a major corporation in San Diego. I thought I had the contract, but at the last minute the client informed me that they had chosen another printer based solely on the competition's lower price. At that precise moment, the client had won and I had lost. The client had found a better price and felt the competitor had the quality and service to back up his price. One month later, I received a call from the client informing me that the printer they had chosen did an awful job printing their brochure. To top it off, the competitor's service was poor and the client no longer trusted the company. Because the competitor's delays forced the client to miss having a brochure on the new product at their only industry trade show of the year, the client lost also.

Outcome Two: Win/Lose

The second and third possible outcomes of negotiation are the win/lose and the lose/win. The difference between the two comes down to which side of the fence you land on. In some negotiations, you will be the winner and your counterpart will lose. In other negotiations, the roles will be reversed. If you have ever lost a negotiation or been taken advantage of by another, you know that the feeling is not pleasant. The real problem in a win/lose or lose/win outcome is that one counterpart walks away without accomplishing his needs or goals. And more importantly, the loser will likely refuse to re-negotiate with the winner. Ultimately, this sets up the potential for a future lose/lose outcome.

An example of a win/lose relationship would be a supervisor who continually asks an employee to work overtime or on weekends but is never willing to give that same employee a day or time off when requested. This one-sided relationship destroys morale and trust.

Outcome Three: Lose/Win

Remember, when you create a lose/win or win/lose, the loser, if given the choice, will most likely refuse to negotiate with the same counterpart again. During a six-week course in Negotiation at San Diego State University, one of our students continually created win/lose outcomes, with himself always in the winner's circle. By the sixth week, there was not one person in the class who would negotiate with him. Creating win/lose or lose/win is not good business!

Outcome Four: Win/Win

In almost all negotiations, the goal we should strive for is to create a win/win outcome. This is an outcome where the needs and goals of both counterparts have been met. Also, both counterparts walk away with a positive feeling and are willing to negotiate with each other again. A supervisor who asks an employee to work the weekend, but then grants the employee's request to take time off to attend his daughter's graduation later in the week is a great example of a win/win outcome. In the negotiation workshops we present, it is rewarding to see the excitement in participants' faces when they both realize they have created a win/win outcome.

Outcome Five: No Outcome

The fifth possible outcome is no outcome: neither party wins or loses. For example, a person who owned a large commercial piece of real estate decided to sell his property. The reason for selling was that the city government was considering rezoning the area where the property was located. The property owner felt the rezoning was going to lower the property value. A real estate agent was called to list the property. In the meeting, the real estate agent, who was a member of the zoning commission, told the property owner that he had received erroneous information and no rezoning would take place. The agent recommended that the owner hold on to the property, rather than sell. The property owner accepted the agent's advice. In this particular negotiation, nothing happened.

Creating a Win/Win Outcome

Creating a win/win outcome is possible. Follow these three keys for success for win/win solutions.

A. *Do not narrow your negotiation down to one issue.* If you do narrow the negotiation to one issue, then you have created a situation where you have a winner and a loser. The most common example of narrowing a negotiation down to one issue is arguing over the price of something. With supervisors, the most typical issue is money. Most supervisors believe the most important thing to employees is money. There are so many other factors that can be brought into the negotiation. Some examples are job assignments, recognition, status, perks, awards, vacation, timing, quality, other goods and services, etc.

B. *Realize that your counterpart does not have the same needs and wants that you do.* If you do not take this factor into consideration, then you negotiate from the framework that my loss is my counterpart's gain. With that attitude, it is virtually impossible to create a win/win outcome.

C. *You must believe point "B" (above) in your heart.* Experience shows that most novice negotiators acknowledge that their counterpart most likely does not have the same needs and wants as they do, but when they get into an actual negotiation, they forget this. For example, most supervisors forget about the power of daily recognition or valued contributions and just focus on what raise they can or cannot give an employee. Supervisors focus on money because that is what they think employees desire the most. In creating a negotiated outcome, in most instances it will be in your best interest to have a cooperative attitude to help develop a win/win atmosphere.

Negotiation Resources

Resource One: Time

Time is a valuable resource for supervisors and managers. Most people think of negotiation as an event that has a definite beginning and ending. Furthermore, we find that most people consider the negotiation to start and end with the actual interactive process between the two counterparts. Nothing could be further from the truth.

Recently, one of our seminar participants asked for advice on what strategy she should use when agreeing on appropriate schedules and deadlines for projects. All the options she had considered dealt with the actual face-to-face meeting. What she had not considered was all the pre-planning and information gathering that creates a powerful negotiation. These included documenting her workload, prioritizing projects, delegating the work properly, and having a clear vision of the goals she wanted to achieve prior to the meeting. Most negotiations, like life, are a continuous process that begins long before the actual negotiation takes place.

Time plays a critical role in negotiations for all supervisors and managers. Most often, negotiations will conclude in the remaining 20% of the time allowed. This element of negotiation is an interesting rule that seems to apply to life in general. It's called the 80/20 rule, or Pareto's Law (named after Vilfredo Pareto, the Italian economist and sociologist who created it). Pareto's Law says, "Twenty percent of what you do produces 80% of the results, and conversely, 80% of what you do produces only 20% of the results."

In negotiation, this means that 80% of your results are generally agreed upon in the last 20% of your remaining time. We consistently see this in the seminars we present. As the participants negotiate with each other, the seminar leader periodically tells the participants how much time they have to conclude their negotiation. Normally, the majority of the negotiations are concluded in the last remaining two minutes. Here are two suggestions that will help you bring time to your side of the negotiations.

- *Have patience.* Because most concessions and settlements will occur in the last 20% of the available time, be patient. Remain level-headed and wait for the right moment to act. As a general rule, patience pays. It may be that the thing to do when you are not certain is to walk away or do nothing.
- *Realize deadlines can be moved, changed, or eliminated.* As a deadline comes near, do not panic. Change your deadline. Have you ever wondered how many of the people who are running to the post office at the last minute on April 15 have refunds coming back to them? Even without an expected refund, people still have the opportunity to file an extension giving them another four months.

Resource Two: Information

Most often, the side with the most information will receive the better outcome in a negotiation. Why, then, do we fail to get adequate information prior to the start of a negotiation? Because, as we mentioned earlier, people tend to perceive the negotiation as the actual interaction between two counterparts. We seldom think about the information that we need until it hits us like a ton of bricks in the actual negotiation.

A negotiation is not an event, it is a process. It starts long before the actual face-to-face encounter. One reason you have to start much earlier is because during the actual negotiation, it is likely that one side or the other will conceal their true interests, needs, and motivations. Your chances of getting this information during the actual negotiation is relatively remote.

How do you get this information? You start early. The earlier you start, the easier it is to obtain information. People will offer much more information prior to the start of any formal interaction. Prior to buying my wife's car, I went to dealerships asking questions about the models we were interested in and the available financing plans, and at the same time I was investigating which dealerships were most willing to deal.

Where do you get this information? From anyone who has any knowledge that will help you in your negotiation. This may be researching facts and statistics, talking to someone who has negotiated with your counterpart in the past, talking to your counterpart, or gaining inside information from friends, relatives, secretaries, etc.

The benefit of gaining your information prior to the negotiation is two-fold. First, with your information in hand, it gives you the opportunity to listen for your counterpart's needs, wants, and motivations. This also includes listening for what is being omitted. Second, as we said earlier, it has been proven that the side with the most information will probably receive the better outcome in the negotiation.

Resource Three: Power

When we discuss power in seminars, I sometimes see disgust written across the face of some participants. The word "power" has had a negative connotation for many years. The association is made because most people, when they hear the word "power," contemplate one side overbearing and dominating the other. I define power as the ability to influence people or situations. With this definition in mind, power is neither good or bad. It is the abuse of power that is bad.

Most people have more power than they think. I believe there is a link between one's self-esteem and the amount of power one feels he or she has. It has been demonstrated that people with high self-esteem feel they have more viable options in negotiations. People with low self-esteem do not perceive themselves as having viable alternatives. This is the same for people who feel they lack the power to act. Powerless people become apathetic, which means they do not stand a fair chance when they take their baggage into a negotiation. When entering into a negotiation, there are some rules to remember about power.

Seldom does one side have all the power. Even in a situation where you are going to banks asking for a business loan, you, the entrepreneur, still have power—the power to decide which bank you will apply to, the power to decide what interest rate you will pay, and the power to decide if you will put up your home as collateral.

Power may be real or apparent. I am reminded of the days when I was a proctor in the Sociology Department at San Diego State University. Cheating was a problem, but I never made a focused effort to stop the offenders. I figured I would use multiple tests on the final and it would all come out in the wash. Unfortunately, I did not have time to scramble the test on the final and I had to resort to Plan B. As I was passing out the tests, I made an announcement that on this final, I would uphold the University's "policy" on cheating. As I finished passing out the test, one bold student asked what the University's policy was on cheating. My response was simple: "If you need to ask, then you do not want to know." This was the first time I ever saw all 60 students with their heads down staring at their own papers! Does the University have a policy on cheating? I do not know. But in this situation, whether the power was real or apparent did not matter—the students perceived that I had the power.

Power only exists to the point at which it is accepted. On a flight home from Europe, all the ticketing agents for the Economy Class had at least a twenty-minute line to check baggage. There were no lines for Business Class and First Class. The Business and First Class ticketing agents were looking off into space like they were mentally rehearsing their policy and procedures manual. Not wanting to wait in lines, I took my baggage and tickets up to the Business Class window and got my seat assignment. (I would have gone up to the First Class counter, but I did not want to push my luck!)

Power relationships can change over time. This is one of the hardest lessons in life I have ever learned. In my youth, I had the same girlfriend from the seventh to the eleventh grade. At the time, I was proud to say I had the power in this relationship. I decided what activities we would become involved in, what friends we would have, and where we would go on our dates. Flowers were not in my repertoire. After all, I did not need them. And then something happened that sent my power into a 180-degree tailspin. Marilyn, my girlfriend, was asked to the senior prom by the student body president. As if that was not enough competition, he was also the quarterback of our football team. Overnight, I was sending

229

cards and roses, and begging for a date. It was my first real-life lesson that win/lose negotiations eventually end in lose/lose.

Test your power. You will never know how much power you have until you test reality. The chances are that you have more power than you think.

Advance Preparation

In negotiations, advance preparation is critical. The more prepared you are, the better off you will be. Also, it will be in your best interest to have a clear set of goals going into the negotiation. You can then set your goals based on the information you collect. The following sheet provides a guideline in collecting the information you will need.

Exhibit 15.2: Negotiation Worksheet

Your Side	Counterpart's Side
Topic:	Topic:
Available Facts:	Available Facts:
Negotiable Issues:	Negotiable Issues:
Position on Issues:	Position on Issues:
Needs of Negotiators:	Needs of Negotiators:
Strategies and Tactics:	Strategies and Tactics:

Listening Skills: A Powerful Key

Unfortunately, not enough negotiators know how to be good listeners. And negotiators who are poor listeners miss numerous opportunities. Statistics state that the normal, untrained listener is likely to understand and retain only about 50% of a conversation. This relatively low percentage drops to an even less-impressive 25% retention rate 48 hours later. This means that the recall of particular conversations will usually be inaccurate and incomplete.

Because listening skills are taken for granted by many negotiators, there will be communication problems. In order to be a good listener, you must attempt to be objective. This means you are going to try to understand the intentions behind your counterpart's communication, and not what you want to understand. With everything your counterpart tells you, you must ask, "Why did he tell me that?," "What does he think my reaction should be?," and "Was he being honest?"

The best negotiators almost always turn out to be the best listeners as well. Why does the correlation exist? Invariably, the best negotiators have been observers of the communication skills, both verbal and nonverbal, of their counterparts. They have heard and noted how other negotiators effectively use word choice and sentence structure. They have also practiced listening for the vocal skills such as the rate of speech, pitch, and tonal quality.

Dr. Lyman Steil, a worldwide expert on listening, states that we all make at least one major listening mistake each day, and for negotiators, mistakes can be very expensive. A study done by Xerox Learning Systems found that the most successful salespeople are the ones who are able to uncover more needs than their less successful colleagues. This is significant because salespeople make their living by negotiating.

231

Hindrances to Effective Listening

Negotiators tend to run into three pitfalls that hinder the effectiveness of their listening.

1. *Persuasion.* Many negotiators think that negotiating is primarily a job of persuasion and persuasion means talking. These people consider talking as active and listening as passive. They tend to forget that it is difficult to persuade other people when you do not know what motivates them.

2. *Overpreparation.* When negotiating, we all tend to overprepare for what we are going to say and tend to use our listening time waiting for our turn.

Many times, while we wait for our turn, we miss vital information we could use later in the negotiation.

3. *Emotional filters.* We all have emotional filters that prevent us from hearing what we do not want to hear. In my early sales career, I seemed to always waste time with clients whom I thought would buy printing from me (but never did). Now, I very seldom have that problem. What experience has shown is that those people whom I used to waste time with had no intention of using my services. If I had been a better listener, I would have been able to pick up on clients' true feelings earlier in my career.

Attentive Listening Skills

Great listening does not come easily. It is hard work. The following suggestions will help you understand the real messages your counterparts are trying to convey. Including them as part of your management skills will lead to more effective, efficient, and productive negotiations.

- *Be motivated to listen.* When you realize that the person with the most information will usually receive the better outcome in a negotiation, you have an incentive to motivate yourself to be a better listener. It is wise to set goals for all the different kinds of information you would like to receive from your counterpart. The more you can learn, the better off you will be.
- *If you must speak, ask questions.* The goal is to get more specific and better refined information. To do this, you will have to continue questioning your counterpart. Your questioning sequence will be moving from the broad to the narrow, and eventually you will have the information to make the best decision. The second reason to continue asking questions is that it will help you uncover the needs and wants of your counterpart.
- *Be alert to nonverbal cues.* Try to not only listen to what is said but also to understand the attitudes and motives behind the words. Remember, the negotiator usually does not put his entire message into words. For example, there is considerable difference between the auditory and behavioral cues emitted by the negotiator. While his verbal message may convey his honesty and conviction, his gestures, facial expressions, and tone of voice may convey doubt.
- *Let your counterpart tell his story first.* Many salespeople have learned the value of this point from the school of hard knocks. One printing salesperson shared an experience where he paid a visit to a new prospect and explained that his company specialized in two- and four-color printing. The

client then told the salesperson that he would not be doing business with this printing company because he only needed one-color printing. The salesperson replied that his company also did one-color printing, but the client had already made his decision. Had the salesperson let the client speak first, he would have been able to tailor his presentation to satisfy the client's needs and wants.

◆ *Do not interrupt while your counterpart is speaking.* Interrupting a speaker is not good business for two reasons. First, it is rude. Second, you are very likely to cut off valuable information that will help you at a later point in the negotiation.

◆ *Fight off distractions.* When you are negotiating, try to create a situation where you can think clearly and avoid interruptions. Interruptions and distractions tend to send negotiations back to square one, or at least create the possibility of a severe setback. Employees, peers, children, animals, etc., all have the possibility of distracting you and forcing your eye off the goal. If you can, create a good listening environment.

◆ *Do not trust your memory.* Write everything down. Any time someone tells you something in a negotiation, write it down. It is amazing how much conflicting information will come up at a later time. If you are able to correct your counterpart or refresh his memory with facts and figures shared with you in an earlier session, it will give you a tremendous amount of credibility and power. Writing things down may take a few minutes longer, but the end results are well worth the time.

◆ *Listen selectively.* With a questioning goal in mind, you can listen for words and nonverbal cues that add to the information you are seeking. When you hear specific bits of information, such as your counterpart's willingness to concede his price, you can expand with more specific questions.

◆ *Give your counterpart your undivided attention.* When negotiating, it is important to look your counterpart in the eye when he or she is speaking. The goal is to create a win/win outcome and have the counterpart willing to negotiate with us again. To do this, our counterpart needs to think that we are fair, honest, and decent. One way to help achieve this goal is to pay close attention to your counterpart. When he or she is speaking, look eyeball-to-eyeball. Watch what message the eyes are sending. What is the nonverbal behavior? Many experienced negotiators agree that with careful attention, you can tell what your counterpart is really thinking and feeling. Is he or she lying or telling the truth? Is she nervous or is he desperate to do the deal? Careful attention and observation of your counterpart will help you determine his or her true meaning.

♦ *React to the message, not the person.* It was mentioned in an earlier point that we want our counterpart to be willing to negotiate with us again. This is not going to happen if we react to him or her and offend his or her dignity. It will be helpful to try and understand why your counterpart says the things he or she does. Elaine Donaldson, a professor of psychology at the University of Michigan, said, "People do what they think they have to do in order to get what they think they want." This is true with negotiators. When we negotiate, we are trying to change a relationship. Your counterpart is trying to change it in his or her best interests. If you were in his or her shoes, you might do the same thing. If you are going to react, pick on the message and not your counterpart personally.

♦ *Try not to get angry.* When you become angry, your counterpart has gained control in triggering your response. In the angry mode, you are probably not in the best frame of mind to make the best decisions. Emotions of any kind hinder the listening process. Anger, especially, interferes with the problem-solving process involved in negotiations. When you are angry, you tend to shut out your counterpart.

If you are going to get angry, do it for the effect; retain control of your emotions so you can retain control of the negotiations. Nikita Khrushchev (Soviet Communist politician, 1894–1971) created quite a commotion when he pounded his shoe on the table at a United Nations conference. The tactic worked well. Later, photos showed us that he still had two shoes on his feet.

It is impossible to listen and to speak at the same time. If you are speaking, then you are tipping your hat and not getting the information you need from your counterpart. Obviously, you will have to speak at some point so your counterpart can help meet your needs and goals. However, it is more important for you to know your counterpart's frame of reference. When you have your counterpart's information, you will be in control of the negotiation. When you are in control, you will be acting and your counterpart will be reacting to your proposals. It is usually better to be the one in the driver's seat.

In conclusion, when you want to improve your listening skills, a good rule to remember is that God gave us two ears and one mouth. We should use them in their respective proportions. To succeed in negotiations, one must understand the needs, wants, and motivations of one's counterpart. To understand those needs, one must hear. To hear, one must listen.

Strategies and Tactics

What follows are five of the fifty strategies and tactics that appeared in Peter B. Stark's book, *It's Negotiable.* Strategies and tactics are the tools of negotiation that help you to maintain or gain leverage.

Strategy One: Principle of Walk Away

I am fond of the saying, "In any relationship, the side with the least commitment to continuing the relationship will have the most power." If you have the ability to walk away from the bargaining table when the tide turns, you will have more leverage.

> Example:
> Recently my wife, Kathleen, bought a daybed for our daughter. The price of the bed was advertised on sale for $177. When she went to pay for the bed, the salesman told her that there was an additional $25 delivery fee. Kathleen was upset about the fee because she had arranged for me to pick up the bed in my company truck. She left the store with the $25 delivery fee still intact because the clerk said that the fee was non-negotiable, whether they delivered it or not. In fact, the clerk said that if they did not charge the fee, they would lose money on the bed.
>
> Kathleen went home and called two other outlets of the same store. To each one, she stated she wanted to buy the daybed advertised on sale, and if she picked it up herself, would there be any delivery charge? In each case, the other outlets said no. Armed with this information, she called the first store and requested to have the delivery charge removed, or she would cancel the transaction and take her business to another outlet. They agreed.
>
> One week later, when we went to pick up the bed, the clerk behind the counter stated that the person Kathleen had talked to did not have the authority to remove the delivery charge. After going back and forth, Kathleen finally said, "Just give me my $177 back and we will buy the bed somewhere else." At that point, the clerk gave in and waived the fee.

If you are always able to walk away, you will retain the ability to create a win/win outcome.

Strategy Two: Principle of Higher Authority

Not being the person who has the final say in a situation can put you in a very powerful position. Someone has to go to someone else to gain final approval. More times than not, I have seen an experienced negotiator work the best deal he could, then run off to a higher authority. Usually, the negotiator will come back from the higher authority with instructions for an even better deal.

Example:
A president of a corporation works the very best deal he can on a piece of machinery. The initial price of the equipment was $450,000. He gets the salesperson to concede to a price of $428,000 with three months of use before the first payment. The president agrees to the deal but needs to take it to his Board of Directors for final approval.

The president comes back from the Board of Directors with the approval to sign the contract at not more than $425,000. He even went back to the salesperson and apologized for the Board being so tough. In this case, the Board could have been real or apparent. One of my students shared this example with me and dubbed the principle "the $3,000 tactic." It worked for him. Best of all, *he* was the Board of Directors, lock, stock, and barrel.

Strategy Three: Principle of Splitting the Difference

When two parties are still apart on an issue and the negotiation seems to be at a stalemate, one can offer to split the difference with the other counterpart.

Example:
Seller: You are selling your car and you do not want to come down any further than $2,000.

Buyer: You want to buy the seller's car, but you do not want to pay any more than $1,800.

Solution: Because you are $200 apart, either the buyer or the seller could offer to split the difference ($200 divided by 2) and do the deal for $1,900.

Strategy Four: Principle of Facts and Statistics

Another powerful technique is that any time you can add facts and statistics to your presentation, you have an added tool that your counterpart will find difficult to handle.

Example:
Peter Ueberroth, the mastermind of the 1984 Los Angeles Olympics, used facts and statistics to his advantage when he negotiated the television rights to the games. Ueberroth studied the ratings and knew them beyond a shadow of a doubt. Several times, the networks questioned Ueberroth on

his knowledge with facts and statistics. Each time, Ueberroth proved he was right. When you can use facts and statistics to your advantage, you add a tremendous amount of power and credibility to your case.

However, if you use facts and statistics incorrectly and your counterpart proves you wrong, it destroys your credibility. When this happens, you will have to fight twice as hard to gain any deal point.

Strategy Five: Principle of Never Saying Yes to the First Offer

Have you ever felt that you paid too much for something? The chances are you felt that way because you did not have to fight hard enough for your outcome. When someone says yes to your first offer, you walk away with one of two feelings. First, you think you paid too much. If that feeling is not enough to make you have buyer's remorse, you probably will think something is wrong with what you just bought.

Example:

Supervisor: "Would you be willing to start for $12.50 per hour?"

Employee: "Sure, $12.50 an hour is great. When do I start?"

In this case, the employee would be better off responding, "Since I currently make $12.50 an hour, I would need to make at least $13.50 before I considered switching positions."

Tips for Success: Negotiations

1. Recognize that everything in life is negotiable! From deciding who takes out the garbage in your house to determining what price you will pay for a product or service to merging your car in rush-hour traffic, everything is negotiable.

2. Go for win/win outcomes. Find out the needs and goals of your counterpart. Yes, you do have a vested interest in helping your counterpart meet his or her needs and goals, especially if you ever have to negotiate with that person again.

3. Aim high. The outcomes will always be better with high aspirations.

4. Have sound strategies and tactics. If you know the strategies and tactics plus the counter strategies and tactics, you will always be able to maintain a balance in the negotiation.

5. Plan ahead and research well. If you wait until you enter the negotiation to do your planning and research, you will be like a ship out at sea without a

sail and rudder. You will move with your counterpart, but without strategic direction.

6. Listen more than you speak. To create a win/win negotiation, you will need to understand the needs and goals of your counterpart. It is impossible to do so without being a great listener.

7. When you do speak, ask great questions. The more you learn and understand about your counterpart's needs, the easier you will find it to create a win/win negotiation.

8. Learn to effectively read nonverbal communication. Remember, only 7% of the total message comes from the spoken word.

9. Utilize strategies and tactics. Strategies and tactics are the negotiator's tools that help to maintain or gain leverage.

10. In most negotiations, you will have the ability to walk away. Remember, the side with the least commitment to the relationship usually holds the most power.

Action Plan: Negotiating for Win/Win Results

Three steps I can take to improve my negotiating skills and when I will begin each step:

Action Step 1:
Target Date for Initiation:

Action Step 2:
Target Date for Initiation:

Action Step 3:
Target Date for Initiation:

Chapter 16

Delivering Extraordinary Customer Service

"There is only one boss—the customer—
and he or she can fire everybody in the company from the chairman on down simply by
spending his or her money somewhere else."

— Sam Walton

As we move toward the year 2000, most of us would agree that the familiar chants of the 1990s—*We do it faster, Our quality is unsurpassed,* and *We do it your way*—have become all too familiar. Everyone who provides us with a product or service is saying that he or she is committed to delivering great customer service. But do we, as consumers, feel that we are being provided that same great service we hear about on a daily basis? And just what *is* it that we have come to expect in the way of customer service?

We recently conducted a training program for the local division of a large international company on the art of providing extraordinary customer service. As we began the training program, we asked each class of participants this question: "In the customer's mind, what constitutes great service?" Throughout the program, there was a consistency in each group's responses to the question. The advice that follows reflects the most popular responses.

What Constitutes Great Customer Service?

Topic One: Treat Customers as Real People

Without exception, treating customers as *real people* was cited as the most important way companies prove that they are committed to providing their customers with outstanding customer service. In today's age of electronic wiz-ardry, it is not uncommon to complete an entire business transaction without ever having spoken with a real live human being. This is great if your needs are routine and you are proficient in navigating through a maze of digital challenges before finally making the right connection to solve your problem.

What we have found in talking with hundreds of consumers, however, is that people are growing increasingly resentful of long waits on the phone and are tired of listening intently to electronic directions, hoping each step along the way they will not "mess up" and have to start the process over again! In other words, if at 11:30 P.M. you are wondering what the balance on your charge card is, accessing an automated system to find out your current balance is a real plus. However, if you have just opened your most recent statement only to find that you have been billed twice for the same transaction, you definitely want to con-nect with a real live person who can assure you that they will fix the problem, right now!

If we listen carefully to today's consumers, they are telling us that they under-stand all the electronic advances companies employ to assist them. However, consumers are also telling us that more than ever, they want to be treated as per-sons with unique needs, rather than as account numbers. Even though customers can deal proficiently with automated systems, what they really value is finally making a connection with a person within a company who values them, treats them with respect, and fixes their problem.

Topic Two: Watch Your Attitude

So many times we hear customers say, "The person I talked with had a lousy atti-tude!" In 1985, a study was completed by the Technical Assistance Research Programs for the White House Office of Consumer Affairs (TARP Study). The group was commissioned by the government to find out why people quit doing business with a company. Their findings were particularly interesting; simply put, most people quit doing business with a company because of an "attitude prob-lem." When asked why they took their business elsewhere, consumers responded with the following information in the TARP Study:

3% Stopped doing business with a company because they moved away.

5% Stopped doing business with a company because they developed friendships with other companies.

9% Stopped doing business with a company because of competitive reasons . . . better pricing, more services, etc. from a different company.

14% Stopped doing business with a company because they were dissatisfied with the products or the service.

68% Stopped doing business with a company because of an attitude of indifference on the part of an owner, manager, or customer service representative.

If you look carefully at the results of the TARP Study, you will find that we have very little control over people leaving because they move away, develop other friendships, or find better pricing elsewhere. We have more control over the quality of our products or service, but only 14% leave because of dissatisfaction in this area. What is especially interesting about the TARP study is that the greatest number of people left because of an attitude problem, which is the *only* area within our control.

So what is it that customers really mean when they talk about an "attitude problem"? Simply put, it is all in the customer's perception. And just what is their perception? It is important to understand that for our customers, *their perception is reality* for them. Whether it be good, bad, or indifferent, their perception is very real for them. And just how do they form their perception? Again, to keep it simple, a customer forms his or her perception when the expected service fails to meet, meets, or exceeds the expectation of what they expected to get. We can go to extraordinary lengths to provide a great product or service, but if our customer meets with a representative of our company who demonstrates a lousy attitude, the customer will leave with the perception that the company does not really care about its customers.

One of the authors recently witnessed an exchange between a frustrated passenger and an irritated passenger service representative. The customer had missed her connecting flight due to the late arrival of her incoming flight. After arranging with the ticketing agent for a later flight on the same airline, the passenger asked to be awarded additional frequent flyer miles to compensate her for the inconvenience of arriving at her final destination four hours later than planned. The agent said, "We don't do that here." The passenger pointed out that on numerous occasions in the past when the same airline had lost her baggage, delayed her flight, or caused her to miss connection fights, the airline had given her bonus mileage points to help compensate her for the inconvenience. The agent again responded, but this time, more emphatically, "We don't do that here." Finally, after arguing futilely, the frustrated passenger said, "Well, thanks a lot!" The agent replied in a rather condescending tone, "It's nothing!" You can bet that not only did the passenger leave with a terrible perception about the airline's attitude toward customers, but that she told anyone who would listen in the lounge while waiting for her flight and then on the plane about her dissatisfaction with the airline. This is an example of the old adage that it only takes one person to ruin a great customer service program.

Topic Three: Fix the Problem the First Time

Customers are quick to acknowledge that from time to time, problems arise. It is not so much the problem that customers have trouble dealing with, but how the problem is solved. No one has time in his or her hectic schedule, nor patience, for problems that just will not go away. Nothing is more frustrating than having to deal on an ongoing basis with a company that just cannot seem to resolve a customer complaint.

Recently, one of the authors called a bank that services a home mortgage to try to report a change of address. After following directions carefully, and successfully pressing just the right combination of numbers, the address change department was reached. She left a voice mail message as directed and assumed the requested change would be made. When the mortgage coupon was mailed to the old address the following month, it was apparent there was a problem. Twice more she repeated the process, never once connecting with a real live human being, and for the next two months, the coupon was again mailed to the old address. Finally, after four months and an adamant plea and veiled threat that were left on the bank's machine, the bank not only changed the address but the name on the account, which had never been requested!

It is estimated that approximately 70% of customers experiencing dissatisfaction with either a product or service will do business with your company again if the problem is resolved in their favor. The reason for their continuing loyalty to your company, even after a problem existed, is that customers build trust with a company that has taken care of their problems in the past. They feel confident that should problems arise in the future, your company will again resolve them to their satisfaction.

Topic Four: Be Honest with Customers

So much of a customer's perception about customer service deals not with the product or service but with the relationship between the customer and the company. Customers enter into a relationship with a company under the basic assumption that the company will deal with them honestly. Companies do not build customer loyalty solely by being honest with customers. Customers expect honesty. Customer loyalty is built when it costs a company something to be honest.

Recently, one of the authors had a new home built. During the construction, the builder presented two choices of materials for kitchen counter tops. The author wanted to know more about additional options for the kitchen counter. The builder said he would research the question and get back to the author at a later date. Two weeks passed, and the author was horrified to see that white tile counter tops had been installed throughout the kitchen. The author contacted the builder immediately, who said, "When I didn't hear from you, I assumed you wanted to go ahead with the standard tile." Upon being reminded that he was to provide additional information on the choices available, he responded with, "You're right. I forgot." After being questioned about what could be done, he hesitated for a moment and said, "We'll make it right. We want you to be happy. We'll tear the tile out and put in what you want." This was an expensive mistake that cost the builder both in terms of labor and product. The builder's willingness to correct the problem, regardless of the cost, gained this customer's loyalty.

Topic Five: Practice the Art of Follow-Up

Customers today expect to be treated with dignity and honesty, and expect to have their problems resolved in a timely manner. What they do not expect, and what companies committed to providing customer service are routinely providing, is the practice of the "follow-up" call. Companies that are dedicated to providing memorable customer service see the follow-up call as one more opportunity to interact with the customer and leave the customer with a positive feeling about the company.

Following a challenging transaction in which the customer experienced difficulty getting his or her needs met, a representative from the company calls to check in with the customer. The company representative asks if the problem has been resolved to the customer's satisfaction. Companies committed to following up after difficult transactions know that this gives them the opportunity to check in with the customer to see if the problem has been resolved to the customer's satisfaction. If the problem has been adequately handled, the customer will most likely be impressed that the company cared enough about business to check back with him or her. If the problem has not been resolved to the customer's satisfaction, the company is provided with yet another opportunity to correct the problem and satisfy the customer. Acknowledging that 96 percent of all dissatisfied customers never bring their complaints to the company for resolution, the follow-up is a great opportunity to correct a problem before a disgruntled customer voices dissatisfaction about your company or product to all who will listen.

One of the authors takes his three children to a pediatrics group. Following the first visit, he was surprised to receive a phone call asking about the health of the child who had seen the doctor the day before. Thinking that something was drastically wrong, he quizzed the doctor. The doctor reassured him that nothing was wrong with the child, but that all the doctors in the practice call the day after they have seen a child in their office. When the author commented about the follow-up call from the aspect of providing great customer service, the doctor noted that doctors in this group are committed to providing great care for all their patients. He noted that unless you call the day after you see a patient, you do not know if the medicine is working, or if the child is experiencing a reaction to an immunization or the prescribed medication. It is noteworthy that this group of doctors has seen over 700,000 patients and has not had one single malpractice suit.

Developing a Customer Service Strategy

When we conduct Customer Service Seminars, we ask the participants, "What is the purpose of business?" The response most frequently made is, "The purpose of business is to make money!" While all of us in service-related fields are attentive to the bottom line and are looking to make a profit, there is much more to the picture than just profits. Certainly, profits are a must in order that we stay in business. There is little arguing the fact that without profits, we will eventually go out of business. However, successful companies in today's super-competitive market know that focus on profits alone will not ensure prosperity. Successful companies, rather than dwelling strictly on profits, focus on how to win over and keep a customer for life. In addition to strategies designed to attract and keep customers, these companies focus on creating an experience in which customers are so satisfied that they tell other customers. No amount of advertising can do for you what happy customers can do by telling others about their positive experience with your company! The following pages will describe strategies designed to attract, win over, and keep a customer loyal to your company for life.

Understanding the Customer Service Triangle

The ultimate goal in creating a service culture should be to focus the energies and talents of every member of the organization on the quality and service they provide to the customer. It is important to note that the quality and service standards evident in a company will be defined and determined not by the organization, but by the perceptions of the customer. Profitable companies know that creating a service culture is much more than just having a "customer service" department that functions well in most circumstances. Companies that have highly effective customer service strategies know that in order to be successful, every employee, regardless of whether he or she has direct contact with customers, must be fully committed to making sure that things turn out right for every customer. If we expect every employee, wherever they are in the organization, to be totally committed to putting the customer first, there must be a clearly defined and easily understood customer service strategy. Such strategies typically consist of three things: (1) a vision of the service we will provide our customers, (2) people who are committed to providing top-notch customer service, and (3) systems that are customer-friendly.

Exhibit 16.1: Customer Service Triangle

Using a pyramid as a model, The Customer is at the center or, more specifically, is the very reason for our existence. Without the customer, ultimately, we have no business. The three points of the pyramid supporting The Customer are (1) Vision, (2) People, and (3) Systems.

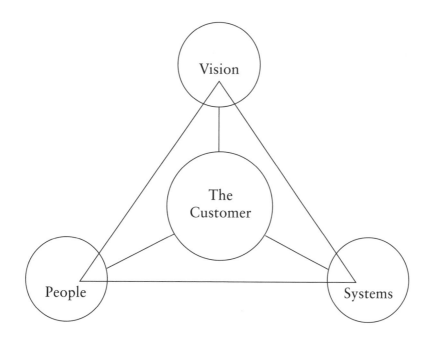

Adapted from Karl Albrecht, 1984.

247

Pyramid Point One: Vision

When it comes to providing quality customer service, you must first have a vision, or a clear mental picture of what that service looks like. It is impossible to deliver extraordinary customer service unless all employees have a clear understanding of the company's standards for and commitment to providing service to its customers. One way to understand vision is to use the analogy of a jigsaw puzzle. Just as you cannot re-create the puzzle without looking at the box top, you cannot expect outstanding customer service unless all employees have a clear mental picture as to what that service looks like.

Defining what you are trying to ultimately accomplish with and for your customers helps your people understand the rhyme and reason of the work they do for your organization. Having a clear vision statement of your goals for customer service has several positive implications. Companies with well-defined customer service vision statements clearly convey to employees "what's important around here." Even employees who do not interact with customers on a day-to-day basis see the "big picture" and make decisions accordingly. Perhaps the biggest advantage of having a vision, though, is that it provides a detailed definition of what good service means as it relates to the company and the customer. When a vision is clearly communicated to employees and consistently used as a measure, the company's chances of getting great reviews from their customers accelerate dramatically. It is estimated that companies with no definition of what good service means have only about a 30% chance of satisfying their customers. Companies that have a general definition increase the likelihood of getting good marks from their customers to nearly 50%. Finally, companies that have a clear vision and use it consistently as a standard for customer service will receive positive reviews from up to 90% of their customers.

Clearly, having a well thought-out customer service vision is critical. If your organization or department does not have a vision, consider challenging the status quo by creating one. Companies that are proud of their vision consider the following when creating their vision:

◆ *Who are our customers and what do they want?* Customers are well qualified and generally willing to provide valuable input that will help the company determine what they want to deliver to customers and what standards are critical in providing both products and service to the customer.
◆ *How will our employees interact with our customers?* Employees have an incredible knowledge base about an organization's customers. Get input

from them about what type of service leaves a lasting, positive impression on customers.

◆ *What are our organizational values?* Acknowledging that an organization's values will drive the vision into action, it is important to take stock of what is valued within the organization. Bringing a vision to reality takes hard work. Without strong values that drive the vision, an organization will quickly find itself slipping back to the old way of doing things, or ways that perhaps benefit the organization, but not the customer.

Once the customers and employees have been polled for their input and the company has examined its core values, it is time to create or write the vision. Based on our experience in helping companies write their vision for customer service, we recommend the following steps for creating a customer service vision:

1. Make it clear, concise and understandable, and write it in everyday language.

2. Make sure the vision clearly conveys actions that must be taken to meet customers' needs, impress them, and win them over for life.

3. The vision must be consistent with organizational values. It must be more than just words on a piece of paper. Reading it, employees should know what to do, how to do it, and why they are doing it. More importantly, they must know that the organization is committed to bringing the "words" into action and will support the employee in the process of delivering the standard of service echoed in the vision.

4. Allow all stakeholders who have a vested interest in the organization to challenge the vision before it becomes "set in concrete." True, a vision is just words. But in some cases even one word makes a tremendous difference. Listen to what people are saying and make changes so that all stakeholders will support the vision and have a vested interest in bringing it to a reality.

Pyramid Point Two: People

The second component of the Customer Service Triangle is people. You can have a great Vision, but without the right people to bring it to life, the whole strategy can backfire. Unfortunately, in reality, it only takes one poor employee to destroy what would have otherwise been great service. We can all remember instances where we encountered a negative, less-than-helpful employee who left us with

249

the feeling that given a choice, we would take our business anywhere else but here. Some organizations currently working on their image with the public are notorious for the lack of service they have provided in the past—the Postal Service, state motor vehicle registries, and some utility and cable companies, to name a few. The impression that a customer leaves with after an encounter with an employee of the company is critical. To help ensure that the customer leaves with a favorable impression, the following advice must be considered:

1. *Hire the right people.* Take great care to hire the kind of employee who can provide the service spelled out in your vision. A person can have degrees, credentials, and expertise, but if he or she is not nice to people, customers will not form a positive impression about your company's service. In the selection process, kindness, caring, compassion, and unselfishness should carry more weight than years on the job, salary history, and educational background. Our clients often remark, "You have such nice people working for you. Not only are they real professionals, but they are nice, too." Hiring these people was no accident. This is just the impression of our organization that we want our clients to have.

   In addition, hire people who demonstrate a high level of personal self-esteem. People who have high self-esteem will treat your customers more positively. It is extremely difficult to treat someone with courtesy, dignity, and respect when you do not feel that way about yourself. Often front-line employees come from the bottom of the available labor pool. They face frequent customer challenges and pressures. Producing goods is different than producing service. Excellent service absolutely depends on welcoming customers' requests and being flexible in response to customers. People who have high self-esteem will be more comfortable in these situations. Great organizations take time to find the right employee to meet their customers' needs.

2. *Place the emphasis on the outcome, not the function.* Everyone in an organization has a function that he or she performs—the job. They may answer phones, take orders, fill orders, schedule work, prepare invoices, etc. Companies that exceed customers' expectations are masters at placing more emphasis on the outcome than the job function. What counts is not only fulfilling the job functions, but fulfilling them in such a way that if the customer erroneously omitted a critical part of his order, the clerk can make arrangements to have the missing parts express-shipped, rather than having the customer complete the usual steps in the ordering process. Looking for

ways to satisfy customers' needs becomes more critical than following company procedures to fulfill one's job functions.

3. *Value those who service the customer.* There is a saying that goes, "If you are not directly serving the customer, you had better be serving someone who is." Unfortunately, often customer service positions hold little value in an organization. Frequently, they are entry-level positions held by people who are anxious to get the experience behind them and move up in the organization. Companies like Starbucks Coffee and Saturn, who know that customers' contacts with representatives make a lasting impact, hire accordingly and continue to place a strong emphasis on the value of the contribution to the company made by the customer service representative. *These companies have figured out that to the customer, the front-line employee is the company.* A company can have a great customer service strategy, but if the front-line employee does not live up to it, the customer leaves disappointed, perhaps not returning again.

4. *Provide training for those who serve the customer, either directly or indirectly.* There is a high turnover rate in customer service positions. People leave these positions because they feel undervalued, overworked, and frequently not even trained to adequately handle customers' demands. Leaders in service-oriented organizations know that it is critical to provide new employees with formal and informal training opportunities. Certainly a new employee must become familiar with the company's product, policies, and procedures. Just as important, though, is that the new employee should become familiar with the company's philosophy regarding customer service. Nordstrom, a company noted for its outstanding personalized customer service, practices both formal and informal training. To help new employees learn the Nordstrom philosophy, the company relies heavily on socialization with peers and supervisors to teach that unique brand of customer service delivered by Nordstrom.

Service leaders also understand that producing exemplary service means ensuring that everyone—not just the customer contact person, but anyone who has an impact on customer satisfaction—has a thorough knowledge of what it takes to get the job done right. To help build this level of understanding, many organizations cross-train their employees and require all employees, regardless of their level in the organization, to spend time on the "front line" interacting directly with customers. When traveling on Southwest Airlines, it is not uncommon to see the pilot taking boarding passes at the gate. All executives at Nordstrom have had time on the floor selling directly to the customer. Every officer at Xerox has spent time resolving customer complaints. Creating employee versatility gives companies a greater service capacity. Requiring employees other than customer service representatives to interact with the customer helps all employees understand the challenges faced by customer service representatives. Further, it says to the customer service representative, "We know firsthand that you have a challenging job and we value your contributions."

Pyramid Point Three: Systems

In addition to having a vision and great people, systems are needed to deliver the service and product to the customers. The service systems are the logistics, policies, procedures, and tools the employees have at their disposal to deliver the service to the customer. Whether a system has been formally designed or just "happened," one thing is sure. Eventually, a system will evolve. When systems evolve on their own, they will usually evolve in a pattern of corporate self-convenience, becoming corporate-friendly rather than customer-friendly. What is the difference? A customer-friendly service system is one that makes things easy for the customer. A corporate-friendly system is one in which systems are designed for the ease of the organization and its employees, rather than the customer. The organization may run smoothly, but customers may not feel that the system is working to benefit them.

You do not have to do much business in today's world to experience high-tech customer service that leaves you feeling frustrated. One of the authors tried to call a mortgage servicing institution and waded through five minutes of electronic transfers before finally getting to talk to a customer service representative, who said that she was sorry that she was not able to provide the information requested. Such requests had to be in writing. Ultimately, customers that do not find a company's systems "user-friendly" will find a competitor whose systems are easy-to-use, understandable, and friendly to the customer, and will do business with them.

The following tips can help you develop customer-friendly systems:

♦ *Develop a service blueprint or plan.* Examine your cycle of service. Start by identifying the processes involved in the delivery of the service and estimate the time needed to deliver the service. Add to the blueprint steps that customers must take to complete their transactions. After developing a service blueprint, many organizations have been able to visualize how unfriendly their systems are. Blueprinting systems show organizations just how many forms, policies, and procedures stand between the customer and the employees' ability to deliver outstanding service.

Strive to fine-tune systems so that the delivery system appears, from the customer's vantage point, almost effortless.

♦ *Listen to your customers.* Once you have developed and implemented service systems, listen continuously to feedback from your customers. Customers' needs and expectations change over a period of time. Value their input and respond accordingly. One industry that has become an expert at meeting customers' ever-changing expectations is the fast-food industry. Not only has it responded to the frantic pace at which we live our lives by delivering fresh, hot, tasty food within 90 seconds of our placing an order, but the "value" meals are competitively priced. For three or four dollars you can have a sandwich, fries, and a drink. This industry knows that continuously seeking customer input and responding to their expressed needs guarantees a place in the highly competitive fast-food market.

♦ *Remember, the customer is ultimately the boss.* Getting people to focus on the customer when designing systems is no easy challenge. It seems to be human nature to design systems that are originally customer friendly, only to see the systems over a period of time be modified to become more convenient for departmental or organizational considerations. During the writing of this book, United Parcel Service announced the start of its "Same Day Delivery Service." Up until this time, customers felt well-served with "Next Day Delivery Service." You can bet that developing systems to support this same-day delivery service was no easy task. You can also bet that competitors will quickly follow suit with similar same-day delivery options. UPS has figured out that ultimately the *customer* is the boss, and if they do not like the service you provide, they can and will fire you!

Managing Customers' Perceptions

Customers make decisions about who they do and who they do not do business with based on their perceptions. What is customer perception? Simply put, the customer's perception is the difference between what the customer expected and what he or she received. When customers interact with a company, they leave with either a positive, neutral, or negative image of their transaction, based on their expectations. The challenge is how to manage the transaction with each and every customer so they all leave with a positive impression about the interaction.

Just how do customers form their perceptions? The following list identifies common methods customers use when forming their perceptions:

253

♦ *Comparison*. Today's informed consumers are competitive shoppers and know price, value, and quality. They compare what you have to offer with your competitors. If your product or service is competitively priced and good value for the money, what may be the deciding factor for the customer is the quality of the service received from customer service representatives in your company. All things being equal, customers want to do business with people who treat them with respect and convey to the customer that their business is valued.

♦ *Initial contact*. When it comes to providing great customer service, first impressions are critical. Often when a customer's first interaction with a company is positive, the customer gains confidence in the organization and does not look for reasons to find dissatisfaction with the company. Initially connecting with an employee who is positive, cheerful, and intent on meeting the customer's needs does a lot to build customer confidence and loyalty.

♦ *Past experiences*. Customers doing business with a company expect a certain type of service based on their past experiences. If the last time they did business with you they battled to get their needs met, they will approach the next encounter with you armed for battle.

♦ *Reputation*. Companies that have great reputations for providing quality services experience fewer customer challenges and more positive interactions with their customers. Why? Because when you have a great reputation, people trust that you will fix problems to their satisfaction.

♦ *Media*. To a large extent, the media helps shape our perceptions as a consumer. We have learned that faster, bigger, quieter, smoother, etc., is better. The media, through advertising, allows us all to be informed, educated consumers. We form perceptions based on a company's ability to deliver what the media says we want and have a right to expect.

Service Ratings Based on Customer Perceptions

Regardless of what we think about the service we provide, what ultimately counts is customer perception about that service. Customers' perceptions are reality for them. Managing our delivery system so that customers' unique needs are met or delivering service that exceeds their expectations is our challenge. First, we need to know what criteria customers use when they rate us and form their perceptions. The following Customer Service Report Card helps us understand how customers rate the service we deliver.

Exhibit 16.2: Customer Service Report Card

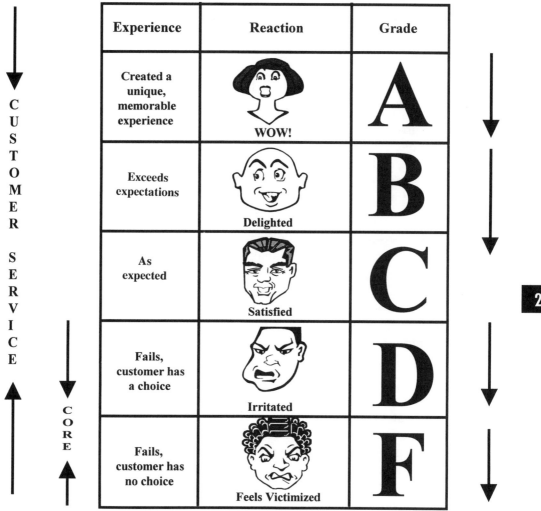

Peter B. Stark & Associates, Inc. 1993

Quality Core Service: The service or product your organization or work team provides to its customers—your "reason for being." Without this core service, your organization or team has no purpose.

Caring Customer Services: The service delivery system, which includes the interactions you have with a customer while you are conducting business. Also included are your policies, procedures, and practices.

Starting at the bottom of the report card, customers award a business "F" when the company fails at delivering both the product and the services, and the customer feels they have no recourse. Waiting half a day for a utility company to turn on the power and then finding out that it will not be turned on until the next day is an example of service deserving "F." The customer cannot call a competitor and has no recourse other than to wait. Fortunately, as the utility industry deregulates and school districts seek to meet community needs with charter and alternative schools, there should be fewer "F" experiences in our lives.

Moving up, a company might be awarded a "D" by a customer if the company failed to provide a core product or service, but the customer had other options. For example, a mortgage company may process a loan application over a month-long period, and then turn down the loan applicant. The applicant will be disappointed, obviously, but will still have other options. There are many other competitors who will be more than willing to work with the applicant in obtaining a loan.

When do customers award a company a "C"? In today's competitive marketplace where customers are continually expecting more for their dollar and more in the way of service, if you deliver all that you say you are going to deliver in the time you said you would deliver the product or service, the customer will still only give you a "C." After all, you just gave him or her exactly what was expected. Competition today is brutal, and you do not get customer points leading to long-term customer loyalty unless you deliver more than the customer expected.

To get a "B," the company must do something that exceeds the customer's expectations. For example, the other evening the authors and their families were having dinner at Marie Callender's, a local restaurant. For whatever the reason, although the service was attentive and pleasant, the dinners were a long time in coming from the kitchen. By the time they arrived, the kids were notably cranky, and everyone was a little disappointed. At the end of the meal, our waiter said, "I apologize for the delay in getting your food to you. We were really backed up in the kitchen tonight. How about a piece of pie, on the house, for everyone?" The offer of a piece of pie to compensate us for our inconvenience was not expected and it left us with a more positive feeling about our dinner at Marie Callender's!

Letter grade "A" is rarely awarded by customers; they reserve this rare distinction for those few memorable experiences when the service they receive far surpasses what they expect. Service of this caliber is so unusual that people often sing the company's praises years after the event actually takes place. What is interesting about memorable customer service is that it often begins with a problem and ends with the company going out of its way to resolve the problem to the customer's satisfaction.

A participant in one of our seminars talked about having electronic difficulties with his late model luxury car. The dealer did not seem to be able to track down the problem, which resulted in the car stalling. Twice the dealer installed new electronic devices, but this did not solve the problem. When the car was taken back for the third time the owner was, in his words, "As close to irate as you can be without blowing up and doing something I might regret later." Sensing the owner's anger, the service manager said, "I am going to be truthful with you. We do not know what is causing the problem. We do understand how upset you are. Here is what I suggest. If you can leave your car with us for a week, we will rent you a similar model, at our expense, and track down the problem." The owner left his car with the dealership for the week. The dealership tracked down the problem, which stemmed from a faulty on-board operating computer. The dealership replaced the computer, at no expense to the owner, and did pay the total bill for the rental car. When we asked the owner if he would continue to do business with the dealership, he was emphatic in his response, "Of course!" When asked why, he responded, "They took care of the problem and if I have more problems, I can count on them to take care of me." That participant was very enthusiastic in his support of this dealership, and it is a great example of a loyal customer providing free advertising for a company!

Dealing with Angry or Difficult Customers

Even if you followed all the recommendations previously given for providing great customer service, the truth is that you would still occasionally encounter an angry or difficult customer. In reality, they are out there and some of their anger has nothing to do with you . . . you just happened to be in a position where they could vent and take it out on you. From experience, we have found the following ten tips to be helpful in dealing with that occasional challenging customer who seems determined to ruin your day.

1. *Develop a positive mental attitude.* When a difficult customer wants to go one-on-one with you, make a decision to stay positive. Say to yourself, "I can handle this. That's what I'm here for. Not just anyone can do this job. I'm the right person for the job." Giving yourself positive messages like these does two things. First, it helps increase your confidence while dealing with challenging circumstances. Second, it helps you convey a more confi-

dent presence in front of the difficult customer. When customers sense you are confident with the situation, they often calm down and become more open to your suggestions for resolution of their problem.

2. *Let the customer unwind.* We sometimes jokingly say, "You can tell an angry customer, but you can't tell them much. Don't try!" Trying to interrupt an angry customer will only escalate the situation. Most likely, the customer has been rehearsing what he or she is telling you long before actually making contact with you. From the customer's perception, he or she has been abused, inconvenienced, or in some other way wronged. This customer needs you to know all the details and does not want you to try to stop the conversation, even if you think you have a good solution. From experience, we advise that in these difficult situations you let the customer unwind.

3. *Respond first with a personal level of interaction.* When customers are "venting" they want two things to happen. First, they obviously want their problem solved. In addition, most angry customers have a need for you to understand how their problem with your organization personally impacted them. Responding with "I understand how upsetting that must have been" or "I'm concerned about what happened; let's look into it" conveys to an angry customer, *I care about not only the problem, but how the problem has affected you.* In today's competitive market, successful service organizations are finding that connecting with customers on a personal level is one way to attract and keep loyal customers.

4. *Reward the customer.* When customers complain, thank them! Research indicates that approximately 96% of all customers who have complaints about either your service or products do not complain directly to you; rather, they take their business to a competitor. Research further indicates that unhappy customers will tell eight to ten people about their dissatisfaction with your organization. This type of advertising is not what your company wants! So, the next time you encounter a complaining customer, thank the person for giving you the opportunity to fix the problem. Remember that once you have fixed the problem to the customer's satisfaction, most of these customers will remain loyal to your organization. The reason? They trust you to take care of future problems.

5. *Keep your cool.* Unhappy customers come in many varieties—some are easier for you to deal with than others. Your response in dealing with an angry customer helps set the tone for the interaction with you. If you lose patience and become angry with him or her, the situation is sure to escalate. If the

customer raises his or her voice, lower yours. Lowering your voice forces the customer to lower his or her voice in order to hear you, and has a general calming effect on a difficult situation. When you need help, ask for it. Some customers may be particularly difficult for you but are not so challenging for other co-workers. When you need their support, ask for help.

6. *Stay objective; do not get hooked.* Some difficult customers, for whatever the reason, delight in the fight. In order to engage you, they dangle a hook, such as, "You folks never do anything right" or "You're always screwing up my account. Can't you get anything straight?" They want the challenge and have put you in a position where you feel you need to defend yourself or your company. Once you do, the hook is set and the fight is on. Make a conscious decision not to bite the hook. To help you avoid the fight, visualize a rusty fishhook baited with something foul and say, "The hook is nasty. I'm not biting!" Instead of defending yourself or your company, ask questions like, "What is it that appears incorrect?" or "Could you give me the information I will need to verify that?" Asking questions refocuses the customer on the problem and gives you the opportunity to address the customer's specific concerns.

7. *Offer alternative solutions.* Before the angry customer begins to interact with you, most have already decided how you are going to resolve the problem for them. The problem is that in many cases, their solution and your solution may vary. When attempting to rectify problems, remember that the greater the number of viable alternatives, the greater the likelihood that one of them will satisfy the customer. In some cases, you will need to tell the customer "No." It is more palatable, for example, to say, "We are not able to do that, but we can credit your account if you return the item, or we could repair the defective product for you. What would you prefer we do?" Customers feel more in control if they are allowed to select from more than one potential solution.

8. *Take immediate action.* Difficult or angry customers want something to happen—right now! Chances are they have been doing a slow burn for some time about their perceived mistreatment. Saying, "Sounds like there might be a problem. We'll look into it and get back to you" will only further incense them. Be specific about what you will do. Even if you cannot resolve their problem immediately, tell the person what action you personally will be taking. Give a specific time frame so he or she knows what to expect, and when it will happen. For example, "I am not able to access that information, but the people in our customer service department will be able

to help you. I think that I have all the details they will need to research this problem. I will give the information to customer service and you can expect a call from a representative within the next four hours. If you still have questions after talking to them, please give me a call. Will this work for you?" Assuring the customer that you are taking some action, even though the entire problem may not be quickly resolved, helps diffuse challenging situations.

9. *Bring the incident to a polite close.* When you have determined an acceptable course of action, review the steps that will be taken to resolve the customer's problem. Check with the customer to see if you can help in any other way. Finally, close the conversation by once again thanking the customer for bringing the matter to your attention and giving you the opportunity to resolve the problem.

10. *Follow-up to ensure satisfaction.* Organizations that are intent on improving their customer service often make it a practice to follow-up with difficult or challenging customers. After the matter of concern has been resolved, they often check back with the customer a week or so later to determine if the actions taken have been satisfactory to the customer. In most cases, the customer is satisfied and pleased that their business matters enough that you would call back to check on the outcome. In those cases where the customer still is not content, remember that this follow-up call gives you yet another opportunity to make it right!

Providing great customer service is not easy. Today's customers are better educated about their rights and more demanding, and are increasingly raising their standards for what is acceptable service. It is getting tougher to impress them with anything less than outstanding, memorable service. Today's successful organizations know that they must rise to the challenge so that their product and their commitment to service set them apart from their competitors.

Attracting customers is easy. Keeping customers loyal to your organization is the challenge. With so many choices, customers will continue to do business with companies that not only provide a great product, but great service. Upholding high levels of service will help ensure that when a customer declares loyalty, it is with your company!

Tips for Success: Customer Service

1. Start first with a clearly defined vision of what customer service in your area of influence looks like. Make sure that each member of your team has the same vision.

2. Help each team member understand both the "big picture" related to customer service and how what they do contributes to creating happy, satisfied, loyal customers.

3. Interview and select new employees cautiously. Make sure those you hire can meet high customer service standards and deliver the service you have spelled out in your vision.

4. Listen to input from your front line people, or those closest to the customers. They know best what the customer expects and often can make specific recommendations to improve service.

5. Be a role model for providing excellent customer service, both externally and internally. The way members of your team treat customers reflects the way you treat customers.

6. Make sure you value and recognize the efforts of those on your team who consistently deliver high quality service. Consistently delivering top notch service in a demanding marketplace is not easy.

7. Look for alternatives when dealing with unhappy customers. The more options you can offer the customer, the more opportunity you have to demonstrate you understand and intend to fix their problem.

8. Stay objective when dealing with angry customers. Don't bite the hook! Listen for facts and look for solutions.

9. Remember this: No matter how great your service is, it only takes one person to destroy great customer service. Watch your attitude and the attitudes of those on your team.

10. Confirm customer satisfaction. Practice the art of following up to ensure satisfaction.

Action Plan: Delivering Extraordinary Customer Service

Three steps I can take to demonstrate exceptional customer service and when I will begin each step:

Action Step 1:

Target Date for Initiation:

Action Step 2:

Target Date for Initiation:

Action Step 3:

Target Date for Initiation:

Chapter 17

Solving Problems Creatively

"The significant problems we face cannot be solved at the level of thinking we were at when we created them."

— *Albert Einstein*

One of the things most supervisors are forced to address early in their supervisory career is problem solving. In fact, you were probably hired or promoted because you demonstrated a good grasp of how to solve problems. Effective supervisors are good problem solvers. This chapter offers some examples and tips to help improve your problem-solving abilities.

It Starts with a Positive Attitude

You all know them—"the people" who take a problem and then blow it all out of proportion. Instead of taking a proactive approach to solving the problem, "they" take a reactive approach and make the lives of those who are in contact with them absolutely miserable. Problems are not only a part of the job, they are a part of life. The only person who truly does not have any problems is a dead person. We suppose that could mean that the more problems we have, the more alive we really are!

A good goal to try and reach for is to become a person who views problems with a positive attitude. After all, no problem gets any easier when your attitude is negative. People who approach problems with positive attitudes have several things in common. They are:

- *Searchers.* These people search for ways something can be done. They are "possibility thinkers." They look for possibilities and solutions rather than focus on why something cannot be done. You do not hear phrases like *It can't be done here, That won't work in our company*, or *They'll never buy into it upstairs.* Instead, you hear possibility thinkers saying things like *Why not try it? Just give it a go!* or *Let's try something new.* Now ask yourself, who would *you* rather work for?

- *Visionaries.* These people do not let problems defeat them. Negative people are usually paralyzed by problems. When problems come up, they see no other solution, while positive people see problems as minor roadblocks. Positive thinkers know that a better road map is needed to get around the roadblock. If the first path ends with a roadblock, they will look for another.

- *Open-mindedness.* These people are also open-minded to new suggestions. Positive people are always willing to learn. As fast as our society is changing, we have to be willing to learn new ways of doing what we have always done before. Being open to new ideas is exciting. Positive thinkers are continually learning and growing.

- *Courageous.* These people are not afraid to take risks. Positive people do not have a "prove it to me attitude" before they try something new. They have the courage to try new things and the willingness to learn from mistakes.

- *Focused.* These people point out the advantages of change *before* they point out the disadvantages. Positive people point out the positive possibilities change can bring. Negative people usually focus on all the possible disadvantages of the change. Most of us have experienced this scenario: You recommend a solution in a meeting and the negative person is always the first to throw cold water on your suggestion.

- *Optimistic.* These people are optimistic that they can find a solution. If you do not think you can find a solution, you are defeated before you even start. Positive thinkers believe that they are bigger than the problem, not vice versa.

Job Function vs. Job Responsibilities

One of the most important things an employee should understand is that there is a significant difference between his or her job *functions* and his or her job *responsibilities.*

Each employee has a specific job function that he or she was hired to do. Job functions are usually well-outlined in job descriptions. For example, an employee who is a welder may have a job description that states that he or she will successfully weld each part onto a main assembly. The employee is evaluated by how successfully the welds hold the parts to the main assembly. There is most likely a quality inspection to help maintain high quality standards.

The difference between function and responsibility is that job responsibilities are much more expansive than job functions. For example, what happens if the welder sees a quality problem on another area of the main assembly? What happens if the main assembly manufacturers do not provide a clean enough surface for the welder to weld to? If the welder solely focuses on the job function, he or she would technically not have to say or do anything that does not relate to the specific job function—welding. But if the welder assumes responsibility for building a quality assembly and satisfying the customer, then the job responsibilities say that he or she must help correct or at least point out any problems that are seen.

This is a powerful concept, particularly when it comes to problem solving in organizations. The minute employees start saying, "That's not my problem because it is not in my job description" is the same minute the organization starts to decay. A company cannot thrive and grow when employees do not take the responsibility to do whatever it takes to satisfy the customer or to uphold a core organizational value. If everyone does not understand what his or her ultimate responsibility entails, the organization will not retain profitability.

Today, there are too many organizations in business willing to do whatever it takes to justify complacency. If you allow people to only satisfy their job function, you are cutting your own throat and then, eventually, the throat of your organization.

Effective supervisors understand the difference between job function and job responsibilities. The acceptance of broad job responsibility allows for better and more creative problem solving. These supervisors also encourage their employees to embrace job responsibility. It is this combination of responsible supervisors and responsible employees that make up creative and innovative organizations.

A Problem-Solving Model

Most people do not like problems and try to get rid of them as fast as they can. Their natural tendency, when faced with a problem, is to pick the first reasonable solution that happens to come to mind. Unfortunately, the first solution may not be the most appropriate one and may even lead to larger problems. The following problem-solving model allows for a larger number of alternatives and increases the probability that the final solution will be the best one.

Step One: Define the Problem

The first step in any problem resolution process is to define what appears to be the problem. Write out a problem statement that describes what is going on.

Step Two: Gather Facts, Feelings, and Opinions

The second step is to gain as much information as possible from as many different sources as possible. This step gives you the opportunity to "get smart" and understand the dynamics of the problem. What is happening? Who is involved? What is the impact of the problem? Who does it affect? What are the causes of the problem?

Step Three: Identify the Real Problem

After you gather the facts, feelings, and opinions, it is important to discover if you are working on the real problem or only a symptom of the problem. This may require restating the problem in a totally different format. Be willing to start over with the real issues if that is what it takes. Why spend valuable time trying to solve something that is not the problem in the first place?

Step Four: Generate Possible Solutions

The next step requires generating as many solutions as possible. In this stage, the goal is to generate alternatives. Avoid any judgment or evaluation of solutions at this point. (Later in this chapter we will discuss brainstorming and fishbone diagrams as ways to generate a variety of alternatives.)

Step Five: Evaluate Alternatives

After you have generated as many alternatives as possible, you want to start deciding which alternative will be the best. Now is the time to be critical about the different alternatives. Be cautious or hesitant when everyone agrees on which alternative to take. When no one is willing to challenge the prevailing viewpoint, you are likely to find yourself in the midst of the *Abilene Paradox*.

The Abilene Paradox occurs when a decision is made and yet there is some concern or disagreement about making the decision. No one wants to speak up and go against the prevailing viewpoint. So, the decision is implemented even though people really believe that it is not the right decision. Critical evaluation and honesty allows for better decisions and will save you from taking a trip to Abilene.

Step Six: Select the Best Alternative

Once you have evaluated all the alternatives, you are then ready to pick the one you think will solve the problem in the best way. Most people start at step one by defining the problem, and then move right to step six by making a choice. If we do steps two through five correctly and thoroughly, step six should be relatively easy.

Step Seven: Gain Approval and Support

Any time you are going to change something, you will always need to rally approval and support. Do not think that the only thing that needs to be done is to select the alternative and then implement it. The negative thinkers will come up with obstacles and adopt a "show me" attitude that must be overcome. It helps if you involve such thinkers in the beginning of the problem-solving process so that they can become part of the solution and not part of the problem.

Step Eight: Implement the Decision

After support has been developed, you are finally ready to implement the decision.

Step Nine: Evaluate the Results

If you do not have a follow-up or monitoring system in place that allows you to check results, the chances for success diminish. If people do not know how the results are being measured or that they are going to be held responsible, problem solving becomes a difficult task. When things go right, recognize success. When things go wrong, go back to step one and start the process again.

These steps in problem solving are known by most experienced problem solvers. Unfortunately, they are frequently not practiced by supervisors. The stresses of the job often pressure managers into circumventing some of these steps, and problem solving suffers as a result. Go through the full problem-solving process and save yourself time in the long run. You will make the best decisions that way.

Cause of Problem or Just Symptom

One of the key questions to address when you are trying to come up with solutions to a problem is whether the cause is really the cause or just a symptom of the problem. For example, a common problem supervisors face is poor quality in production. When asked what the cause of this quality problem is, many supervisors respond that the cause is a lack of motivation among workers.

Once you identify a cause, the next question is, "Is that really the cause or just a symptom of the problem?" In this particular example, poor quality is probably not the true cause of the problem, but just a symptom. Some of the true causes that can be manifested through the disguise of motivation are:

- The employee has not had the proper training.
- The importance of high quality has not been communicated.
- There is a lack of coaching and counseling when poor quality occurs.
- There are no consequences for poor quality.

One of our clients was dealing with the problem of poor attendance at their educational seminars. They believed that the possible causes of the poor attendance might be:

- The fees were too high.
- The time of the seminar was wrong.
- They were not spending enough effort on marketing.

After they looked at their organization's two-year track record, it seemed clear that they were not having any problem recruiting and enrolling new members. The problem they were having was retaining people once they were enrolled in the organization. After a careful look at their programs and the feedback given to them by participants, it became clear that poor attendance was a symptom of the real problem, which was the poor quality of the educational programs and materials. This realization allowed the client to rethink programming and re-design materials to be more well-suited to their customers' needs. This change resulted in an overall increase in attendance and more repeat customers.

Cause-and-Effect or Fishbone Diagram

One simple and effective technique used to identify causes of problems is the cause-and-effect diagram. It is also referred to as the fishbone diagram. Begin by writing the problem on the right-hand side of the paper and drawing a box around it. Then, draw a straight line and an arrow that points to the box with the problem inside. Start adding what you feel are the main causes of the problem along either side of the straight line.

Exhibit 17.1 illustrates an example of the fishbone diagram. "Low Sales" is stated as the problem. Potential causes are listed on either side of the straight line—Economy/Environment, Quality of Product, Aesthetics of Product, Sales People, Delivery Schedules, and Price. The economy could be one cause. Poor quality or missed delivery schedules might be another. Sales people not doing certain things might be still another cause.

Once the major possible causes are identified, you can begin to note possible reasons or implications of the various causes. For example, one of the causes of low sales could be the sales people. What could contribute to sales people being the cause? Maybe they are not properly trained *or* they are not following up with customers *or* they are not calling on enough new accounts.

Use the cause-and-effect or fishbone diagram to analyze problems and their causes. This is also a useful technique to use with your department or team. When a small group contributes to creating the diagram, you will come away with a number of perspectives and some good ideas. Once the primary causes are clearly identified, research is conducted to confirm the cause. When the cause or causes of the problem are clear, brainstorming for solutions comes next.

Exhibit 17.1: Cause-and-Effect or Fishbone Diagram

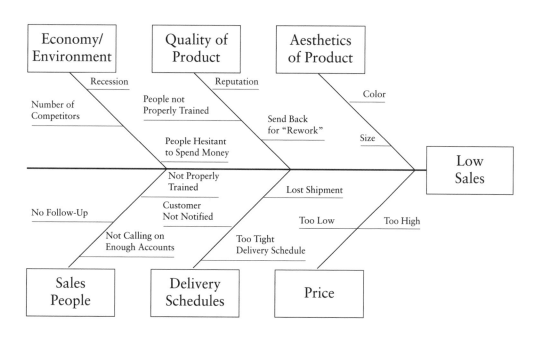

Brainstorming for Solutions

Brainstorming is a process where people use their collective and creative thinking power to generate ideas. The objective is to generate a list of ideas, topics, or solutions related to a specific subject or problem. There are several advantages to the brainstorming process.

1. It involves everyone who may know something about the problem, because the more people you have participating, the better your chances of coming up with the most inclusive list of alternatives.

2. Brainstorming promotes creativity. Every idea is accepted; wild ideas are encouraged.

3. Third, it generates a large numbers of solutions.

It would be helpful to check the seven steps for successful brainstorming, listed in Chapter 12.

Roadblocks to Problem Solving

Even when an organized problem-solving model like our nine-step version is used, people often encounter certain conceptual blocks that inhibit the problem-solving process. These conceptual blocks relate largely to individual thinking processes and to the ways problem solvers use their minds when facing problems. Improving your problem-solving skills is often thought of as gaining more information. However, being exposed to more information alone will not improve problem-solving skills. The entire process, including the way we think, must be considered.

Conceptual Blocks

Conceptual blocks are mental obstacles that constrain the way the problem is defined and the number of alternative solutions we find to be relevant. These blocks are largely unrecognized or unconscious, so the only way individuals can be made aware of them is to be confronted with problems that are unsolvable because of them. The following conceptual blocks can hinder our problem-solving ability.

◆ *Unilateral thinking.* Beginning with a single problem definition, unilateral thinking then pursues that train of thought until a conclusion is reached. No alternative definitions are considered. All the alternatives generated are consistent with the original thought pattern. It is very similar to digging one hole and drilling for oil. If you do not hit pay dirt, keep drilling deeper. In contrast, multi-lateral thinking is thinking that generates alternative ways of viewing a problem and thus produces multiple definitions. Instead of drilling the oil well deeper, multi-lateral thinkers drill wider; they pick different places to drill for oil.

♦ *One-thinking language.* Most people think about things by only using words. In fact, it is impossible to think without using words. When it comes to solving problems, however, other thought languages are available, such as our senses, emotions, and verbal imagery. The more languages we are able to involve in the problem, the more opportunity we have to develop creative solutions.

♦ *Past experiences.* A major obstacle to innovative problem solving is that individuals tend to define present problems in terms of problems they have faced in the past. Current problems are usually seen as variations of some past condition. Alternatives proposed to solve the current problem are alternatives that have proven successful in coping with past problems. This becomes limiting when you are facing a completely new set of problems.

♦ *Forest or trees.* Can you differentiate the forest from the trees? Another conceptual block is the inability to differentiate or separate the major problem from irrelevant problems or background information. Inaccurate, misleading, or irrelevant information must be filtered out to correctly define the problem and to generate appropriate alternative solutions.

♦ *Artificial constraints.* Just as difficult as it is to filter out noises and to add missing details, it is also difficult for many people to avoid ignoring information. That is, they often constrain or place boundaries around problems; they are then unable to use information before them. The following questions illustrate this point.

Q. How many animals of each species did Adam take with him aboard the Ark?

Q. If you had only one match and you entered a room to start a kerosene lamp, an oil heater, and a wood-burning stove, which would you light first?

Q. Do they have a Fourth of July in England?

Q. Two men played chess. They played five games and each man won three times. How do you explain this?

Q. A mama bull (mb), papa bull (pb), and a baby bull (bb) were in the barnyard. Which one did not belong there?

How long did it take you to answer these five questions? Now, check the following "correct" answers to see how you used the "hidden" information.

A. None. Adam did not take animals on the Ark. Noah did.
A. You would light the match first.
A. Yes. Everyone has a fourth of July. Not every country celebrates it as a holiday.
A. They did not play each other.
A. There is no such thing as a mama bull.

♦ *Fear of asking questions.* Some people are afraid to ask questions for fear of being perceived as ignorant or naive. Yes, asking questions is a risk. But in the long run, the person who does not ask questions is the one who appears ignorant.
♦ *Biases against thinking.* There is a particular conceptual block in our culture against the kind of thinking that uses the right hemisphere of the brain. Left hemisphere thinking is associated with logical, analytical, linear, or sequential tasks. Thinking using the left hemisphere is apt to be organized, planned, and precise. The emphasis in most formal education is toward left hemisphere thought development.

A number of researchers have found that the most creative problem solvers are able to solve problems in both the right and left hemispheres, switching from one to the other as needed. Creative ideas arise most frequently in the right hemisphere, but must be processed by the left.

Conceptual blocks cannot be overcome all at once because most blocks are a product of years of habit-forming thought processes. Overcoming them requires practice and thinking in different ways over a long period of time.

Tips for Success: Problem Solving

1. Be optimistic in approaching the problem, and remember this: for most things, somehow, somewhere, there is a better way.

2. Focus your energies on what *can* be done, rather than on what cannot be done.

3. Recognize that your job responsibilities are always much larger than your job function when it comes to solving problems.

4. Generate as many possible solutions to the problem as you can think of through brainstorming.

5. Evaluate and select the best alternative.

6. Determine whether you are solving the real problem or only a symptom of the problem.

7. Gain approval and support from each team member who is involved before implementing the decision.

8. Transform yourself from a unilateral thinker to a multi-lateral thinker. Multi-lateral thinking generates alternative ways of viewing a problem.

9. Challenge "sacred cows" where knowledge justifies it.

10. Ask questions. The more information you have, the better you will be at solving problems.

Action Plan: Solving Problems Creatively

Three steps I can take to expand my problem-solving skills and when I will begin each step:

Action Step 1:
Target Date for Initiation:

Action Step 2:
Target Date for Initiation:

Action Step 3:
Target Date for Initiation:

Chapter

18

Cultivating an Empowered Workforce

"Within each of us is the ability to create an organization/department of our own choosing."

— Peter Block

While we were looking for a quote to start off this chapter, the words from Peter Block, author of *The Empowered Manager*, struck a positive chord with us for two reasons. First, it is controversial. There are managers and supervisors who will read the quote today and strongly respond, "That's not true. I will never be able to change the way upper management operates our organization." Second, intertwined in this quote is the very essence of empowerment. If you believe it, you have the ability to become empowered and make a difference to your organization. If you disagree with the quote, you will find it difficult to lead the life of an empowered individual or manager. The goal of this chapter is to define what empowerment really is; explore what characteristics comprise an empowered manager or supervisor, and describe what possible actions a manager or supervisor can take to create an empowered and empowering work environment.

What Is Empowerment?

It is important to provide both individual and organizational definitions for the concept of empowerment. The reason for splitting up the definitions is because empowerment was an individual concept long before it became the organizational buzzword of the late 1980s and 1990s. Individually defined, empowerment is the ability to make a decision and take action responsibly. When organizations and others are involved in the picture, the definition changes slightly. Organizationally defined, empowerment is the process of increasing the power of others by allowing them to make decisions and take responsible actions.

Where Does Empowerment Begin?

One of the great quotes that emerged from a recent training program on empowerment is, "I will become empowered when my boss decides to empower me." This thought-provoking statement raises the question, "Where does empowerment really begin—with the individual, with the individual's manager, or with the organization?"

Many employees believe that empowerment starts when the organization and the manager make the decision to empower an individual. This might have some validity, but it does not account for the situations where multiple employees work for the same manager and some employees are empowered and some are powerless. Most employees, when asked, say that they know of many situations where the empowerment levels of employees working for the same boss differ dramatically.

Different individuals working within the same organization can have different levels of power, and some departments in unempowered organizations can be quite powerful. This is because empowerment starts with the individual, not with the manager or the organization. About one-half of the employees in our in-house seminars for the Department of Defense's Logistics Defense Contract Agency claim that they are empowered.

Building Empowered Relationships

♦ *Support your boss.* The more your supervisor is convinced of your genuine support, the more freedom and flexibility you will have in the relationship because he or she will trust you. Also, as you support your supervisor, your supervisor will feel a mutual obligation to support you.

♦ *Produce significant results.* It does not matter what your job is, if you do not produce results, you will slowly begin to feel like a mouse in the clutch of a boa constrictor. If we do not produce, the people we are responsible to will place safeguards and constraints on us to make sure we will do exactly what they want. But as you exceed expectations in the area of results, you will slowly see the constraints fade away.

- *Take initiative and responsibility to solve problems.* Empowered individuals ask two questions when problems occur. The first question they ask is, "Where do we want to be?" Their second question is, "How do we get there?" With these questions they can focus their energy on proactive, positive solutions. Unempowered employees ask two different questions. The first question an unempowered employee asks is, "What went wrong?" The second question is, "Who is to blame?" Unfortunately, entire days can be wasted on these two questions with nothing accomplished.

- *Build self-confidence.* Without a deep-seated level of confidence in yourself, your boss will find it difficult to have confidence in your ability to get things accomplished. The more confidence you have, the more flexibility and leeway you will have in all your relationships.

- *Turn in assignments early.* Turning in assignments ahead of schedule will help to build trust because you are doing more than is expected. This becomes a positive "surprise element."

- *If in doubt, check it out.* When making decisions, use good judgment. The goal of an empowered employee is to take reasonable risks, not to commit suicide! Do your research, ask the opinions of others you work with, and then verify your decisions with your boss prior to implementation.

- By supporting your boss, producing significant results, taking initiative and responsibility to solve problems, building self-confidence, turning in your assignments ahead of schedule, and checking out decisions when you are in doubt, you will be well on the way to increasing your power in the relationship you have established with your supervisor.

277

Five C's of Empowerment

If empowerment does start with the individual, it is important to address the characteristics it takes to become empowered. The following model sheds light on the topic.

Exhibit 18.1: Empowerment Model

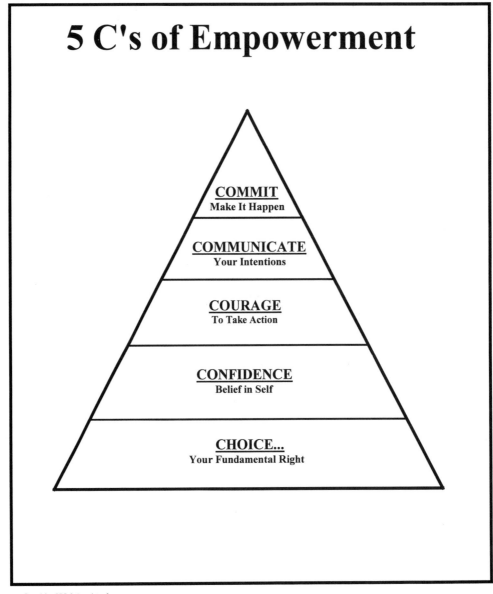

5 C's of Empowerment

COMMIT
Make It Happen

COMMUNICATE
Your Intentions

COURAGE
To Take Action

CONFIDENCE
Belief in Self

CHOICE...
Your Fundamental Right

Level One: Choice—Your Fundamental Right

If you are to become empowered, the most important thing you need to do is believe that you have a choice in everything you do. Let's look at an example. Recently we spoke with a manager who was not treated with dignity or respect by the senior managers in her organization. When we recommended that it was in her best interest to leave and find a job where people valued her talents and contributions, she responded that she was not able to do that. When we explored her remarks in more detail, she shared four reasons why she could not leave: (1) the economy and job market were bad, (2) she had five years invested in the company, (3) she was not sure if she would get a job that paid as well, and (4) the company was close to her home. The sad part is that this manager does not believe she has a choice in leaving. It is sad because if you have ever made the decision to go out and find a new job, then you know that you *do* have a choice. Until we recognize that we have a choice in almost everything we do, it will be difficult to advance the concept of being personally empowered.

Level Two: Confidence—Belief in Yourself

Once we believe that we have a choice in the matter, the second step is having the confidence to know that we can have a positive impact on the outcome. In the example listed above, the manager needs to believe that she will find a new and better job when she decides to take action. It is that belief that will drive her actions to find not just a new job, but a great job.

Level Three: Courage—Taking Action

The knowledge of choice and the positive belief in self are not enough. You need to have the courage to take action. Courage is the power to let go of the familiar. One example of taking action would be if this manager decided to send out ten resumes each week to prospective employers. Taking action can be scary but it has a positive impact on your self-esteem. Taking action is the only way you can effectively change or control your environment.

Level Four: Communicate Your Intentions

In this specific example, it may not be in this manager's best interest to tell her bosses that she is actively looking for another job. But let's take a look at communication from another angle. An empowered individual would communicate to her boss that she does not feel she is treated with dignity and respect. An empowered individual might also ask if he or she has done anything specific to warrant such treatment. It is certainly a better option than doing nothing, which is what an unempowered individual would do.

Level Five: Commit—Make It Happen

Empowered individuals do not just talk about what they are going to do, they make a commitment to make things—or changes—happen. Empowered individuals have a key characteristic called character. We define character as the willingness to continue on with the task, long after the feeling to do so has left you. In this specific example, the manager goes home in the evening and needs to choose between watching television or sending out five of the resumes to complete her weekly goal. Committed to finding a new and better job, she begins the tedious task of sending out more resumes.

Empowerment starts with you. If you can put the Five C's to work on every decision you make, you will have the foundation in place to create an empowered work environment.

Role of Power in Empowerment

In our seminars, we ask participants the question, "When you give your power away to subordinates, why do you always gain power in return?" There is one strong reason. By giving subordinates decision-making power and the power to take action, you are also telling them that you have trust in their ability. Any time we allow someone else to make a decision for us, we are putting a piece of our career into that person's hands and that takes trust. Most employees do not want to undermine the trust that their supervisor has in them, so they will work hard to exceed expectations. What is wedged deeply into this concept of empowerment is your belief and trust in your employees' ability. If you do not trust your employees, it is not likely that you will give them the freedom to make a decision or take action without your approval. A secondary consequence of your distrust of employees is that they most likely will also begin to distrust you. Empowerment will not be successful without trust. The following model describes the process of trust a manager or supervisor can create with employees.

Exhibit 18.2: Building Trust Model

Building Trust

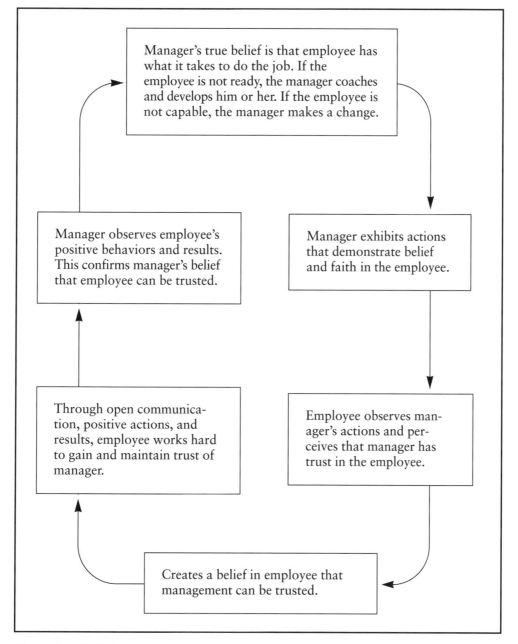

Copyright PBS & Associates, Inc., 1994.

To be a successful empowering manager or supervisor, it is important that you believe that employees are trustworthy. If you have an employee whom you cannot trust, it is important that you spend time with this employee to coach, train, and develop the individual. If these actions do not improve your trust in this employee, it may be better to move the person to another position or help him or her leave the organization. What is critical is that you do not change your belief about employees being trustworthy based on your problem with this one employee. If you do not trust people, people will not trust you and empowerment will never take place in that environment.

A Need for Organizational Empowerment

There are several reasons why empowerment is timely for organizations. Some of the reasons include:

- The environment is changing rapidly and we no longer have the luxury of having every front-line decision sanctioned by a manager.
- Everyone is being asked to do more with less; as a manager, you simply do not have the time to do all the things you used to do.
- Many employees currently feel alienated from their jobs.
- When employees feel that they have no influence or control over their environment, it creates stress.
- Employees value having power and the ability to make a difference in their work environment.

Giving employees the power to make decisions and to take actions in their work environment can solve many of these current work issues.

Does It Really Make a Difference?

Recently, the authors had to travel to Indiana to work with a client. When we returned the rental car to National Rental Car Company, we were told that the bill was $356 for three days. It was a shock to hear the price was so high, as we had rented the car for $49 per day and were expecting a bill closer to $160. The rental agent explained that the reason the bill was so high was because we rented the car in Detroit and were returning the car to a different location. Therefore, there was a $200 drop-off fee. We told the rental agent that we were unaware that the drop-off fee was so high and were confident that the client would be unwilling to pay this exorbitant travel expense. We were actually thinking that this drop-off fee would have to come out of our own pockets. The rental agent said, "I can see on the computer that you are a frequent renter. I will go ahead and waive the drop-off fee this time." We expected to see the title "Sales

Manager" on her name tag. Surely, only a manager would have the power to waive this type of fee! No, the name plate indicated that the agent was only a sales representative. That's giving the front line the power to satisfy the customer!

Success Tips: Empowerment

1. Empower yourself. You will never be able to empower your team members if you do not feel you have the personal power to take action and make a difference. If you follow the Five C's, you will be personally empowered.

2. Trust your people. Remember, the foundation block of organizational empowerment is trust. If you do not trust your people, then you will not be able to pass on the power to make decisions and take action.

3. When trust is lacking, begin to coach, train, and develop your employees. Giving employees responsibility is scary for both you and the employees. Not giving employees a chance because of your belief that you cannot trust them is a self-fulfilling prophecy.

4. Set boundaries. Remember to take reasonable risks, but do not commit suicide. Setting boundaries helps ensure that you do not overempower employees too early in the process.

5. Provide open and honest communication. Employees need the best information available and supervisors need to build trust by being totally honest at all times.

6. Clarify and communicate your strategic direction and goals. Employees need to be clear on what your expectations are for their responsibilities in meeting strategic goals.

7. Make your values clear. Send a clear message of what is important and employees will find it easy to be empowered.

8. Delegate, delegate, delegate. If you cannot delegate as a manager, you cannot grow as a manager. Managers who do not delegate run head-on into the Peter Principle, reaching their own level of incompetence. Stave off the Peter Principle. Delegate!

9. Set a specific time to follow up. To delegate and then forget about the delegated task is not good management. To delegate and then micro-manage the accomplishment of the task is also not good management.

10. Learn to forgive. Everyone makes mistakes. Your reaction to the mistakes will determine if employees will continue to take risks and make empowered decisions. If they believe your reaction to any mistake is not worth the risk, they will refuse to make decisions.

283

Action Plan: Cultivating an Empowered Workforce

Three steps I can take to encourage my staff to be empowered and when I will begin each step:

Action Step 1:
Target Date for Initiation:

Action Step 2:
Target Date for Initiation:

Action Step 3:
Target Date for Initiation:

Chapter

19

Creating a Motivating Environment

"What I do best is share my enthusiasm."

— Bill Gates

A frequent complaint from many supervisors is that their employees lack motivation. Supervisors feel that this lack of motivation is responsible for most of the problems they encounter, from tardiness to a lack of productivity. The big question is, "How do I motivate my employees?" This chapter will define motivation and explore how to use it in the workplace.

One of the first questions we need to address is, "Is it really possible to motivate anyone?" Most people will agree we can motivate ourselves, but many of us have tried a myriad of different ideas and we still have not created motivation in another person. This is because you cannot motivate anyone! What you can do is create an environment that is conducive to motivating someone. You can also create an environment that will demotivate someone. Motivation is an internally-generated phenomenon. It is a feeling that each of us develops internally and it causes us to act. As supervisors, our focus should be on how we can create an environment and develop a relationship with our employees that fosters the action of motivation.

What is Motivation?

Motivation can best be described as the internal drive to fulfill a need. Each of us has specific needs. These needs translate into drives that we act upon through specific behaviors. Drives are action-oriented and provide an energizing thrust toward goal accomplishment. As we act on the behaviors (through drives), we satisfy our needs. As our needs are satisfied, the intensity of the drive subsides.

A more succinct explanation is that "people do what they think they have to do in order to get what they think they want." As supervisors, if we truly want to create motivated individuals, we have to fully understand their needs and goals. If we can understand the needs and goals of our employees, we have a good possibility of showing them the appropriate behaviors that will help them satisfy their needs. And those appropriate behaviors will be the behaviors that satisfy our needs and goals.

There is a big difference between internally generated motivation and just getting someone to move. Technically, the term *motivation* can be traced to the Latin word *movere*, which means to move. Motivation is an *inner state* that energizes and activates—or moves—a person toward a goal. Historically, supervisors have been quite effective in providing the external motivation to get employees to move: "If you don't work faster, you will be fired." Most likely, the employee will begin working faster because he or she does not want to lose their job. However, is the increase in productivity due to an inner push, or an outside threat from the supervisor? The supervisor was able to move, not motivate, the employee. Most likely, the employee will produce just enough not to be fired, but the employee will not produce what he or she would be truly capable of if internally motivated.

Historical Perspective of Motivation

The traditional human relations approach to management generally failed to recognize the importance of the underlying psychological process of motivation. The approach was based on these three simple assumptions:

1. People are primarily economically motivated, but secondarily desire security and good working conditions.
2. Providing the above rewards to people will have a positive effect on the motivation and morale of employees.
3. There is a positive correlation between morale and productivity.

With these three assumptions, the motivational problem facing management was relatively easy to solve. All management had to do was devise monetary plans, ensure security, and provide good working conditions; morale, motivation, and maximum productivity would result.

Unfortunately, the human relations approach to motivation did not work in practice. It became evident through research and experience that such a simplistic approach to motivation fell short of providing a meaningful solution to the complex motivational problems managers and supervisors faced.

Maslow's Hierarchy of Needs

Abraham Maslow, in a classic paper published in 1943, outlined the elements of a new overall theory of motivation. Drawing chiefly from his clinical experience, he came to believe that a person's motivational needs could be arranged in a hierarchical manner. In essence, he believed that once a given level of need became satisfied, it no longer served to motivate. The next higher level of need had to be activated in order to motivate the individual.

Maslow identified the following five levels in his need hierarchy.

1. *Physiological needs*. This most basic level in the hierarchy, physiological needs, includes our human primary needs. The needs of hunger, thirst, and sleep are some examples. According to the theory, once these basic needs are satisfied, they no longer motivate. In other words, if you are hungry, you will be motivated to satisfy your hunger before other needs. When your hunger is satisfied, you can move on to other needs.

2. *Safety needs*. This is the need to ensure that you are safe from danger, that you are safe from natural elements, and that you can get your physiological needs met in a safe way.

3. *Belongingness needs*. These are the needs for affection and affiliation, as well as the need to feel connected or a part of a group. Emotional needs for family and friends are included here.

4. *Esteem needs*. The esteem level represents the higher needs of humans. The need for achievement, power, growth, accomplishment, and status can be considered part of this level.

5. *Self-actualization needs*. This level represents the culmination of all the lower, intermediate, and higher level needs of humans. People who have become self-actualized are self-fulfilled and have realized their full potential. Another way to describe self-actualization is that you could look back at your life, from any point in time, and feel that you have accomplished your purpose in life, and have done what you intended to do.

Maslow did not intend that his needs hierarchy should be directly applied to work motivation. In fact, he did not study the motivating aspects of humans in organizations until about twenty years after he originally proposed his theory.

Despite this lack of intent on Maslow's part, Douglas McGregor and others popularized the Maslow theory in management literature.

McGregor's Theory X and Theory Y

Starting around 1960, people began to examine and discuss Douglas McGregor's Theory X and Theory Y styles of management. Theory X represents the old-style, authoritarian type of management and is based on three primary assumptions about human beings. The major assumptions of Theory X are:

- The average human being has an inherent dislike for work and will avoid it if possible.
- Because of this inherent dislike for work, most people will perform only if coerced, controlled, directed, or threatened with punishment.
- The average person prefers to be directed, wishes to avoid responsibility, and has very little ambition to work.

Prior to the 1950s, Theory X was widely accepted and, with few exceptions, universally practiced. In the 1950s and 1960s, many researchers were starting to challenge McGregor's Theory X thinking. McGregor summarized the new thinking of the day in Theory Y. The major premises of Theory Y are:

- The expenditure of physical and mental effort in work is as natural as play or rest.
- People will exercise self-direction and self-control in the service of objectives to which they are committed.
- Commitment to objectives is a function of the rewards (both internal and external) associated with achievement.
- The average human being learns, under proper conditions, not only to accept but to seek responsibility.

Herzberg's Two-Factor Theory of Motivation

Herzberg extended the work of Maslow and developed a specific "job content" theory of work motivation. In the late 1950s, Herzberg conducted a motivation study of about 200 accountants and engineers. The professional subjects in the study were given the following directions by an interviewer:

"Think of a time when you felt exceptionally good or exceptionally bad about your job, either your present job or any other job you have had. This can be either the long-range or the short-range kind of situation, as I described it. Tell me what happened."

Responses obtained from this critical incident method were interesting and fairly consistent. After tabulating these reported good and bad feelings, Herzberg concluded that job satisfiers were related to job content and job dissatisfiers were related to job context. The satisfiers were labeled *motivators* and the dissatisfiers were called *hygiene or maintenance* factors. Taken together, they became known as Herzberg's two-factor theory of motivation.

Updated in a *Harvard Business Review* article in January/February 1968, Herzberg's theory is closely related to Maslow's need hierarchy. The hygiene factors, like the medical term, are preventive and environmental in nature, and they are roughly equivalent to Maslow's lower level needs. These hygiene factors prevent dissatisfaction, but they do not lead to satisfaction. In effect, they bring motivation up to a theoretical zero level and are a necessary "floor" to prevent dissatisfaction, as well as serving as a take-off for motivation. By themselves, hygienic factors do not motivate. Only the motivators (or satisfiers) motivate humans on the job. According to Herzberg's theory, an individual must have a job with a challenging content *and* the individual must feel connected to the purpose of the organization in order to be truly motivated.

Exhibit 19.1 defines the dissatisfiers as hygiene or maintenance factors and the satisfiers as motivators.

Exhibit 19.1: Two-Factor Theory of Motivation

Hygiene or Maintenance Factors	Motivators
Company policy	Achievement
Supervision	Accomplishment
Relationship with supervisors	Recognition
Work conditions	Work itself
Salary	Responsibility
Relationship with employees	Advancement
Status	Growth
Security	

Herzberg's two-factor theory cast a new light on the content of work motivation. Up to that point, management had generally concentrated on the hygiene factors. When faced with a morale problem, the typical solution was higher pay, more fringe benefits, and better work conditions. Herzberg was the first to say that the hygiene/maintenance factors are absolutely necessary to maintain the human resources of an organization. However, once the basic needs are satisfied with the hygiene factors, which is the case in almost every organization that exists today, adding any more hygiene factors will not motivate the employees. Only a challenging job that has the opportunities for achievement, recognition, responsibility, advancement, and growth will motivate people. Herzberg is telling supervisors: If you are trying to motivate your employees with items listed in the hygiene column, you are shooting blanks; it will not work.

Herzberg is right. Most supervisors have witnessed this firsthand. For example, an employee is given a raise as a motivational ploy. The raise usually motivates the employee, but only until the first paycheck arrives. Then it is back to square one again. What we can learn from Herzberg's theory is that achievement, praise, and recognition are the three most powerful motivators we have in our supervisory "tool kit."

Creating a Motivational Environment

The best supervisors have the most productive people, and these people are happy. The real challenge for supervisors is to design incentive systems that encourage high performance *and* also engender high employee morale. To accomplish this objective, supervisors should employ two general approaches to employee motivation.

A. *First, they should examine the overall system of rewards in their organization from the employees' point of view to ascertain its potential for motivation.* This is best done by asking the question, "What do my employees expect when they complete a task?" This expectancy theory basically proposes that people regulate how much effort they put into their work based on what they expect to get out of it. More specifically, this theory states that employees will be motivated to perform well if they believe that meaningful rewards or recognition will result from their hard work, and that there is a reasonably high probability that hard workers can become high performers.

B. *The second approach focuses on shaping employee behaviors so they are consistent with the expectations of management.* This is referred to as operant conditioning or reinforcement theory. Behaviorists argue that if we want to understand why employees do the things they do, we should examine the events that occur after a behavior that encourages or discourages similar future behaviors.

Expectancy Theory

Managers should examine the motivational potential of their organization's reward system for supervised employees. Too often, managers examine opportunities for rewards only from an organizational level. For example, it is common practice to compare pay and benefit programs with industry averages. If the organization does well in these comparisons, managers often conclude that the system will motivate the employee. This conclusion is based on the false premise that all employees are motivated by the same reward opportunities.

1. The big question we need to ask is, "Are the rewards offered important to each individual in my department?" Employees bring a wide variety of personal values and needs to the work environment. For example, an employee who has marginal skills and heavy financial obligations will be primarily concerned about job security, salary, and benefits. An employee who is sharing responsibility for child care with a working spouse will probably be less concerned about job security and more concerned about flextime or the availability of an on-site childcare facility. While the prescription to link work outcomes to the expectations of employees seems obvious, it is frequently violated, especially when employee feedback is not encouraged.

2. Once you have identified what is important to each individual, the second question you should ask is, "Are highly-valued rewards linked to good performance?" One way employees judge fairness is by calculating a job-input-to-job-output equity ratio. This means that they add up everything they are contributing (including experience, training, effort, and recognition), and measure it against the rewards they receive.

3. This brings us to the third diagnostic question, "Is the employee capable of achieving the desired outcome?" Because good performance requires both high motivation and adequate ability, an attractive and equitable reward system is useless unless all organizational obstacles to personal performance are eliminated. For example, if a worker is rewarded for submitting reports on time but other departments refuse to provide the information needed on a timely basis, then the motivation system will be nullified.

Taken together, these three diagnostic questions emphasize the importance of the supervisor's role in providing people with a motivating environment. Supervisors should work to ensure that the organization's reward structure is consistent with established behavior principles and then facilitate workers' efforts to obtain rewards within the system.

Operant Conditioning

The process whereby managers and supervisors use rewards and punishment to shape behavior is called *operant conditioning*. Operant conditioning uses a variety of techniques involving the presentation or withdrawal of positive and negative reinforcers or no reinforcement whatsoever. Operant conditioning theorists have argued that the best way to change an employee's behavior is to change the supervisor's behavior. Unfortunately, many supervisors do not behave as though they believe their daily interactions with work group members influence worker attitudes and behaviors.

Positive Reinforcement

Positive reinforcement consists of linking desired behaviors with positive outcomes. When an employee does something you like, you should respond in a manner that is rewarding to that person. How can you motivate a marginal employee to improve? The following six-step model shapes behavior with positive reinforcement.

Step One: Describe the Goal or Target Behavior

The target should always be related to performance. What, specifically, must the individual do to become a high performer? Answers such as work faster, be dependable, or take initiative are too general. "Answer the phone in a more professional manner" should be replaced with, "When you answer the phone, say: 'This is XYZ Enterprises, Donna speaking. How may I direct your call?'" State the goal or target behavior clearly.

If the target behavior is actually a complex chain of behaviors, divide it into a chain of smaller successive behaviors. It is best to find a smaller series of steps you can reward instead of waiting to reward the individual when the entire task is completed. In other words, acknowledge small successes.

Step Two: Check the Technical Skill Level

Make sure the individual possesses the technical skill required for the job. If low performance is due to lack of natural ability or training, provide the training and information to set the employee up for success.

Step Three: Select a Meaningful Reward

A manager once gave an employee a two-week, all-expenses-paid trip to Hawaii for two. The employee found it difficult to even muster a "Thank you" to the manager who presented the reward to him. When the manager asked why he did not seem pleased, he responded, "I have a fear of flying. Also, my wife and I are not getting along right now and the last place I want to be is stuck on an island with her for two weeks." The company replaced the vacation package with something the employee wanted—a complete set of Craftsman tools from Sears. Make sure that you know your employees well enough to provide an appropriate reward that will be meaningful to that person.

Step Four: Provide Positive Reinforcement

All positive reinforcement should be directed toward moving the employee closer to the target behavior you desire. If the employee receives the same reward at performance level two as at performance level five, the supervisor's reinforcement actually discourages improvement. This is what happens when everyone in the organization is given the same raise reward.

Step Five: Administer Immediate Rewards

Administer rewards immediately following each improvement in behavior. In animal studies, one can imagine how little learning would take place if a reward was delivered two hours after a desired behavior had occurred. While this principle appears obvious in animal research, it is frequently violated in everyday management practice. Most managers and supervisors give positive feedback at the worst possible time—when they want to, not when the employee will be most reinforced by it. Feedback on the negative consequences of an employee's performance is often delayed for months by the supervisor. No wonder we have problems with motivation!

Step Six: Use Intermittent Reinforcement

As the desired behavior becomes a reality, change from a continuous reward structure to an intermittent reinforcement schedule. Administering a reward every time a given behavior occurs is continuous reinforcement. Administering rewards on an intermittent basis means administering the same reward each time, but not every time it is warranted. Neither approach is clearly superior, but they both have trade-offs. Continuous reinforcement represents the fastest way to establish new behavior. In contrast, partial reinforcement is a very slow process and it is resistant to extinction. For example, an employee who is praised every time an accurate report is written will quickly learn that you value accuracy. But what happens when you are on vacation and there is no one to offer that praise? That behavior becomes prone to extinction.

In contrast, partial reinforcement, although slow, is resistant to extinction. The huge number of repeat gamblers in Las Vegas is illustrative of one partial-reinforcement outcome. Some people stay motivated to win long after they should have stopped an unsuccessful behavior!

Meaningful Recognition

Feeling appreciated and recognized are two of the most powerful motivators available to the supervisor. The question then becomes, "What is meaningful recognition?" Recognition is meaningful when tailored to the individual being praised. Instead of the usual "grip and grin" so many managers employ to thank someone for the job they have done, the manager should tap into the uniqueness the individual brings to the job.

This uniqueness is not unlike the work of an artist who paints. The painting is a unique contribution, in many ways a gift that the artist is giving to society. It represents his unique way of seeing reality. If the artist is good enough, the painting might even have a commodity value.

Lewis Hyde, a poet and essayist, describes this concept when he states, "It is the cardinal difference between the gift and commodity exchange that a gift establishes a feeling-bond between two people, while the sale of a commodity leaves no connection."

If we only value and recognize the commodity side of our relationship with employees—the dollars we pay them—then we are undervaluing the uniqueness and giftedness they bring to their jobs. Human work is not just a commodity. If we feel we are just a commodity and that anyone qualified can do our job, we begin to lose our motivation.

Our motivation intensifies when we and others recognize the gifted nature of our work. Try to value the uniqueness of each employee, recognizing that his or her work is a gift. Every employee has different strengths we need to recognize. We cannot forget that motivation is a feeling. Recognizing people's unique strengths helps tap into that feeling.

Recognition Suggestions

The following suggestions for recognition in Exhibit 19.2 were generated by seminar participants. It has been well-documented that two of the strongest motiva-

294

tors available to supervisors are recognition and praise. If you are able to customize these ideas or suggestions, they will help you build a more motivated workforce and it will cost nothing more than your thoughtfulness and time.

Exhibit 19.2: Suggestions for Recognition

Brainstorming Results: Ways to Recognize Employees	
Ask employees for their opinion	Go to lunch with employee
Write a thank-you note to employee	Bring doughnuts or food
Put a letter of recognition in employee's personnel file	Recognize or praise employee or team in a group meeting
Have your boss say thank you or send letter of appreciation to employee	Give employee a plaque or something suitable for public display
Do something unexpected (buy a coffee mug, bring flowers, etc.)	Write article about accomplishments in company newsletter
Assign a special parking place	Give employee time off with pay
Award "Employee-of-the-Month"	Provide employee with business card
Award "Employee-of-the-Year"	Recognize someone via electronic mail
Increase employee's responsibilities	Listen—really listen—to employee
Recognize employee's birthday or work anniversary	Share a reward you receive with your employees
Give employee a special project	Teach employee something new
Take employee to lunch	Send employee to training
Take employee to lunch with your boss	Have employee train or teach others
Post a memo of recognition in a public area (company bulletin board)	Have employee fill in for you during your absence
Attach a "Post-it" that says "Great!"	Call to say "Job well done"

295

Ensuring High Motivation

There are many ways to build employee motivation. You can develop an environment that makes internal motivation a reality in your employees' lives. We suggest:

1. *Set high expectations with clearly-defined objectives.* When you ask people the question, "What accomplishment are you most proud of?" most will describe an accomplishment requiring significant effort to complete. Many managers think that pushing mediocre employees to higher accomplishments requires too much effort. No doubt it does require tremendous effort. But the problem with allowing mediocre or poor employees to continue at their present levels is that the cycle of low motivation also continues. There is nothing motivating about mediocre performance. It takes guts to set higher standards and then hold your employees to them. As employees rise to meet the new standards, increased feelings of motivation are fostered in the workforce.

2. *Reward people for meeting high expectations.* If you set high standards for your employees, then you need to celebrate and recognize success when achievement occurs. One of the biggest complaints from employees is that they work incredibly hard to meet deadlines, and then no one recognizes them for their extraordinary effort. As you recognize and reward people for accomplishment, you must be sure the rewards you are bestowing are important to the recipients. As we learned earlier in the chapter, different things motivate different people.

3. *Praise and recognize your employees often.* This statement sounds so easy, and yet it is incredibly difficult to practice on a steady basis. It is easy to find things that seem more important to do, like manage the cash flow, solve a customer's problem, pick up a new job, answer an employee's question, or complete a report. However, if time is not taken to praise and recognize your employees, motivation and morale will wane. Then you *will* have a lot more things to do!

4. *Explain the "big picture."* People are motivated when they feel they are making a significant contribution to the organization. Many times, employees do not understand how significant their contribution really is. One way to highlight the importance of an employee's contribution is to ask the question, "What happens when the employee does not do his or her job?" Often, when the employee does not do his or her job properly, it adversely affects someone else. That someone is usually another employee, depart-

ment, or customer. You need to demonstrate how each employee's contribution is connected to the overall purpose of the organization.

5. *Find out the needs and goals of your employees.* Different things motivate different people. If you are going to successfully motivate your employees, you need to find out what is motivating to each employee. Employees may be motivated by challenge, recognition, promotions, responsibility, or learning something new. Once you identify what motivates your employees, you need to merge that individual's needs and goals into your needs and goals and then into the needs and goals of the organization.

6. *Develop your self-esteem and the esteem of others.* People with high self-esteem are more motivated and productive. We feel best about ourselves when we have challenged ourselves and have accomplished something. This means that you constantly have to set goals for yourself. Keep your employees involved in the goal-setting process. It is important for supervisors to remember that, by position alone, your behavior and actions have a tremendous impact on the way employees feel. Take the responsibility to help others feel heightened self-esteem.

7. *Get others involved in the goal-setting process.* If people are not involved in setting goals that affect their job performance, there is a strong chance that they may not be committed to the goals. Employees resent it when management sets goals that affect them without soliciting their input and then holds them responsible for achieving those goals. The problem with a goal not being "our goal" is that if we do not see the importance of achieving the goal, it is hard to find the motivation to act on the task. We tend to spend our energies on other tasks we perceive as more important; we tend to spend our energies on our own goals.

8. *Develop a positive mental attitude.* Being around a negative person is not motivating. Negative people tend to take energy away, not instill motivation. If your attitude is negative, it is probably a reflection of your vision. If things are getting worse, what is exciting and motivating about a negative future? Be positive—people will gravitate toward you, rather than push away from you.

9. *Develop a "that's no problem" attitude.* Have you ever worked with someone who could take a small problem and then blow it all out of proportion so everyone can "enjoy" it? There are some people who spend a lifetime looking for problems and then complain about them, rather then solve them. It does not take much of a person to handle life—or a job—when everything is going right. It does take a special kind of person to success-

fully handle an environment when things go wrong. The most valuable employees are the ones who can look at problems and come up with solutions. They say, "We have a problem, but that's no problem." Leo Buscalia, a professor at the University of Southern California, states it the best when he says, "The most successful people in life are the ones with the greatest number of viable alternatives."

10. *Be a positive role model.* If you want to be a motivator, you need to be motivated. You cannot demand top performance from your employees if you are unwilling to give your very best effort. When employees witness your willingness to contribute extraordinary effort, they are much more willing to go the extra mile.

Tips for Success: Motivation

1. Remember, motivation is something internally generated. It is impossible to motivate someone else. However, you can create an environment where people find it easy to become motivated.

2. Do not try to use money or any of Herzberg's other maintenance factors as motivators. They do not work.

3. Make the reward meaningful to the employee. People are motivated by different rewards. Tailor your praise, recognition, or other motivator to the specific recipient.

4. Link your rewards to *good* performance.

5. Make sure that the employee is capable of doing the task you are asking him or her to do.

6. Administer rewards and feedback *immediately following* the positive behavior you desire.

7. Choose one idea each day from "Recognition Suggestions" (Exhibit 19.2) and pass it along to the people in your work group.

8. Maintain high expectations. Low or mediocre expectations that are accomplished are not motivating.

9. Get your employees involved in the goal-setting process. When it is also their goal, the opportunity for successful accomplishment increases.

10. Be motivated! You will never motivate anyone unless you are highly motivated yourself.

Action Plan: Creating a Motivating Environment

Three steps I can take to create an environment for internal motivation and when I will begin each step:

Action Step 1:

Target Date for Initiation:

Action Step 2:

Target Date for Initiation:

Action Step 3:

Target Date for Initiation:

Chapter 20

To Be a Leader

"Management techniques are obviously essential, but what matters is leadership. Leading the whole organization needs wisdom and flair and vision and they are another matter; they cannot be reduced to a system and incorporated into a training manual."

— Anthony Ja

The writer makes an interesting point. It is difficult to be considered a leader if you have no followers. What makes this point so significant is that you *can be* a supervisor or manager and have no followers—all you need is employees. To take this point one step further, you can be considered a supervisor even if you are ineffective in your ability to direct the actions of your employees. However, this is simply not the case for a leader. A leader must have followers.

Leader or Supervisor?

Over the last twenty years, countless theorists have attempted to define and differentiate leadership from management. Some have made statements such as "managers manage things, whereas leaders lead people" or "management is about efficiency, but leadership is about effectiveness." Others say that leaders possess "charismatic" or "heroic" qualities that allow them to influence people toward positive change. In contrast, managers maintain the status quo.

When we ask supervisors and managers to make distinctions between the two terms, the responses invariably paint a more positive picture of the functions a leader fulfills than of the functions a manager or supervisor fulfills.

A typical list of the differences between leaders and managers/supervisors was generated by a group of participants at several of our seminars. The compiled information is outlined in Exhibit 20.1.

Exhibit 20.1: Differences between Leader and Manager/Supervisor

Leader	Manager or Supervisor
Builds Trust	Manages Things
Motivates	Controls
Empowers People	Maintains Power
Develops Vision	Assigns Goals
Has Integrity	Plans
Develops Commitment	Demands Compliance
Coaches and Counsels	Disciplines
Asks	Tells

When people look at this list, there is no question in their minds which role they would like to play in the organization. They want to be the leader! But our problems begin in this discussion when we ask the question, "Wouldn't a good manager motivate his or her employees?" The answer is most definitely "Yes." "Wouldn't a good manager also build trust with his or her employees?" Once again, most likely "Yes." On the other side of the coin, "Wouldn't a good leader also plan and even force compliance or discipline in some instances?" The reality of this discussion is that good managers and good leaders will probably rely on both sets of skills or behaviors at different times.

Let's look at an example to illustrate the value of being able to employ both leading and managing skills. A young man worked as an ambulance driver for two years and was then promoted to the position of field training officer. This meant that most of his time was spent working with people new to emergency medicine. As a field training officer, part of the job was motivating new employees to continually learn new aspects of emergency medicine. Another part was to coach and counsel people when things did not go right. He was also responsible for having a vision and developing a plan for every call they responded to. People said he was a great leader in very traumatic situations. Once a nervous rookie said to him, "I feel calm when I work with you." The young man not only felt comfortable leading his partners, but also leading bystanders, police and fire personnel, and the patient's relatives. He encountered few situations where he lacked the confidence that he could handle the situation. However, on any given moment, he might change roles and become incredibly directive—many times even forcing compliance in the process. If the situation warranted it, he might be *telling* the patient what to do, *telling* the bystanders what to do, and even *telling* his partner exactly what to do. Do these telling/directive behaviors make him any less of a leader? We feel strongly the answer is "No." Both sets of behaviors are required by both leaders and supervisors at different times.

There is one significant difference between a leader and a manager that needs to be addressed. The one significant difference between a leader and a manager deals with where their power source is based.

Leadership, unlike management, is not a formal position. It is a relationship. Managers receive their power and authority from the organization. This is what we call legitimate or position power. Leaders hold no position power per se. Their power base comes voluntarily from the followers. Ideally, we would like both of these power bases to be held by one person. That is, the manager should also be the leader. In this scenario, the manager would have both the power of the organization and the power of the people. In the event that this is not the case, a leader potentially has more power. The reason is that the manager takes the power from the organization and then diffuses that power down through his or her employees. The opposite is true for the leader. The leader has the followers' power invested in him or her. This infusion of power from the followers creates an incredibly powerful source for action.

From time to time, managers say that with formal authority they can always fire a negative informal leader. This is most definitely true. The only thing you can almost guarantee is that another informal leader will crop up and almost always have more power than the one who was fired.

The goal for all of us would be to perfect the skills and traits of both the leader and the manager. When we have the power sourced from both directions, we have the ultimate opportunity to create positive change for our organizations. The bottom line is that leadership and management are two distinctive and complementary systems of action. Both are necessary for success in our increasingly complex business environment.

Types of Power

There are four distinctly different types of power a leader or manager may possess. Each type of power has different qualities and carries different weights in our efforts to lead people.

Type One: Power of Position

This is formal authority, giving you the sacred right to tell someone else to do something. There are times when we do not agree with our boss and we may even express our disagreement to him or her. Then we go ahead and bow to our boss's demands. We may have responded to the power of the position. Most people respond to this power base because they practice a simple management concept called "I want to keep my job!"

Type Two: Power of Competence

To be successful as a leader or manager, you need the competence to do the job. John P. Kotter, a Harvard Business School professor, states that effective leaders seem to have life experiences that demonstrate their competence. These life experiences may consist of industry and organizational knowledge, relationships in the firm and industry, reputation and track record, and even formal schooling (although Kotter stated that very few of these competence characteristics were developed by our educational system). According to Kotter, most of our competence is developed on the job as a part of our post-educational career. The more competent others perceive us to be, the more likely they will be to follow us.

Type Three: Power of Personality

If you have ever worked with someone who has rubbed you the wrong way, then you know the power of a personality. Personality defines the specific skills and behaviors you utilize to help build relationships. The easier it is for others to talk to you, listen to you, and work with you, the easier it will be for them to respond to your wishes.

Type Four: Power of Character

This component is your "credit rating." Do the people you interact with perceive you as trustworthy, credible, and honest? Do they perceive you as having high personal morals, sincerity, and strong ethics? You acquire this power from the trail of promises you have kept and the expectations you have fulfilled or exceeded. To put this another way, you have done what you said you were going

304

to do and therefore people trust you. What is interesting about this component is that you get no credit for being truthful when it costs you nothing to tell the truth, for being honest when it costs you nothing for being honest, for being dependable when it costs you nothing to be dependable. The measure other people use to determine your character is how far you are willing to go to maintain your standards of honesty, dependability, trustworthiness, and credibility.

As we look at these four bases of power, one is clearly managerial—the power of position. The other three fit under the realm of leadership. However, these three components also need to be developed simultaneously by managers and supervisors. Of the four components, the power of character is the most powerful of all. If people do not trust you or do not perceive you as credible, it will affect every other aspect of your relationship.

Many people feel that the power of personality is equally powerful to that of character. They back this up with examples of "charismatic" personalities. One way to differentiate between the power of personality and the power of character is to ask the question, "Have you ever met a salesperson that you liked, but did not trust?" If you did not trust the salesperson, you probably did not buy his or her product or service. If his or her character was the most powerful factor, you probably would have made the purchase. You may even have some friends that you like, but do not trust. It is in these feelings where we find the difference between character and personality.

We have looked at the value of the four types of power and we have also discussed the importance of both managing and leading. Now, let's take a look at what we consider to be more "managerial-oriented" activities as well as activities considered to be more "leadership-oriented."

Managerial-Oriented Activities

Management, by definition, is getting things done through others. The science of management developed during the 20th century because organizations grew incredibly large. The goal was to be able to mass produce something in the most efficient way possible. Management practices and procedures were largely developed to cope with large, complex organizations. Without order and consistency, outputs such as quality, productivity, and profitability are adversely affected. To control these outputs, pay attention to these critical "managerial" functions:

M-O Activity One: Planning

Planning is the science of setting goals and targets for the future, and then deciding what steps you will take to achieve those goals. You can have the greatest dreams and goals in the world, but without the plan to turn the goals into a reality, you will not get far.

M-O Activity Two: Budgeting

Budgeting is the part of the planning process where finances are allocated to help achieve the plans.

M-O Activity Three: Organizing

Organizing means creating a formal structure that can accomplish the plans.

M-O Activity Four: Staffing

Once we have the plan and the organization in place to support the plan, the next managerial function would be to staff the jobs with qualified individuals, communicate the plan to those individuals, and delegate responsibility to carry out the plan.

M-O Activity Five: Controlling and Problem Solving

Controlling involves looking for variations from the plan. Managers look for the deviations—formally and informally—by means of reports, meetings, and other tools. Once deviations are identified, we then plan and organize to solve the problems.

A great example of an organization that thrived on management strategies in the 1950s and 1960s but did not make the leadership transition required in the 1970s is ITT. Under Chairman Harold Geneen's leadership, ITT was managed in a highly-disciplined manner. That meant continuously producing detailed plans and budgets aimed at achieving financial objectives set mostly by Geneen. Geneen established elaborate control mechanisms—financial control systems and regular business review meetings—and then he paid strict attention to the data produced by those mechanisms. During Geneen's tenure, ITT bought dozens of companies and applied the same management principles to each. In the process, ITT's revenue went from $811 million in 1960 to $6.36 billion in 1970. Geneen's claim to fame was that he led ITT to 60 consecutive quarters of profitability and growth. This is an incredibly impressive performance.

However, the problem with Geneen's style of management is that it does not work particularly well in the kind of volatile and unpredictable business environment we now experience. Tight, structured, and disciplined procedures restrict and limit new ideas and approaches. With an emphasis on very disciplined management but very limited leadership, ITT took a huge fall in the last decade. Between 1975 and 1985, ITT's financial performance was among the worst of all large corporations, eventually leading to major divisions being sold in the mid 1990s. Today's constantly changing and competitive environment requires flexibility, adaptability, and innovation.

Leadership-Oriented Activities

While management focuses on coping with complexity, leadership is about creating positive change. Part of the reason leadership has become such a desirable quality in the last twenty years is because of the rapid changes and innovation we discussed in the first chapter. The net result of these changes is that doing what was done yesterday—or even doing it 15% better—is no longer a prescription for success. Major changes are necessary to survive and compete effectively in today's environment.

An example of an organization that made the transition from management to leadership quite successfully is the United States Armed Forces in the 1991 Gulf War. In peacetime, a military can usually survive with good administration and management up and down the hierarchy, coupled with good leadership at the very top. In times of war, a military needs good leadership at every level of the organization. Under the direction of General Norman Schwarzkopf and General Colin Powell, the United States military performed in a way that rallied not only the troops, but the entire country.

Steven Covey, author of *The Seven Habits of Highly Effective People,* says, "The leader is the one who climbs the tallest tree, surveys the entire situation, and yells, 'Wrong jungle!' But how do the busy, efficient producers and managers often respond? 'Shut up! We're making progress!'" To help you focus on ways to make sure you have followers to lead, we have summarized aspects critical to your leadership development.

L-O Activity One: Developing a Vision

Leading an organization to positive change, whether it is a company or a small work unit, begins with a vision. A vision is a clear mental picture of a desired future outcome. If you have ever put together a large 1,000-piece jigsaw puzzle, the chances are that you used the picture on the top of the puzzle box to guide the placement of the pieces. That picture on the top of the box is the end result or the vision of what you are trying to turn into a reality. It is much more difficult—if not impossible—to put the jigsaw puzzle together without ever looking at the picture. An organization without a vision is like a person trying to put together a jigsaw puzzle without ever seeing the picture on the box.

Effective leaders will create and articulate a clear vision for their organization or unit. A good vision is clear and compelling. It works like a magnet, pulling people toward it.

There are at least four benefits of a clear vision.

A. *It ensures that all employees are moving in the same direction.* This means that all employees are working towards the same end result.

B. *It helps to overcome adversity.* Employees are more willing to tackle problems that get in the way of achieving the vision.

C. *It helps to create motivation.* If the leader is committed to and excited about his or her vision, the excitement is contagious. Employees will be more motivated to work toward the vision and will tend to focus on the positive rather than dwell on the negative.

D. *It provides a guide for decision making.* A clear vision will help employees determine the right path when it comes to problem solving and decision making. For example, if the vision for your department includes providing superior customer service, employees will make decisions that support that vision. When it comes to deciding whether an employee returns a customer's call now or waits until tomorrow, a vision of superior customer service tells the employee to make the call now.

L-O Activity Two: Aligning People

In management, we staff the organization to fulfill certain functions. Leadership involves connecting and aligning people to the true purpose of the organization. This means communicating the vision and helping the employees see how they fit into the vision. The employee is a piece of the puzzle and he or she helps to create the overall picture. He or she needs to know how critical each piece is to the overall success of the organization.

One example that brings this point to life is an event that took place in an electrical assembly plant. The plant was having severe quality problems. A team of lead personnel was assigned responsibility for manufacturing a replacement wiring harness for the instrument panel on an F-14 fighter jet. When we asked them the question, "What happens when you do not do your job correctly?" they collectively responded, "The wiring harness comes back from the military for rework." Then we asked, "How does the military find out if it is not working properly?"

To find that answer only through pilot experimentation would mean a terrible ride for a pilot traveling at 1,500 miles per hour and then having his or her instrument panel fail! To help the lead employees see their true organizational purpose, we had pilots from the Miramar Naval Station come down and talk to the employees about the importance of their assembly-line job.

One of the pilots said it best when he asked, "Can I go over to the box of wiring harnesses, pick out one, install it on my jet, and then take you (pointing to a lead person) for a ride?" The end result of that day was a change in purpose. No longer did the lead employees feel they were solely in the electrical manufacturing business. They now realized that when they did their jobs correctly, they were also in the business of saving pilots' lives.

L-O Activity Three: Motivating People

In a true management capacity, controls are in place to identify problems. At the end of the month, we have reports that tell us how we did on productivity, quality, and profitability. The problem of relying solely on the controls is that we find out we have problems at the end of the month when it is too late. The problem has most likely already done its damage. What we need is to have each individual inspired and motivated to do things right the first time. If we are solely using controls, we are pushing the employee to conform. Having to push an employee does not satisfy his or her basic human needs for achievement: a sense of belonging, recognition, self-esteem, and a feeling of control over one's life. Such feelings touch us deeply and create a powerful response.

Good leaders create a motivating environment. They articulate the vision and help align employees to the role they play in fulfilling the vision. They also give employees the power to be involved and make decisions that affect their work. Leaders solicit and value the feedback of their employees. Leaders also help employees realize the vision by providing coaching, feedback, and role modeling. These activities help employees grow professionally and personally, which enhances their confidence and self-esteem.

L-O Activity Four: Empowering People

Empowerment, by definition, means to give another person the authority and power to act. This means that the employees who work for you actually have the ability to get things done themselves. The opposite of empowerment is "micro-management." When we "micro-manage," we oversee every action and decision our employee makes.

What is important to note about empowerment is that is starts with you, not with someone above you. Before you can empower someone else, you have to feel that you have the power to change aspects of your own life and your area of influence. This is the feeling that you can control your own destiny. Developing a vision and then taking action will help you take a proactive stance in becoming empowered.

To empower your staff, you must also understand that power is not "zero-sum" based. Zero sum means that there is only a certain amount of power to go around, and if I give up power, I lose and someone else gains. If I gain power, then you lose power. The problem with seeing power as a finite source is that you spend your time and energy protecting what power you do have. This is time that could be more productively spent turning your vision into a reality or motivating your staff. The goal is to gain the confidence and understanding that when you empower others, you are taking a risk, developing trust, and creating an enlarged power base. In a sense, you are giving away power to gain power. The opposite is also true. If you do not trust your employees, if you do not give them the capacity to act, then they will most likely not invest their power in you or your vision. By not giving away power to your employees, you lose your own power.

L-O Activity Five: Clarifying Values

The values that you carry with you are the basis for governing your decisions and behaviors. Values influence the relationships you enter into, the significant others you choose, the careers you develop, the family you raise, and millions of other decisions you are faced with each day. In many ways, values are like a moral compass that guides you through life. As a leader, it is important to clarify what values your organization or department is going to represent. What will you be known and remembered for?

One organizational value is being honest with your customers and employees. This sounds easy to live by until a decision comes up where, if you are honest, it costs you thousands of dollars. If you are true to your values, the values will be non-negotiable. When you have this value consistency, people will perceive you as having integrity. Without value consistency, you will be perceived as a hypocrite. Essentially, when you clarify values *and* you live by those values, you are "walking your talk." Exhibit 20.2 illustrates this concept.

When espoused values (words) and values in use (actions) meet and are consistent, you demonstrate integrity. If espoused values and actions do not meet or are in conflict, you demonstrate hypocrisy.

Exhibit 20.2: Walking My Talk

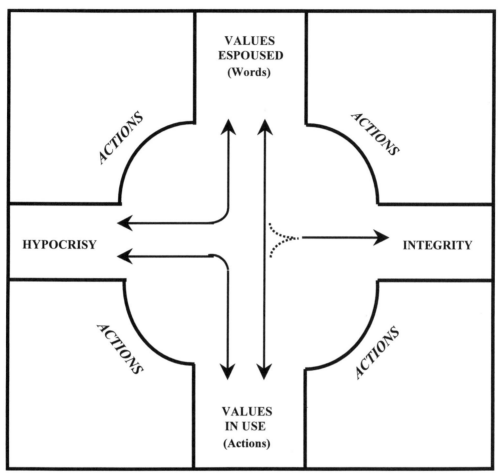

COPYRIGHT: PBS & Associates, Inc.

L-O Activity Six: Building Trust

It sounds so simple: all you have to do is build trust with your employees. We know that this is no easy task. Here are five ways you can develop trust:

A. *Do what you say you are going to do.* When you tell people you are going to do something and then do not do it or do something different, people begin to doubt your word. Do what you say you will do and you will gain credibility and trust.

B. *Provide just a little more than expected.* Whether it is additional support and counseling for an employee, going the extra mile for a customer, or going a little out of your way to help a co-worker or fellow supervisor, exceeding others' expectations builds trust and loyalty.

C. *Be consistent.* If you are consistent, people can predict what actions you will take. When people are unsure of how you will act or react, they tend to proceed cautiously, or not at all.

D. *Increase responsibility.* One of the fastest ways to build trust with people is to increase their responsibility. By increasing someone's responsibility, you are taking a risk. When you take a risk and people fulfill or exceed your expectations, you develop trust in them. Your trust in them fosters their trust in you. It is a reciprocal relationship, and it is critical for good business and personal relationships.

E. *Accept honest mistakes.* Supervisors and managers tend to forget that their value lies in their experience. Their experience comes from making mistakes and learning how to proceed so the same mistakes do not happen again. If we do not have the capacity to accept mistakes, then people in our area of influence will refuse to make decisions or take risks. Try not to see failure as failure, but only as a learning experience. Help people learn and grow from their mistakes. Ensure their self-esteem and people will go out of their way to please you.

L-O Activity Seven: Mentoring

Mentoring is just a fancy word for a coach. The power of mentoring is two-fold. It not only builds up the esteem of the person being mentored, it also builds the esteem of the mentor. The reason this concept works so well is that most of us have a deep-seated need to help someone else. By helping someone else grow, we feel good in the process. To share something we know costs us very little except our time.

L-O Activity Eight: Willingness to Learn

If leadership is about creating positive change in the organization, then being a leader is about continuous learning. As fast as things are changing, it is almost impossible to maintain any type of expertise. As long as we have a willingness and a desire to learn, we have the ability to adapt to new environments.

Becoming a Better Leader

There are many practical reasons for becoming a better leader. After reading the following paragraphs, you will be able to cite additional ideas that are even more relevant to your work structure.

- *Recognize that the world is rapidly changing.* You can decide that you are going to help create change and learn from it, or you can try to resist change. Because of global competition and the rapid increase of information and technologies, many large organizations are eliminating layers of middle management and supervisors in order to be more responsive to change and to their customers. Knowing this, middle managers need to look forward and see how their talents and energies can be re-applied in the organization. Many managers in large organizations are finding out that change is the one thing they can count on. Your ability to adapt to change will significantly impact your organizational success.

- *Develop a positive mental attitude.* No one wants to follow someone with a rotten attitude. Enough said!

- *Look for freedom, not at what you cannot change.* Where are you going to spend your energy? Complaining about things you cannot change, or creating the things you can? If you feel your destiny is in someone else's hands, you do not have to take responsibility for your actions. Focus on what you can do and take responsibility. There is power in responsibility.

- *Lead with your heart and head.* We recently heard a manager say that he did not care about people's emotions. He went on to say, "We have a job to get done!" Unfortunately, people are the ones who are going to get that job done. And people have feelings. In fact, everything about motivation and the desire to do good work is based on a feeling. If we do not consider people's feelings, it is impossible to be an effective leader.

- *Reach out to people who have different perspectives.* It is easy to communicate with people who think just like you. It is difficult to effectively communicate with someone who has a differing viewpoint. However, if we only have the ability to communicate with people who think like us, we are preventing ourselves from learning new and valuable information.

- *Become comfortable with the unknown.* One of the prerequisites to becoming empowered is to feel comfortable with the unknown. This means having the ability to deal with ambiguity. As fast as our environment is changing, it is impossible to know all the facts or have all the answers all the time. If you think you know everything, you are obsolete.

- *Develop a leadership "tool kit."* No one can have all the answers. What you can develop is a "tool kit" of resources that can help to solve problems. If you only have a hammer, you tend to see every problem as a nail. Collect information, and then learn and practice leadership and management techniques. Remember, good leaders never stop learning.
- *Look for multiple right answers.* With information and the environment changing as rapidly as it is, we can no longer afford to look unilaterally for one right answer. Become multi-lateral in your thinking. Search for possibilities—not just one solution.
- *Substitute effectiveness for perfectionism.* If you wait until all the available information is in to make your decisions, you probably waited too long. In today's environment, we no longer can afford the luxury of waiting until something is absolutely perfect. We need to ask the question, "What's the goal or purpose?" If we can satisfy the goal, then we are effective.
- *Develop the flexibility of a sapling.* San Diego is full of beautiful eucalyptus trees. Unfortunately, it seems like every time there is a rain or windstorm, some of the biggest trees blow over. Fortunately, eucalyptus trees are great at dropping seeds that start new saplings. What is amazing is that the wind and the rain do not bother the saplings. They are pliable and just blow with the wind. The large trees are not so adaptable. They snap because they are not able to sway with the changing wind. In today's environment, supervisors need to be like saplings.

In closing, we leave you with a few simple thoughts about leadership: True leaders understand that success does not depend on their titles, but on the values they uphold and the choices they make on a daily basis. True leaders know that leadership is not achieved through technical expertise, but rather is based on an emotional connection or relationship with followers. It is our hope that the insights we presented in the previous chapters will help you with the technical expertise and "people smarts" you need to be not only a great supervisor, but an *outstanding leader!*

Tips for Success: Leadership

1. Recognize that leadership is not a formal position, it is a relationship. If you want to be a leader, you need to earn followers.

2. To be effective, you need to have strong skills in both areas—leadership *and* management.

3. As a leader, your greatest source of power comes from your character. The more others trust you, the more power you will have.

4. Create a compelling, positive leadership vision for yourself and for your work group. A vague vision is not motivating to you or to your people.

5. Help your employees see how they contribute to bring the vision to reality.

6. Empower your employees. Give them the freedom to act and make decisions as necessary to get the job done.

7. Clarify the values you will use to guide you and your work group. Values are the basis for governing your decisions and behaviors.

8. Increase responsibilities for your employees. If you are doing your job, your employees should be growing by taking on added responsibilities.

9. Develop a willingness to learn. With the economy and business environment changing so rapidly, you need to continuously learn and relearn.

10. Reach out to people who have different perspectives. If you surround yourself with people who think just like you do, eventually your work group's strengths will become its weaknesses.

Action Plan: Earning Followers in Your Role as a Leader

Three steps I can take to improve my leadership skills and when I will begin each step:

Action Step 1:
Target Date for Initiation:

Action Step 2:
Target Date for Initiation:

Action Step 3:
Target Date for Initiation:

Bibliography

Albrecht, Karl. *The Only Thing That Matters*. New York: HarperCollins Publishers, 1992.

Belasco, James, and Stayer, Ralph. *Flight of the Buffalo, Soaring to Excellence, Learning to Let Employees Lead*. New York: Warner Books, 1993.

Bennis, Dr. Warren. *On Becoming a Leader*. Reading, MA: Addison-Wesley Publishing Co., 1989.

Bennis, Dr. Warren, and Nanus, Burt. *Leaders, The Strategies for Taking Charge*. New York: Harper & Row Publishers Inc., 1985.

Block, Peter. *The Empowered Manager: Positive Political Skills at Work*. San Francisco, CA: Jossey-Bass, 1987.

Branden, Nathaniel. *How to Raise Your Self-Esteem*. New York: Bantam Books, 1988.

de Pree, Max. *Leadership Jazz*. New York: Dell Publishing, 1992.

California Department of Fair Employment and Housing. *DFEH-161*. Sacramento: State of California, 5/97.

Fournies, Ferdinand F. *Coaching for Improved Performance*. Bridgewater, NJ: Fournies & Associates Inc., 1978.

Fournies, Ferdinand F. *Why Employees Don't Do What They're Supposed to Do*. Blue Ridge Summit, PA: Liberty Hall Press, 1988.

Fritz, Robert. *The Path of Least Resistance*. New York: Fawcett-Columbine, 1989.

Kotter, John P. *The Leadership Factor*. New York: The Free Press, 1988.

Kouzes, James M., and Posner, Barry Z. *Credibility: How Leaders Gain and Lose It, Why People Demand It*. San Francisco, CA: Jossey-Bass Inc., 1993.

Kouzes, James M., and Posner, Barry Z. *The Leadership Challenge*. San Francisco, CA: Jossey-Bass Inc., 1988.

Mackenzie, R. Alec. *The Time Trap*. New York: McGraw-Hill Book Company, 1975.

Oncken, William, Jr., and Wass, Donald L. "Management Time: Who's Got the Monkey?" *Harvard Business Review*, November/December 1974, pp. 75–80.

Raines, Claire. *Beyond Generation X*. Landam, MD: Crisp Publications, 1997.

Sheehy, Gail. *Pathfinders*. New York: Bantam Books, 1982.

U.S. Bureau of the Census. *Current Populate Reports, series P-25, No. 990 in the Statistical Abstract of the United States*, 1987.

U.S. Bureau of Labor Statistics. *Handbook of Labor Statistics*, June 1985.